**SCHOLASTIC**

# 500+
## Fabulous Month-by-Month
# TEACHING IDEAS

### Instant Activities and Reproducibles
### for the Themes and Topics You Teach

New York • Toronto • London • Auckland • Sydney
Mexico City • New Delhi • Hong Kong • Buenos Aires

**Teaching** *Resources*

This book is a compilation and update of a series of previously published titles:
*Fresh & Fun September* by Bob Krech; *Fresh & Fun October* by Deborah Rovin-Murphy and Frank Murphy;
*Fresh & Fun November* by Deborah Rovin-Murphy, Frank Murphy and Nancy Sanders;
*Fresh & Fun December* by Bob Krech; *Fresh & Fun January* by Pamela Chanko;
*Fresh & Fun February* by Joan Novelli; *Fresh & Fun March* by Jacqueline Clarke;
*Fresh & Fun April* by Jacqueline Clarke; *Fresh & Fun May* by Jacqueline Clarke;
*Fresh & Fun Summer* by Pamela Chanko

Cover design: Maria Lilja
Interior design: Kathy Massaro
Interior art by Shelley Dieterichs, except page 163 by James Hale
Copy editor: Eileen Judge
ISBN-13: 978-0-545-17659-0 • ISBN-10: 0-545-17659-X

Compilation copyright © 2010 by Scholastic Inc.
All rights reserved. Published by Scholastic Inc.
Previously published work included in this book: pp. 97–126 © 2000 by Bob Krech;
pp. 155–184 © 2000 by Joan Novelli; pp. 185–274 © 2000 by Jacqueline Clarke.

Printed in the U.S.A.

6 7 8 9 10    40    16 15 14 13 12

# Contents

*E*very teacher knows that the school year—and teaching time—goes by so quickly, and that with each changing season and each new month, students' interests also change. But each month also brings new opportunities for teaching and learning. This book is a treasury of hundreds of terrific month-by-month teaching activities and ideas that will add sparkle to every school day, while connecting with your curriculum, supporting the standards, and tapping into your students' ever-changing interests.

Best of all, many of these irresistible and easy-to-do activities and ideas come from creative teachers across the country. They've used them successfully in their very own classrooms and share them here with you in this terrific collection of ideas, activities, games, projects and reproducibles that will boost learning in math, reading, writing, science, social studies, art, and more.

*500+ Fabulous Month-by-Month Teaching Idea*s takes you and your students from September to the summer months, with a host of fun and motivating activities—including pocket-chart poems, calendar activities, read-aloud plays, math story mats, and more—all organized according to the unique opportunities and themes that each month naturally presents: weather and seasons, holidays, the life cycle of plants and animals, nutrition and health, prominent people and historical figures, and so much more. For example, September activities take advantage of the excitement that the start of the new school year brings, focusing on themes like Back to School, Community, and Transportation. November is a natural time to teach about Thanksgiving and Native Americans; it's also when Children's Book Week takes place, so you'll find lots of great literature activities, too. December and January abound with ideas for learning about everything from special winter holidays to hibernation, to civil rights and Martin Luther King, Jr. April and May cover rain showers and spring flowers, life cycles, Earth Day, and much more.

Throughout the book, you'll find a variety of month-specific ideas to inspire and motivate students of all learning styles—all year, including:

✤ Hands-on math, science, and social studies activities

✤ Collaborative book-making projects

✤ Fun and easy no-cook recipes

✤ Creative art projects

✤ Songs and poems

✤ Pocket-chart activities

✤ Read-aloud mini-plays

✤ Movement activities

✤ And so much more!

Plus, throughout the book, you'll find these great features:

**TEACHER SHARES:** Hundreds of terrific teacher-created-and-tested activities help boost learning in math, reading, writing, science, social studies, art, music and more.

**BOOK BREAKS:** In each month's activities, you'll find numerous book suggestions sprinkled throughout, that link great literature to the curriculum to help you enhance and extend the activities and learning at hand.

**COMPUTER CONNECTIONS:** Throughout, you'll also find a variety of Web site suggestions that will support and extend the activities.

**TIPS:** Insightful Teaching Tips will help you make the most of the activities and ideas.

**REPRODUCIBLE SEND-HOME ACTIVITY CALENDARS:** Each month features a reproducible calendar that you can send home to families. They're full of fun activities that kids can do with their family—and are a great way to reinforce the home-school connection!

**READY-TO-USE REPRODUCIBLE ACTIVITY PAGES:** Handy reproducible pages provide you with ready-to-go activities that are fun-filled and highly motivating.

**REPRODUCIBLE THEMATIC STATIONERY:** Each month also features reproducible fun and festive thematic stationery that kids will love.

**Reaching All Learners**

Your students learn in different ways—some are more verbal, others prefer written expression. Some are comfortable working in groups, others like independent projects. And some children's strengths may lie in music, art, movement or other modes of expression. To help you meet your students needs and encourage all of their strengths, you'll find all these learning modalities woven into the activities in this book. perspective.

# Supporting the Standards

Mid-continent Research for Education and Learning (McREL), a nationally recognized, non-profit organization, has compiled and evaluated national and state curriculum standards. Many of the activities and teaching ideas in this book are designed to support students in meeting the standards in language arts, math, science, social studies, art and music. The K–2 benchmark standards for reading, writing, math and science are listed below. Standards for other curriculum area activities, including social studies, art and music, can be found at McREL's online database: www.mcrel.org/standards-benchmarks.

## Math

**Uses a variety of strategies in the problem-solving process**
- Draws pictures to represent problems
- Uses discussions with teachers and other students to understand problems
- Explains to others how she or he went about solving a numerical problem
- Makes organized lists or tables of information necessary for solving a problem
- Uses whole number models such as manipulative materials to represent problems

**Understands and applies basic properties of the concepts of numbers**
- Understands that numerals are symbols used to represent quantities or attributes of real-world objects
- Counts whole numbers
- Understands symbolic, concrete, and pictorial representations of numbers
- Understands basic whole number relationships
- Understands the concept of a unit and its subdivision into equal parts

**Uses basic procedures while performing the processes of computation**
- Adds and subtracts whole numbers
- Solves real-world problems involving addition and subtraction of whole numbers
- Understands basic estimation strategies
- Understands the inverse relationship between addition and subtraction

**Understands and applies basic and advanced properties of the concepts of measurement**
- Understands the basic measures length, width, height, weight, and temperature

- Understands the concept of time and how it is measured
- Knows processes for telling time, counting money, and measuring length, weight, and temperature, using basic standard and non-standard units
- Makes quantitative estimates of familiar linear dimensions, weights, and time intervals and checks them against measurements

**Understands and applies basic properties of the concepts of geometry**
- Understands basic properties of and similarities and differences between simple geometric shapes
- Understands the common language of spatial sense
- Understands that geometric shapes are useful for representing and describing real world situations
- Understands that patterns can be made by putting different shapes together or taking them apart

**Understands and applies basic and advanced concepts of statistics and data analysis**
- Collects and represents information about objects or events in simple graphs
- Understands that one can find out about a group of things by studying just a few of them

**Understands and applies basic and advanced concepts of probability**
- Understands that some events are more likely to happen than others
- Understands that some events can be predicted fairly well but others cannot because we do not always know everything that may affect an event

**Understands and applies basic properties of functions and algebra**
- Recognizes regularities in a variety of contexts
- Extends simple patterns

# Reading

**Uses the general skills and strategies of the reading process**
- Uses mental images based on pictures, meaning clues, basic elements of phonetic and structural analysis self-correction strategies
- Understands level-appropriate sight words and vocabulary
- Reads aloud familiar stories, poems, and passages with fluency and expression

**Uses reading skills and strategies to understand and interpret a variety of literary and informational texts**
- Knows the basic characteristics of familiar genres
- Knows setting, main ideas, main characters and events, sequence, and problems in stories
- Understands the main idea and supporting details of simple expository information
- Relates stories to personal experiences.
- Relates new information to prior knowledge and experience

# Writing

- **Uses the general skills and strategies of the writing process:** prewriting, drafting and revising, editing and publishing, evaluating own and others' writing, organizing written work, and writing in a variety of forms and for different purposes

- **Uses the stylistic and rhetorical aspects of writing:** uses descriptive words to convey basic ideas and declarative and interrogative sentences in written compositions

- **Uses grammatical and mechanical conventions in written compositions:** uses conventions of print and spelling, complete sentences, parts of speech, capitalization and punctuation

- **Gathers and uses information for research purposes:** generates questions about topics and uses a variety of sources to gather information

# Science

*Earth & Space Science*
**Student understands that:**
- short term weather conditions can change daily, and weather patterns change over the seasons
- water can be a liquid or a solid and can be made to change from one form to the other, but the amount of water stays the same
- Earth materials consist of solid rocks, soils, liquid water, and the gases of the atmosphere
- rocks come in many different shapes and sizes
- the Sun and Moon move in regular patterns

*Life Science*
**Student understands that:**
- plants and animals closely resemble their parents
- differences exist among individuals of the same kind of plant or animal
- plants and animals have basic needs
- plants and animals have features that help them live in different environments
- plants and animals need certain resources for energy and growth

*Physical Science*
**Student understands that:**
- different objects are made up of many different types of materials and have different observable properties

- things can be done to materials to change some of their properties
- the Sun supplies heat and light to Earth
- electricity in circuits can product light, head, sound, and magnetic effects
- sound is produced by vibrating objects
- light travels in a straight line until it strikes an object
- things near the Earth fall to the ground unless something holds them up
- the position of an object can be described by locating it relative to another object or the background
- the position and motion of an object can be changed by pushing or pulling

*Nature of Science*
**Student understands that:**
- scientific investigations generally work the same way in different places and normally produce results that can be duplicated
- learning can come from careful observations and simple experiments
- tools can be used to gather information and extend the senses
- in science it is helpful to work with a team and share findings with others

# September

## Back to School

## Community

## Transportation

## Apples

# September
## Teaching Ideas

Could there be a more exciting month for teachers and students than September? We experience it like no one else—the anticipation…the butterflies…the smells of new crayons, pencils, and erasers…old friends and new classmates…new teachers and books. Most of all, there is the promise of a brand new school year filled with possibilities.

These September activities will help you get a great start on a productive and memorable year by providing you with ideas, books, games, songs, poems, and activities that will help you create a truly sensational start-of-the-year experience for your students. The activities and ideas are organized in four popular, multidisciplinary theme units. **BACK TO SCHOOL** provides some great ways to get things started and help students get to know one other while learning key skills and concepts. **COMMUNITY** focuses on the classroom community—how you and your students can work together to create a welcoming environment. It also allows you to look beyond, into the larger communities of neighborhood, country, world, and future. (See "Your Community in the Future" on page 21.) **TRANSPORTATION** is an excellent vehicle (pun intended) for all kinds of learning! Children start by looking at ways they get to school, then go further to explore other ways people get around in the world, including trains, planes, boats, and more. **APPLES**—September is the time you'll find them everywhere. They're a great springboard for delving into math (see "Apple Fact Families," page 32), reading, science, and, of course, food!

Most of the ideas for September, though organized by themes, naturally integrate a number of disciplines and learning styles. They can work together or stand alone. In the pages that follow, you'll find:

- a reproducible send-home activity calendar
- literature connections
- a collaborative class book
- hands-on science and math activities
- a math story mat
- a collaborative class banner
- a no-cook recipe
- songs to sing
- an interactive poem
- art projects
- and lots more to make September a sensational experience for you and your students!

Name _____

# September Activity Calendar

Choose _____ activities to do each week this month.
Ask an adult in your family to initial the square in the box of each activity
you complete. Bring this paper back to school on _____ .

| Monday | Tuesday | Wednesday | Thursday | Friday |
|---|---|---|---|---|
| Write the word *September* on a sheet of paper. Cut apart the letters. Make new words! **bee** **see** **pet** | Say the word *September*. Find ten things around you that start with the same sound: sssssssssssss. | Look at the words on this page. Find one that rhymes with *pet*. Find one that rhymes with *ball*. | September 3 is Aliki's birthday! Celebrate with one of her books. Try *We Are Best Friends* (Greenwillow, 1982). | Autumn is also called *fall*. What other words name seasons? |
| Look at a calendar. Find the first day of fall. How many weeks away is winter? | Find out when the sun will rise tomorrow. Is this before or after you wake up in the morning? | Find out when the sun will set today. Is this before or after you go to sleep at night? | Count the letters in your first name and last name. Write a number sentence to show how many letters there are in all. | Count the letters in a family member's first and last name. How many more or fewer letters in your name? |
| Read a book with someone in your family. Take turns retelling the story. Include a beginning, middle, and end. | Collect a pile of leaves. Sort them by color. Sort them by shape. How else can you sort them? | Look at this leaf. Find a matching leaf on this page. | Look at the words on this calendar. Circle all of the capital letters. | *Ladybug* is made from two words: *lady* + *bug*. Find another word on this page that is made from two words. |
| September 15 is author Tomie De Paola's birthday. When is your birthday? Does it come before or after Tomie's? | Tape a leaf to paper. Color all around the leaf. Lift up the leaf! What shape do you see? | The Mayflower's voyage to America lasted from September 16, 1620 to December 20, 1620. How many days was the trip? | Happy birthday, Johnny Appleseed! (September 26) Name five things you can make with apples. What's your favorite? | Turn *September* into a tongue twister! Make up a sentence using as many words as you can that start with s. |

# Teacher Share

## Lift-the-Flap Class Album

**H**elp students learn the names of new classmates by making a collaborative lift-the-flap class album.

◎ Take a photo of each student. Glue each photo to a sheet of sturdy paper. Let students write their names beneath their pictures. (You may wish to laminate the pages at this point.)

◎ Tape a strip of paper over each name to make a flap.

◎ Put the completed pages together with O-rings to make a book.

◎ Let students take turns using the class album at school and taking it home to share with families.

*Jackie Clarke*

## TIP

The first few times you try this activity, go around the circle, giving each student a turn in order. After a while, make the game more exciting by letting children pass the ball randomly around the circle so the pattern is not so predictable.

MUSIC, SOCIAL STUDIES

## "Learn the Names" Song

Help students learn one another's names at the beginning of the year with "Learn the Names," a song you can sing to any tune you like, such as the first part of "Twinkle, Twinkle, Little Star" or "This Old Man."

◎ Form a circle and give one student—for example, Jon—a ball. As Jon holds the ball, the class sings, "This is Jon, this is Jon, everybody knows that this is Jon."

◎ Jon passes the ball to the student on his right and the class then sings the song again, substituting that person's name.

◎ Continue, until you've substituted each child's name in the song.

## Bedtime for Frances
### by Russell Hoban (Harper, 1960)

Many primary classes begin the year reviewing or learning the alphabet song for the first time. You can expand on this with Frances the Badger's help. In this story, Frances sings a very silly alphabet song that she makes up as she goes along. (Children universally howl when Frances sings, "T… is for tiger, U is for underwear down in the dryer.") Using the rhythm of Frances's song, have students create short phrases or sentences that feature a word that begins with a targeted letter. Put these together on a chart and create your own silly alphabet song.

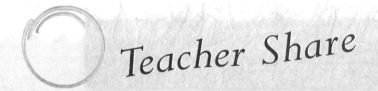

### Teacher Share

MATH

## M & M Sorting Game

It just may be that "M & M" stands for "Motivating Manipulative." For a start-the-year math activity that also gives every child a chance to share, try an open-ended sorting activity that lets students explore on a variety of levels.

◎ Bring students together in a circle. Give each child an individual-size bag of M & M's® candies and a sheet of centimeter graph paper.

◎ Have students pour out their M & M's® on the paper and sort or organize as they like; ask them to be prepared to make a statement about their particular sort. Do a sort yourself and make some example statements, such as, "I have four reds," or "I have more blue than yellow."

◎ When children have sorted the candies and thought of their statements, have them move out of the circle, leaving their sorting papers where they are.

◎ One at a time, have children share their statements with the class. Let students take turns finding the matching paper. Follow up with the best part: eating those "Motivating Manipulatives"!

*Daphne Snyder*

You can also use colorful cereal pieces shaped like O's for this activity. Be sure to check for food allergies before letting children eat the candy or cereal pieces.

# Teacher Share

## Mingo

The name of this get-to-know-you game is a combination of the words *bingo* and *mingle*. To play, give each child a copy of a Mingo board (see page 18) and a pencil. Have children walk around the room and try to find someone who qualifies to initial or sign his or her name in each box. Play until someone gets four in a row (across, down, or diagonally), or until children fill their boards (better for having children get to know one another). To encourage children to mingle with as many classmates as possible, tell them that they can only sign someone's Mingo board one time.

*Monica Orloff*

## Classroom Portrait Quilt

Here's a project that can help build class unity and identity. Give each student a 4- by 5-inch sheet of white drawing paper. Have children draw self-portraits on the paper. Remind them to include all their features—for example, eyes, ears, nose, and hair—and to concentrate on just the head and shoulders, not the whole body. Have children write their names on their portraits, then carefully cut them out and glue them to 4- by 5-inch pieces of colored construction paper. Have children arrange their portrait quilt squares side by side on a large sheet of craft or bulletin board paper. Label with the class name and display proudly in the hall or on the front door.

## Book Break

## Lilly's Purple Plastic Purse
### by Kevin Henkes (Greenwillow, 1996)

This story opens with Lilly describing all the things she loves about school. Soon, though, she has a serious falling-out with her teacher. The relationship is artfully repaired in the end. Read and discuss the story. Let children share likes and dislikes about school. Reflect on these comments as you plan for the year ahead.

SCIENCE

# Scientific Popcorn Party

Welcome students to a new school year with a popcorn party. Bring in a hot-air popper, unpopped popcorn, and a tea kettle and hot plate. Before beginning, give each student a popcorn kernel to examine. Ask: *Why do you think popcorn pops?* Discuss responses, then tell students you are going to give them a demonstration that will provide more information.

◎ Fill the kettle with water and bring it to a boil. Guide students to notice the steam escaping. Ask students to explain what is happening. (*As the water heats up it turns to steam, which rises out of the kettle.*)

◎ Explain that each popcorn kernel has a tiny bit of water hidden inside it. Ask: *Now that you see what happens when water is heated, can you guess why popcorn pops?* At this point many students will begin to understand that as the popcorn kernels are heated, the water expands as steam and literally pushes open the kernel and pops it.

◎ Now, you can finally make that popcorn and enjoy it with your new students! Share a popcorn poem, too! (See "Popcorn," right.)

### Popcorn

Pop, pop, popcorn,
popping in the pot!
Pop, pop, popcorn,
eat it while it's hot!
Pop, pop, popcorn,
butter on the top!
When I eat popcorn,
I can't stop!

—Helen H. Moore

# Teacher Share

MATH

## Knots on a Counting Rope

**K**eeping track of the number of days of school has to begin right away (especially if you want to celebrate that 100th day of school later on). Here's one fun and physical way to do it. Using a long piece of rope or clothesline (30 feet should be enough), tie a knot for each day of school. Let children paint every fifth knot yellow and every tenth knot red. Through this pattern, children can practice counting by ones, fives, and tens. The rope really helps children "take hold" of math skills and concepts, letting them see and touch patterns and relationships found in simple counting.

**Kathleen Lindsay**

## TIP

You can also use a class mascot as a story starter. Any time children are at a loss for a story idea (or just feel like a familiar topic), they can tell a story about the day from the mascot's point of view. Even simple events, such as watching a bird from a window, will take on new meaning when told from a fresh perspective.

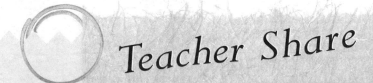

# Teacher Share

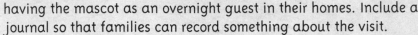

LANGUAGE ARTS, SOCIAL STUDIES

## A Friend for Everyone

On the first day of school, introduce the class to someone who will be everyone's friend—a class mascot, a stuffed animal of your choice. (Or, have children vote on a mascot.) Ask the class how they think their new friend feels on the first day of school. Let children take turns having the mascot as an overnight guest in their homes. Include a journal so that families can record something about the visit.

*Mary Sheffield*

ART

## Pop-Up Name Tags

Have students make unique name tags for their desks or cubbies. Give each student an 8 1/2- by 11-inch sheet of oaktag. Have children fold and cut it in half widthwise. On one half of the paper have students write their names with markers in large, colorful letters, adding detailing as they like. Have them decorate the second half of the oaktag, then fold it in thirds to form a prism-like base. Have students tape the flaps in place, then glue their name tag to one side. This becomes a portable and very visible name tag. Students can take them along to classes outside the classroom so other teachers (art, music, etc.) can quickly learn their names.

### Book Break

## Kindergarten Rocks!
by Katie Davis (Harcourt, 2005)

Dexter is just fine about the first day of school, but Rufus, his stuffed dog, "is an eensy teensy beensy bit scared"—about the bus, his teacher, lunch, and so on. Young children will enjoy the speech-bubble exchanges that follow Dexter through his day, and will feel reassured when they find out that this young boy's day is going so well, he forgets all about his stuffed animal friend.

ART

# Line Design

This quick but rewarding art project lets every child start the year with a successful experience. Give each student a sheet of white drawing paper and a black crayon. Have children place their crayons, ready to draw, at any spot on the paper. Explain that you will say "Begin" and count to five. As you count to five, tell children to move their crayons across the paper in any pattern they wish. The only rule—they may not lift the crayon during the entire five count. Model this for the class to see.

   After students create their own line drawings, guide them in noticing the spaces and shapes they created with one line. Have children make the spaces and shapes stand out by filling them in with crayons, paints, and markers. They can use solid colors, stripes, spots, zigzags, and so on. Display students' artwork for everyone to appreciate.

# Teacher Share

LANGUAGE ARTS, ART

## Quick as a Cricket

In *Quick as a Cricket* by Audrey Wood (Child's Play International, 1990), a young boy compares himself to different animals—for example, "I'm as happy as a lark." After reading the story, invite children to describe themselves in a similar way, comparing some trait or attribute an animal might have to one they find in themselves. Guide children by writing the prompt on the board: I'm as _____ as a(n) _____.
Give each student a sheet of 11- by 17-inch white drawing paper. Have students copy and complete the sentence and illustrate it. Bind pages together for the first collaborative book of the year—a book that tells something special about each child in your new class.

*Betsy Alexander*

Name _____  Date _____

# Mingo

| | | | |
|---|---|---|---|
| Flew on an airplane | Has a birthday this month | Watched fireworks | Read more than five books this summer |
| Made a new friend over the summer | Went to a birthday party this summer | Climbed a tree this summer | Played a board game this summer |
| Rode a bike this summer | Went to camp this summer | Wrote to a friend or relative this summer | Played a sport this summer |
| Tried a new food this summer | Went to an aquarium or museum this summer | Took a train somewhere this summer | Traveled out of the state this summer |

SOCIAL STUDIES

# Class Constitution

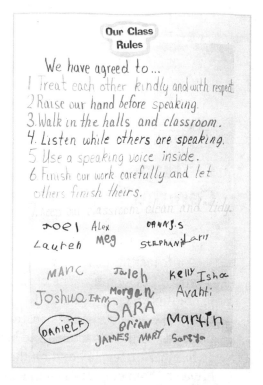

Every community has rules or laws. It pays big dividends down the line to establish your class rules for the new school year right from the first day. Begin by discussing with your class why rules are necessary. Talk about rules in the community such as laws against speeding, dogs running loose, and littering. Ask: *How are these rules helpful?*

Let students share reasons they think school is important. Guide them to recognize that one goal is to help each child grow as a learner. Ask: *What kinds of rules will help that happen?* List students' suggestions on the chalkboard or chart paper. Try to state these rules in a positive way. For example, if a student suggests "Don't yell" as a rule, work with the class to rephrase this along the lines of "Use a quiet, indoor voice."

Don't forget: As part of the class, you, too, have a voice in creating the rules. If you feel something important is not being addressed, chime in and get it on the chart. After the rules have been written up in rough draft form and reviewed, edit them together. Write a final copy of the rules on chart paper. Have students sign the chart, indicating that they helped develop the rules, understand the rules, and will do their best to follow them. Post the chart and refer to it as needed throughout the year.

SCIENCE, ART

# Recycling Robot

Juice boxes are very popular with kids. Use these to help the class start thinking about recycling in their community, and how they can help. Have students collect and rinse out juice boxes after their lunches or snacks. (Cut the juice box corners open to make rinsing them out easier.) Once you have about five boxes for each student, explain that these materials can now be used as "robo-bricks." Working together in groups, have students assemble the robo-bricks with masking tape to create a recycling robot. Then have them create a sign with a recycling message on it for their robot to hold. Students can change the message throughout the school year as they learn more about ways to reduce waste and protect their environment.

Even with class rules, conflicts happen between children in school as they do in any community. A simple conflict resolution process can be found in the revised edition of Naomi Drew's *Learning the Skills of Peacemaking: A K-6 Activity Guide to Resolving Conflicts, Communicating & Cooperating* (Jalmar Press, 1995). It includes the simple but effective win/win guidelines—for example, "Take time for cooling off if needed. Find alternative ways to express anger," and "Brainstorm solutions together and choose a solution that satisfies both—a win/win solution."

# Teacher Share

ART, SOCIAL STUDIES

## Classroom Community Wreath

This is a quick and easy art project that can help kids feel a sense of belonging—one of the keys to creating a class community. Give each child half a sheet of construction paper. Let students team up to help each other trace one hand on the paper. Have children cut out the hand shapes and write their names on them, making the letters as fancy as they like. Cut out a large, doughnut-shaped oaktag ring. Let children take turns gluing their hands to the oaktag ring to create a wreath. Remind them to make sure everyone's name shows. Display the wreath on the classroom door to welcome students to class.

*Kristin Kissell*

**TIP**

For more information on words with Hispanic origins, check *The Complete Teacher's Almanack: A Practical Guide to Every Day of the Year* by Dana Newman (The Center for Applied Research, 1991).

SOCIAL STUDIES

## A Community of Words

September is Hispanic Heritage month. To help students recognize Hispanic influence on our United States community, focus attention on some interesting words in our language that have Hispanic origins. Begin by sharing words such as *patio, canyon, bronco, taco, mosquito, burro, buffalo, breeze, tornado, siesta, key,* and *alligator.* Write these on a chart. Provide students with magazines, and ask them to see if they can find pictures to illustrate any of the words. Keep the chart up, and add to it throughout the month as students come up with more words of similar origin.

MATH

# How Old Is This Class?

Communities can be new or ancient or somewhere in between. Age can be reported in different ways. It is not unusual to find statements in advertising like this one: *We have more than one hundred years of combined experience.* Well, how many years of combined experience does your class community have?

◎ Give each child some multilink or Unifix cubes. Ask children to take the number of cubes that matches their age and connect these to form a rod or train.

◎ Bring children together. Let each child take a turn displaying his or her train while the rest of the group figures out how old that child is by counting the cubes.

◎ When everyone has taken a turn, ask: *If we were to add up all the years of the ages in the class, what would the total age of the class be?* Take estimates first, then guide students in connecting the individual trains into one giant class train. This represents the total age of the class, but it is tough to count. Ask the class for good counting strategies, and use ideas such as breaking up the giant train into fives or tens to count more efficiently and find out "how many years old this class really is."

SOCIAL STUDIES, SCIENCE

# Your Community in the Future

Have students describe their community—for example, sharing information about transportation, services, housing, recreation, shopping, and so on. Help them recognize the parts of their community that provide basic needs (shelter, food, etc.). Ask them to consider how science plays a part in providing for these needs and wants. For example, discuss electricity, water power, heat sources, use of computers. Then, start students thinking about the future. Ask: *How do you think the things we talked about may change in 20 years?* Have them focus particularly on how science will help initiate this change. Have students draw a picture or map of what they envision their community of the future will look like. This can also be an excellent story starter, although the results might sound a little like science fiction!

Use the easy-to-make mini-books in *20 Manipulative Mini-Books* by Kathleen M. Hollenbeck (Scholastic, 2004) to explore homes, transportation, jobs, goods and services, natural resources, and more. The mini-books provide great nonfiction reading practice and offer a variety of formats (including lift-the-flap, turn-the-wheel, and slide-a-story strips) to keep readers engaged.

For more on building community, check these titles:

◎ *Build a Caring Classroom Kit* (Scholastic, 2009). This kit features six picture books and lessons to help foster sharing, kindness, cooperation, and classroom community.

◎ *Conflict Resolution Activities That Work!* by Kathleen M. Hollenbeck (Scholastic Professional Books, 2000). Students participate in reading, writing, and role-playing activities to create a positive classroom environment.

## *Teacher Share*

MATH, SOCIAL STUDIES

## Meet-Your-Shape Match

**H**ere's a quick way to help your students get to know one another and practice some geometry at the same time.

◎ Prepare different colored cutouts of the shapes you want students to learn about or review in your geometry study this year.

◎ Cut these in half. Make enough so that each student will get one half of a shape.

◎ As students enter the classroom on the first or second day of school, hand each one half of a shape. Let children find their matches and spend time talking to find other ways they are alike.

*Jackie Clarke*

## Teacher Share

### SOCIAL STUDIES, LANGUAGE ARTS, TECHNOLOGY

## E-Mail the Mayor!

When learning about community helpers, students may come up with some specific questions or comments about the jobs that mayors, police officers, firefighters, judges, and others do. These folks can't always come in, and it is difficult to arrange field trips to see them all, so head for the computer and send e-mail. Your students will learn more about their community helpers and the communication capabilities of e-mail.

◎ Start by obtaining the e-mail addresses of community helpers. You may find this information on your town's or city's Web site or by calling the various offices.

◎ Compose group letters to find out more about community helpers. Copy the letters into e-mail messages and send.

◎ Share responses with the class as they come in, then place them in a binder so that children can revisit them on their own.

*Ruth Melendez*

**TIP**

Your students can compose e-mails offline, then copy and paste the letters into the e-mail messages. This saves time online and, depending on your Internet account, may save money.

---

### Book Break

## Miss Rumphius

by Barbara Cooney (Viking, 1982)

Share this gem of a book to inspire a class discussion about the many ways people can help make their community a better place to live. What's Miss Rumphius's way of helping? She beautifies the landscape with the red and purple flowers she plants. For another look at how communities come together, share *And to Think That We Thought That We'd Never Be Friends* by Mary Ann Hoberman (Crown, 1999), a colorful, cumulative rhyming story that tells a lively tale of how one community came together.

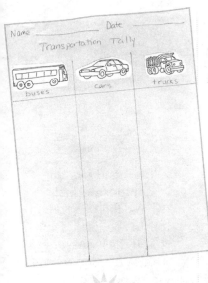

## TIP

As a variation, have students keep track of cars by color. Make a new record sheet with pictures of different colored cars across the top. Let children make tally marks for each color car they see.

MATH, SOCIAL STUDIES

# Transportation Tally

Invite students to watch buses, cars, and trucks go by to learn about using tally marks to record data. Start by showing students how to use tally marks to keep track of something—or count something—by dropping pennies into a can. For each penny you drop in, make a tally mark on the chalkboard. Have students do the same on paper. When you get to the fifth penny, show students how to cross the bundle to form a group of five. Circle two bundles to show a group of ten.

After a little practice like this, give each student a Transportation Tally record sheet. (See sample, left.) Ask: *What do you think we're going to keep track of with this record sheet?* (how many buses, cars, and trucks go by outside) Bring students to an outside area where they can safely observe local traffic. Have students keep tallies of what goes by for five or ten minutes. Depending on the amount of traffic in your area, you may have each student keep track of all three forms of transportation, or you may assign some students to keep track of buses, others cars, and others trucks. When you return to the classroom, let students report and compare data. Extend the activity by graphing data.

MUSIC, LANGUAGE ARTS

# Wheels on the Bus

"Wheels on the Bus" is a great song to sing early in the year. Most students are familiar with it and enjoy its swinging cadence and opportunities for hand motions and noisemaking. *Raffi Songs to Read: Wheels on the Bus* (Crown, 1988) is a very appealing book version. The final page of this attractively illustrated book has all the verses and the music. A little different is Maryann Kovalski's *The Wheels on the Bus* (Little, Brown, 1987), which surrounds the song with a story about a grandmother taking her two grandchildren shopping. While they wait for their bus they sing about it.

Since there are so many versions out there already, could one more hurt? Certainly not! Sing the original version with your students.

> The wheels on the bus go round and round,
> Round and round, round and round.
> The wheels on the bus go round and round,
> All around the town.

Repeat the verse for wipers ("swish, swish, swish"), driver ("Move on back"), people ("up and down"), and horn ("beep, beep, beep").

Then invite children to think up new verses. Kids will enjoy singing their new song as much as the original.

MATH

# Main Street Math Story Mat

Math story mats are a fun way for students to practice math skills and concepts with manipulatives in an engaging story context. Use the reproducible story mat and patterns (see pages 29–30) to let children "act out" the math activity below.

◎ Give each child two copies of the story mat. Have children tape the story mats end to end to make one long street. Ask them to draw a traffic light at one end. Have children cut out and color the pattern pieces (buses, taxis, cars, trucks).

◎ Have children listen as you read "A Busy Morning on Main Street" aloud. (See below.) Reread the story, this time having children use the transportation patterns to act out the story as it unfolds. Repeat the process with the second story, "Red Light!"

## A Busy Morning on Main Street
It is a very busy morning on Main Street. There are three buses taking children to school. People are going to work, too. There are four cars and two taxis. Trucks are starting to make deliveries. There are five trucks. How many buses, cars, taxis, and trucks are on Main Street all together? All the taxis have driven away. How many vehicles are left on Main Street?

## Red Light!
The light has turned red on Main Street. The traffic is stopping. A bus pulls up to the light. A truck is right behind it. Here come two taxis behind the truck. There are two cars behind the taxis. How many vehicles are stopped at the red light? Which is first in line at the light? Which is second? Which is third? Which is fourth? Which is fifth? Which is sixth?

SCIENCE

# A Boat Can Float

Bring in a small plastic tub or, for even more excitement, a kiddie pool. Fill it halfway with water. Assemble a variety of commonly found materials, such as sponges, pieces of wood, foam containers, crayons, and so on. Have students predict which objects will float and which will not, then test them. Keep a chart and record which float and which do not. Invite students to work with partners to create boats that will float. Allow time for them to decorate their boats and give them a try.

### TIP
After students have successfully answered the questions in each story, invite them to team up for a new story mat activity. Have one child tell a new story while his or her partner uses the patterns to act it out on the story mat—for example, one child might rearrange the vehicles to form a new order at the red light, and use ordinal words (*first, second, third,* etc.) to tell about the new line. Have children switch places so that each child makes up and acts out a story.

MATH

# The Money Boat

Bring out that tub or kiddie pool, and once again fill it about halfway with water. Give students a set of coins. (For example, if you are teaching the value of pennies, nickels, and dimes, provide those coins.) Mark off a tape line on the floor about four feet from the pool. Float an empty margarine tub in the pool. This is the target "money boat." Have students use an underhand toss to try to get their coins into the tub. Whatever lands in the tub, they count up and record as their score. Children can play on teams, with each team trying to get the highest score. Or, play cooperatively as a class. Have each child add up his or her total, then have students work together to find the total class score.

### Book Break

# Tooth-Gnasher Superflash
## by Daniel Pinkwater (Dutton, 1977)

There are cars, and then there are CARS! When the Popsnorkle family goes shopping for a new car and takes a test drive in the Tooth-Gnasher Superflash, they try out all of its special features, to the delight of young readers. This, after all, is a car that can fly, hop, and turn into a dinosaur!

SOCIAL STUDIES, LANGUAGE ARTS

# Signs and Symbols Share

Most children recognize popular fast-food restaurant signs and stop signs. In fact, much of a child's earliest language experience is with signs and symbols, including those designed to regulate transportation. (*stop sign, yield sign, deer crossing*) Give students a weeklong homework assignment. Ask them to look around as they go places, and to record as many signs and symbols as they can. Have them report back on Friday and share what they found. Discuss why some road signs do not have words. (*It's easier and quicker to understand an image than words.*) Talk about why other signs do. (*It's hard to convey every idea with just a picture.*)

MUSIC

# Song of the Train

"Song of the Train," is a great poem for class involvement. Give each child a copy of the poem. (See page 28.) As you read the poem with the class, practice increasing the speed with each verse so that the train is just starting out in the first verse, picking up speed in the second, and moving along quickly in the third. Add noises and motions, and you'll soon think there is a real train in the room!

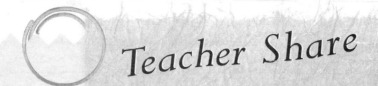

## Teacher Share

MATH

## How Did They Get There?

Provide students with round counters, such as pennies, and some counters of a different shape, such as counting bears. Then pose this question: *Twelve children went to school. They used nine wheels. How did they get there?* Let students use the manipulatives—pennies for wheels and counting bears for people—to find solutions. This is a very open-ended challenge with lots of possible solutions—for example, *four students went in a car with four wheels, seven went in a bus with four wheels, and one rode a unicycle.*

*Wendy Weiner*

### Book Break

## Freight Train

by Donald Crews (Greenwillow, 1978)

This Caldecott Honor book is a favorite with young children. After sharing the story, discuss differences between freight trains and passenger trains. Ask: *What kinds of things do you think a freight train might carry?*

MATH, ART

## Transportation Shape Search

Cut out a variety of basic shapes (circles, triangles, squares, rectangles, trapezoids) in different colors. Let students explore these as you discuss their distinctive features. Next, take a look at pictures of trains, buses, and planes from magazines or books. Ask the class to look carefully and see if they can recognize any of the basic shapes in these objects. Give each child a sheet of 11- by 17-inch white construction paper and a variety of precut shapes or shape templates and colored paper. Ask children to create pictures of a type of transportation, cutting shapes from the colored paper and gluing them on the white paper. They may create pictures of familiar forms of transportation or invent a new way for people and things to get from one place to another!

Name _____  Date _____

# Song of the Train

Clickety-clack,
Wheels on the track,
This is the way
They begin the attack:
Click-ety-clack,
Click-ety-clack,
Click-ety, *clack-ety,*
Click-ety
Clack.

Clickety-clack,
Over the crack,
Faster and faster
The song of the track:
Clickety-clack,
Clickety-clack,
Clickety, clackety,
*Clackety*
Clack.

Riding in front,
Riding in back,
*Everyone* hears
The song of the track:
Clickety-clack,
Clickety-clack,
Clickety, *clickety,*
Clackety
Clack.

—David McCord

## Try This!

Say the words in the poem that start with the letters *cl*. List more words that start with the same letters. We did one for you!

**clown**

Say the words in the poem that end in the letters *-ack*. Write more words that end in the same letters. We did one for you.

**quack**

*500+ Fabulous Month-by-Month Teaching Ideas* © 2010 Scholastic Teaching Resources

# Main Street Math Story Mat

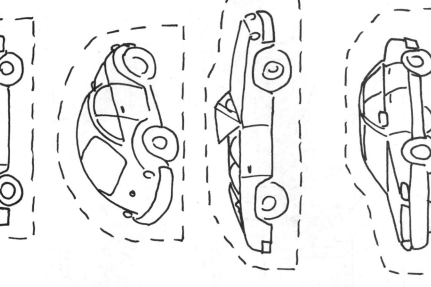

Main Street Math Story Mat
Patterns

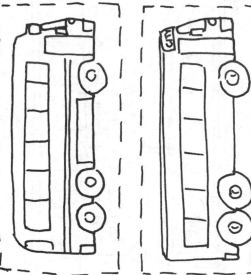

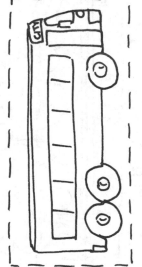

SCIENCE

# Apple Sprouts

Students can observe the beginning stages of an apple tree's growth with this activity. Give each child a few apple seeds, a resealable plastic bag, and a paper towel. Guide them in following these steps.

◎ Moisten the paper towel with water. Fold the paper towel in half and place it inside the plastic bag.

◎ Place the apple seeds inside the bag on top of the paper towel. Close the bag partway, leaving an opening so that air can circulate inside.

◎ Place the bags in a refrigerator for six weeks.

◎ Bring out the bags, and spritz the paper towels with water to keep them moist but not soggy.

◎ As seeds begin to germinate, tiny roots and little shoots will appear.

◎ Plant the sprouts one inch deep in paper cups filled with potting soil. Keep in a sunny spot. Cover the cups loosely with plastic wrap to retain moisture and help seedlings survive over weekends.

**TIP**

This activity was adapted from *Early Themes: Apples, Pumpkins, and Harvest* by Ann Flagg (Scholastic, 1999). This book includes reproducibles, poetry, hands-on math and science activities, learning centers, a poster, and much more.

SCIENCE, MATH

# Apple-Snack Science

Let children explore one of the ways people preserve food by drying apples. They'll discover the science of evaporation and strengthen math skills at the same time.

◎ Peel apples and slice them into rings. Ask children to predict how much the apples weigh. Record estimates, then weigh the apples.

◎ Have children team up to string apples. Give each team a length of string and some apple rings. Have children string the apples, then predict how much the apples will weigh after they dry.

◎ Clip the strings of apples to a clothesline strung up in the classroom. Cover with cheesecloth to protect the apples from dust.

◎ Ask students what they think will happen to the apples. (*They'll shrink and wrinkle as water evaporates.*) Let them record changes they observe.

◎ Weigh the dried apples. Compare with the weight of the apples before they dried. Ask students to tell what they think caused the change in weight. (*loss of water*) Let children enjoy their apple snack!

Check for food allergies before serving the apple snacks.

# Rain Makes Applesauce

by Julian Scheer (Holiday House, 1964)

"The stars are made of lemon juice and rain makes applesauce. I wear my shoes inside out and rain makes applesauce." And so goes the Caldecott Honor book, *Rain Makes Applesauce*, a bouncy rhyme combining fanciful illustrations with child-inspired nonsense sentences. Each silly phrase ends with the refrain, "and rain makes applesauce." Children will enjoy this as a read aloud, read along, poem, story, or song. They will love finishing each stanza with a hearty, giggling, "And rain makes applesauce!"

**TIP**

Be sure to check for food allergies before serving the snack.

### SCIENCE

## No-Cook Applesauce

Mix up this no-cook snack with your students to reinforce predicting, measuring, and other skills.

◎ Gather the following ingredients: one apple and two teaspoons of honey for every two students; cinnamon.

◎ Peel and core the apples. Cut them into quarters and chop into small chunks.

◎ Place the apple chunks in a blender and mix. Add the honey and mix until smooth.

◎ Pour into serving dishes (small paper cups work well) and sprinkle with cinnamon.

As you mix up the applesauce, ask questions to guide a discussion—for example, *Why do you think we cut the apples into chunks? How do you think the applesauce will change when we add the honey? How many cups of applesauce do you think one apple will make? Ten apples?*

### MATH

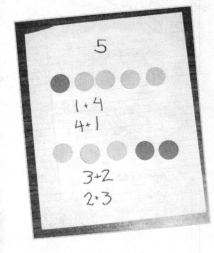

## Apple Fact Families

Provide each student with two-color counters and a sheet of white paper. (Counters that are red on one side and yellow on the other are best for this activity.) Tell students they will use these counters to represent red and yellow apples. Have students construct sets of apples on their paper for a given target number. For example, if the target number is 8, students might show 6 yellow and 2 red. Have them write an equation underneath for each of the sets they create. Challenge them to create as many sets and equations as possible for each target number.

SCIENCE, SOCIAL STUDIES

## Apple Facts Tree

Can you remember the first apple you ever saw? Not likely. We grow up with apples everywhere and never think much about them. Learn more about this favorite fruit with a mini research project.

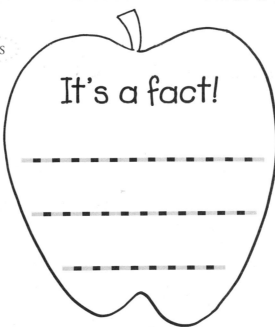

It's a fact!

Apple Fact pattern

◎ Gather resources on apples. (See Tip.)

◎ Enlarge and copy the "Apple Fact" pattern above. Have children write one fact on each apple.

◎ Prepare a simple tree with branches on the bulletin board and have children add their apples to the tree. Add a title, such as "Pick a fact about apples."

MATH

## How Many Apples Does That Weigh?

Your class can explore how to use a balance scale, and the idea of standard measure, by using apples. Use a pan balance and a bag of apples from the store. (Smaller apples work best.) Put a book

**TIP**

Explore nonfiction and learn more about apples with these titles.

◎ *Apples* by Gail Gibbons (Holiday House, 2000). Simple text and bright, appealing illustrations explore the history of apples and how they grow. Illustrates and identifies different varieties and provides fun facts.

◎ *Apples* by Inez Snyder (Children's Press, 2004). A cover bursting with bright green apples invites readers inside to learn about how apples grow. A table of contents and index offer opportunities to teach features of nonfiction.

in one side of the balance. Ask the class to estimate how many apples they think the book weighs. Test it to see. Weigh other items from around the room in terms of apples. Always have students estimate an answer first. To explore further, use a pound weight to find out how many apples are in a pound. Finally, have students estimate how many apples they think *they* weigh. (You can find out by weighing a pound of apples, and then multiplying the number of apples in a pound by the number of pounds the student actually weighs.)

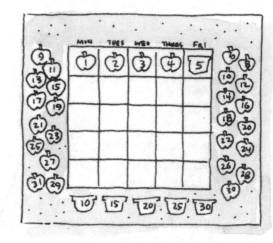

MATH

# Apples in a Basket

Apple cutouts and a simple calendar are great tools for teaching skip counting and patterning as part of your daily calendar activities.

◎ Staple a large blank calendar to your bulletin board. Write the odd numbers from 1 to 29 on red cut-out apples and the even numbers from 2 to 30 on green apples. Write the multiples of 5 (*5, 10, 15, 20, 25, 30*) on six bushel-basket cutouts. All of the cutouts should fit inside a calendar square.

◎ Each day, ask a student to place the appropriate odd or even apple on the calendar date. Every fifth day, have a student place an apple basket on top of, but not completely covering, the apple for that day. Ask: *How many apples do you think a basket represents?* Explain that each basket represents a multiple of five. Students can also skip count by twos using the green apples.

SCIENCE, LANGUAGE ARTS

# Apple Observation

Good observation skills are necessary for any scientist. Help students develop this skill with this apple activity.

◎ Give each child an apple to examine and then draw. Remind students to really look at the apple and to draw what they see, not just what they think an apple might look like.

◎ Ask students to draw five lines leading out from the apple to make an observation web. At the end of each line, have them write the words *hearing, touch, smell, sight,* and *taste.* Invite students to use their senses to explore the apple in greater detail, writing words at the end of each line that describe how the apple sounds, feels, smells, looks, and tastes.

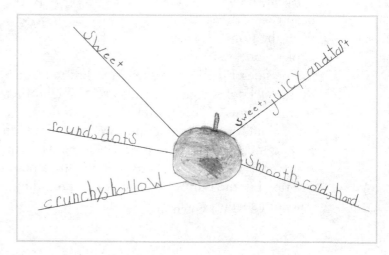

Book Break

# Cider Apples

### by Sandy Nightingale (Harcourt, 1996)

*Cider Apples* is a charming story of how young Holly helps save her grandparents' apple orchard on a magical New Year's Eve. Beautiful illustrations and a happy ending make for a great apple-inspired read aloud. You may want to bring in some apple cider for students to enjoy as they listen.

LANGUAGE ARTS, ART

# "All About Apples" Collaborative Banner

Use a little apple knowledge and the awesome imaginations of young children to create this collaborative banner.

◉ Give each student a copy of the banner template on page 36. Read the sentence frame aloud: *What can you do with an apple? You can _____ .*

◉ Brainstorm possible answers together, then have students complete the sentence. The blank space is purposefully large to give children room for any idea they might have—whether it's "make applesauce" or "put an engine in it and fly to the moon."

◉ Have students illustrate their pages, then arrange them in banner formation. Glue banner pages to a long strip of craft paper and display!

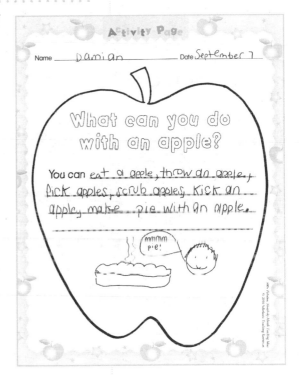

**Book Break**

# Johnny Appleseed: The Legend and the Truth

### by Jane Yolen (HarperCollins, 2008)

Richly textured pages share the history and facts behind the legend of John Chapman, also known as Johnny Appleseed.

**TIP**

Check for food allergies before serving apple cider.

Name _____     Date _____

# What can you do with an apple?

You can _____

_____

_____

_____

# October

# October
## Teaching Ideas

*O*ctober is a month that is rich with special topics. Plus, it's a month when K–2 children have settled into the classroom routine, and learning really begins to stick!

These activities will help you plan lessons that take advantage of children's enthusiasm for topics unique to October. They will support your curriculum while filling your classroom with the feel of October and a new season.

There are four October topics: FALL, EXPLORERS, FIRE SAFETY, and HALLOWEEN. Each topic is filled with activities that connect every corner of your curriculum—from reading and writing to science, movement, and art. Many of the activities naturally integrate several disciplines. For example, "Leaf Lineup" combines science and math as children sort leaves by shapes, sizes, and colors. (See page 42.) "Firefighter Relay" combines social studies and physical fitness as children explore the history of fire safety and simulate an old-fashioned firefighting technique. (See page 58.) Other special features in October include:

- a reproducible send-home activity calendar
- computer connections
- hands-on math and science activities
- literature connections
- collaborative bookmaking projects
- an easy-to-learn "piggyback" song
- ready-to-use reproducible activity pages
- a mini-book to make
- a no-cook recipe to make and enjoy
- a reproducible mini play
- and many more October treats!

Name _____

# October Activity Calendar

Choose _____ activities to do each week this month.
Ask an adult in your family to initial the square in the box of each activity
you complete. Bring this paper back to school on _____ .

| Monday | Tuesday | Wednesday | Thursday | Friday |
|---|---|---|---|---|
| Write the word *October* on a sheet of paper. Cut apart the letters. Make new words! **be** **Boo!** **too** | Talk with an adult in your family about fire safety. Check your smoke detectors together! | Make a map of your fire escape route at home. Practice it! | Look at a calendar. Name the special days people celebrate this month. | Say the word *Halloween.* Take turns with a family member saying words that start with the same sound. |
| Author Donald Sobol was born on October 4. What famous mystery books did he write? | Think of something mysterious that happened in your family. Tell a story about it! | Draw a picture of your lunch today. Write a sentence about what makes a healthy lunch. | Take a survey: What is each family member's favorite lunch? | Look at a lunch food label. Tell something you can learn from the label. |
| How many letters in the word *October?* Which months have more letters? fewer? the same? | Say the word *cat.* Say the word *bat.* List five new words that rhyme. | Tell someone in your family a story about something that happened to you this week. Trade places! | Look at this pumpkin. Find a matching pumpkin on this page. | Look at the words on this calendar. Can you find three that rhyme with *hat?* |
| Ask someone to help you look up the word *explorer* in a dictionary. How are you an explorer? | Draw a picture of a pumpkin. Give your pumpkin a face that shows how you feel today. | Ask someone to shine a light on a wall. Put your hand halfway between the light and the wall. What happens? | Use a flashlight to make shadow pictures on a wall. Tell a story about your shadows. | Turn *October* into a tongue twister! Make up a sentence using as many words as you can that start with *o.* |

# Teacher Share

Fall for
a Good Book
Name Ethan          Date October 5
I fell for the book
my mother the cat
I like this book because
it was funny and
silly
I give this book a   4   leaf rating.
Color in from one to five leaves to show
your rating. (Five is the highest)

### LANGUAGE ARTS

## Fall for a Good Book

**K**ick off your fall theme, and integrate language arts at the same time, with an activity that celebrates reading.

◎ Create a large tree using brown bulletin board paper to make a trunk and branches. Display the tree in your reading corner.

◎ Give students copies of page 45. Have them complete the book review form for books they read, then color the leaves in fall colors, cut them out, and staple them to the tree, in the "air," and on the ground.

**Cheryll Black**

### TIP

When you run out of room on the tree display, "rake the leaves" to get ready for a whole new set of leafy reviews!

### MUSIC, MOVEMENT

## Leaf Song

Teach your students this fun fall song based on the familiar tune, "Twinkle, Twinkle, Little Star."

> Crinkle, crinkle, colored leaves
> Falling, falling from the trees
> Red and yellow
> Orange and brown
> Falling, falling to the ground
> Crinkle, crinkle, colored leaves
> Falling, falling from the trees.

Incorporate dramatic play by having students cut red, yellow, orange, and brown leaves out of construction paper. As they sing the song, have them hold up the leaves as their colors are named in the song, crinkling the paper to create sound effects. Students can let the leaves fall to the ground at the end of the song.

### TIP

As a variation, graph the leaves by color, shape, and size. Ask questions to guide a discussion of the data:

⊚ Which colors are least and most common?

⊚ Which shapes are least and most common?

⊚ Are most leaves small, medium, or large in size?

# Teacher Share

MATH, SCIENCE

## Leaf Lineup

Turn students into super sorters with this activity. Gather children together around a basket of leaves. Choose a handful of leaves and place them in one of two lineups by color or size. (The size lineup can feature leaves of different colors but the same size. The color lineup should have leaves of different types but the same color.) Ask children what the leaves in each lineup have in common. (*same size or same color*) Let children take turns choosing leaves from the basket to place in one of the lineups.

**Kathleen Cronin**

LANGUAGE ARTS

## Fall Word Wall

You can teach phonics, spelling, and conventions of language in one activity. Invite students to make a classroom word wall with favorite fall words. Start by letting students suggest words they associate with *fall*. Record these on a chart. Use the words from the list to start word walls and teach mini-lessons. For example, the word *leaf*

changes to *leaves* when you make it plural. Make a list of other words whose endings change when you make them plural. Use the word *tree* to teach the phonogram *-ee* (*see, three, bee*). Use the word *fall* to explore words with multiple meanings. Name color words. Your list will grow week by week. See what other great teaching opportunities "fall" out of your word wall activities.

# Why Do Leaves Change Colors?

by Betsy Maestro (HarperCollins, 1994)

"Look at the leaves! It's autumn, and leaves are turning red and yellow, gold and brown." Diagrams and beautiful illustrations help answer the title's question!

## Teacher Share

LANGUAGE ARTS

### Meet My Leaf

Strengthen observation skills and descriptive writing with an activity that lets students "make friends" with a fall leaf.

- Have students bring in one fall leaf from home. (Or go on a leaf hunt at school.)

- Ask students to study their leaves, looking for details such as color, shape, size, number of points, and any other distinguishing details.

- Encourage students to look for interesting details—for example, *looks like a heart.*

- Give each child a copy of the "Meet My Leaf" activity sheet. (See page 46.) Have them complete the information, then glue their leaves in the oval space (adding googly eyes, if available).

*Barbara Gauker*

Activity Page

Name Sasha          Date _____

Meet My Leaf

Name red maple
Color(s) green and Brown
Shape half star
Size medium
Number of points 12 points
Other details it has a lot of veins

**TIP**

Challenge the whole class! Before gluing their leaves to the paper, invite students to put all of their leaves in a pile. Let students try to match leaves to the descriptions.

## I Am a Leaf

(Hello Reader, Science)

by Jean Marzollo (Cartwheel, 1999)

"Now fall has come. My work is over. My green goes away…Red! Yellow! Orange!" Follow the life cycle of a leaf through summer, fall, winter, and spring in this cyclical story. Vibrant, collage-style illustrations and an easy-to-read format make this book a perfect choice for young children.

## Computer Connection

View spectacular photos of fall foliage, and learn facts about fall leaves, at these Web sites:

The Miracle of Fall (The University of Illinois Extension): www.urbanext. uiuc.edu/fall color/index.html

Vermont Fall Foliage: www.vermontfall foliage.com

State of Maine's Official Fall Foliage Site: www.state.me.us/ doc/foliage/

# Teacher Share

### MATH

## Leave It to Math

Cut out yellow, red, brown, and orange leaves (use almond-shaped pieces of construction paper about two inches long). Have each student draw a picture of a leafless tree on white paper. Put students into groups of two or three. Give each group one pile of 30–40 construction-paper leaves. Have students in each group take turns rolling a die. They count out the number of leaves indicated on the die and glue them on their tree. The game is over when there are no leaves left in the pile. The winner is the person who has the tree with the most leaves. (For a change, play to have the fewest leaves on the tree.) After the game, have students decorate the background of their trees. Make a fall display!

*Natalie Vaughn*

### Book Break

## Autumn Across America

(Seasons Across America)
by Seymour Simon (Hyperion, 1993)

*Is fall the same all across America?* Ask this question before sharing this book with your students. Seymour Simon does a great job of explaining the different ways that fall looks and feels in different parts of America. After reading, discuss how fall looks and feels in your region and compare it to other parts of America.

### ART

## Leaf Print Paintings

Have students make leaf printings by covering the top sides of real leaves with orange, yellow, or red paint. Have them gently press each leaf on white construction paper, then paint favorite fall activities to complete the pictures.

# Fall for a Good Book

Name _____ Date _____

I fell for the book

_____

I like this book because

_____

_____

I give this book a _____ leaf rating.

Color in from one to five leaves to show
your rating. (Five is the highest.)

Name _____ Date _____

# Meet My Leaf

*500+ Fabulous Month-by-Month Teaching Ideas* © 2010 Scholastic Teaching Resources

Name _____

Color(s) _____

Shape _____

Size _____

Number of points _____

Other details _____

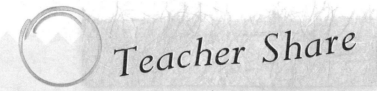

MATH, SOCIAL STUDIES

## Little, Medium, Big

Christopher Columbus sailed on three ships—the Niña, the Pinta, and the Santa Maria. Use this information to practice the concept of size. Precut six squares for each student in the following sizes and colors: 2 by 2 inches (white); 3 by 3 inches (white); 4 by 4 inches (white); 3 by 3 inches (yellow); 4 by 4 inches (orange); 5 by 5 inches (brown). Have students follow these directions to turn the paper into sailboats.

◎ Fold the yellow, orange, and brown squares diagonally to make triangles. Tuck the top part of each triangle under to make it look like the bottom of a ship.

◎ Fold each white square once diagonally to make a triangular sail.

◎ Have students attach the small sail to the small boat, the medium sail to the medium boat, and the large sail to the large boat. (They can tape the sails to toothpicks, then to the boats.)

◎ Let students write the names on their boats (*Niña, Pinta, Santa Maria*) and arrange them in size order.

**Bonnie Webster**

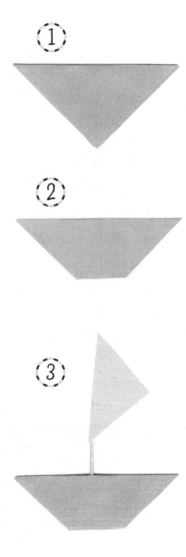

SCIENCE

## Sink or Float Boats

Explore the concepts of sinking and floating (*buoyancy*) with this hands-on activity. Remind students that Columbus sailed to the New World with three ships, the *Niña, Pinta,* and *Santa Maria.* Ask students if they think these ships were well built. Invite students to build their own mini-ships out of clay or aluminum foil. Explain that they will test the strength of their boats by floating them in water and adding marbles one at a time until the boat sinks. Ask students to predict how many marbles it will take to sink their boats. Fill a tub with water and let students take turns testing their predictions. Discuss how the shape of their boats affected how well their ships performed.

SCIENCE, MATH

## Make a Speedy Sailboat

Invite students to explore the ways things move by making three boats with different-shaped sails. Give students clay, toothpicks, construction paper, and tape. Have them pair up to make three mini-ships, each with a different-shaped sail: triangular, square, and rectangular. (Tape the sails to the toothpicks.) Have children take turns launching their ships in a tub of water. *What happens when they blow on the ships? Which sail works best?*

## Book Break

## Picture Book of Christopher Columbus

(Picture Book Biography)
by David A. Adler (Holiday House, 1992)

Children will learn about Columbus's journey through life and to the New World. The last page lists important dates and events.

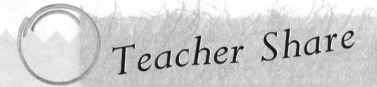

# Teacher Share

SCIENCE, SOCIAL STUDIES

## Moving in the Right Direction

**S**trengthen map skills with this activity. Show students a compass rose. (Most globes have one printed on the surface.) Discuss how a compass rose works, and point out directions (north, east, south, west, northeast, and so on). Invite students to use a globe to tell the directions that Columbus sailed on his way to the New World and back to Spain. (*southwest, then west, on his way to the New World; northeast, then east, on his way back*) Next, discuss where Columbus was planning to sail. (*Asia*) Which direction *should* he have sailed?

*Ronnie Yankovich*

LANGUAGE ARTS, SCIENCE

# "Let's Go Exploring!" Mini-Play

Explore rhyming words and give children a chance to express their dramatic flair with the mini play on page 53. Copy the play on chart paper. Read it through with children, then invite them to find three words that rhyme and belong in the same word family (*kings, rings, things*). Let children name other words that fit in the same word family (*-ing*). Give each child a copy of the play and assign parts. Let children rehearse, then perform their play for an audience. Repeat the play several times so that children can play different parts.

SOCIAL STUDIES

# Lost and Found

Many explorers got lost on their way to discovering new places. Discuss with students how using coordinates on a map helps people find locations. Demonstrate how to use coordinates on a map, then let children take turns using coordinates to identify a location. Have the rest of the class use the coordinates to find and name the place. Give students copies of the game board on page 54. Have students cut out the ships and secretly place them on different coordinates on the grid. Pair up students and have them sit opposite their partners with a folder blocking each other's grid. Have them take turns calling out coordinates (such as A, 3) to try to locate their partner's ships. Students play until one child's ships have all been found.

| Book Break |
| --- |

# Encounter

## by Jane Yolen (Harcourt, 1992)

Use this book to introduce the concept of seeing Columbus landing in the New World through the eyes of the natives. This book has an excellent afterword that will help you discuss the controversial side of Columbus's landing in the New World. As a challenge, invite students to write a journal entry as if they were a native seeing Columbus's ships.

**TIP**

When using your class compass, make sure there is no metal nearby. (Does the table you are working on have metal in or under it?) Also make sure the magnet you used to magnetize the needle is at least two feet away from the bowl.

# Teacher Share

SCIENCE, SOCIAL STUDIES

## Making a Compass

Ask students to point their pencils to the north wall of your classroom. You will probably get pencils pointing in four different directions! Explain that one instrument aviator Amelia Earhart used to help her find her way was a *compass*. Inform students that a compass is an instrument with a magnetized needle that points north. Explain that by knowing where north is, an explorer can use a compass to find other directions. Follow these steps to make a class compass. You will need a sewing needle, bar magnet, bowl of water, and small piece of paper.

◉ Stroke the "eye" end of a needle across the magnet 50 times, going in the same direction each time. (For counting practice, have students count for you.)

◉ Fill a bowl with water. Place the piece of paper on the water. Set the needle on top of the paper, and gently move the paper to cause it to spin slightly. If the paper gets stuck to the side of the bowl, gently nudge it toward the center again.

◉ Explain that when the needle and paper have completely stopped moving, the sharp end of the needle will be pointing north. You can prove this compass is really pointing north by setting a manufactured compass nearby. (Don't set the two compasses too close to each other because they will interfere with each other.) Compare your findings with students' earlier predictions about which way was north.

*Bob Krech*

## Book Break

# Follow the Dream: The Story of Christopher Columbus
by Peter Sis (Knopf, 2003)

A *New York Times* Best Illustrated Children's Book award-winner, this easy-to-read picture book biography tells the story of Christopher Columbus. Use the illustration of Columbus's September voyage log to inspire students' own explorer logs. (See Explorer Calendar Journals, page 51.)

MATH

# Message in a Bottle

Create a learning center where students can explore problem solving. Use ten small plastic milk bottles or any small plastic containers. Label each bottle with a number. Tuck a small piece of paper with a math problem inside each bottle. Fill a tub or basin with water and float your math message bottles inside. Have students pull out a bottle and solve the problem inside. Provide a key for self-checking.

*Teacher Share*

LANGUAGE ARTS

## Explorer's Backpack Alphabet Game

**P**ractice alphabet skills with a variation on a familiar game.

- Have students form a circle. Teach them the sentence, "I'm going exploring, and I'm going to bring a _____."

- Have the first student repeat the sentence and complete the blanks, by filling in a word that starts with the letter *a*—such as *apple*.

- Let the next child repeat what the first child said, and then name something that begins with a *b* for example, *I'm going exploring, and I'm going to bring an apple and binoculars.* Repeat this pattern all around the circle. Record responses to make a class alphabet book.

*Jackie Clarke*

MATH, LANGUAGE ARTS

## Explorer Calendar Journals

Discuss the reasons explorers kept logs. (See Book Break, page 50.) Invite students to keep their own explorer log, using the reproducible on page 55. Discuss possible entries with students (weather, new foods they've tried, something interesting they did, etc.). Set aside time each day for students to record an entry. This size journal is a fun change from the usual notebook-size format. Students can record an entry with just a sentence or two, making this a great writing activity for even your most reluctant writers.

LANGUAGE ARTS

# Discover a Friend

Discuss how explorers are like reporters. (*They ask questions to discover information.*) Have your students discover a friend with this activity. Divide your class into two groups. Students in one group are "explorers" and the others are the "discoveries." Place identical stickers on pairs of index cards. Give half the index cards to the explorers and the matching halves to the discoveries. When students find their matches, have the explorers ask the discoveries questions to learn more about them—for example, they may ask about favorite foods, books, and so on. Have students switch places and repeat the activity.

## Book Break

# DK First Atlas
DK First Reference Series
(DK Children, 2004)

Detailed and colorful maps help young readers explore their world and make sense of geographic concepts.

LANGUAGE ARTS

# Exploring Bats Bulletin Board

Students can find favorite places to explore–including unusual places like caves! Make a copy of the bat pattern, below, for each student. (Enlarge it first.) Show students how to fold the bat's wings to cover its belly. Have students color the back and front of the bat, leaving the belly uncolored. Have students write the following sentence starter on the belly: *I want to explore....* Discuss with students places they think would be exciting to explore, then have them complete the sentence. Students can illustrate their sentences, then use their bats to make an explorers' display, complete with a cave background.

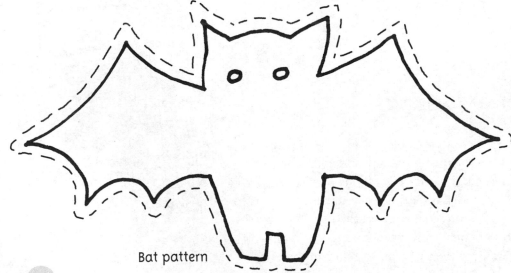

Bat pattern

# Let's Go Exploring!

by Deborah Rovin-Murphy and Frank Murphy

**Characters:** Explorer 1 ☆ Explorer 2 ☆ Explorer 3 ☆ Explorer 4 ☆ Class

**Explorer 1:** I'm going exploring!

**Class:** Where will you go?
What will you find?

**Explorer 1:** I'm going to the ocean,
I'm going to the sea,
To find some pretty seashells
You can share with me!

**Explorer 2:** I'm going exploring!

**Class:** Where will you go?
What will you find?

**Explorer 2:** I'm going to the forest,
I'm going to see the trees,
To find some leaves
and pinecones.
Won't you join me, please?

**Explorer 3:** I'm going exploring!

**Class:** Where will you go?
What will you find?

**Explorer 3:** I'm going to the mountains,
To the top I'll climb.
I hope to find
a mountain goat.
Can you come next time?

**Explorer 4:** I'm going exploring!

**Class:** Where will you go?
What will you find?

**Explorer 4:** I'll see dinosaurs,
I'll see kings,
I'll catch a star
from Saturn's rings,
I'll find fossils
and dragon's teeth.
Come to see these many things.

**Class:** Where will that be?

*(Explorer 4 reaches behind him/herself
and pulls out a book.)*

**All Explorers:** We're going exploring
in the library!

Name _____  Date _____

# Lost And Found

| | ① | ② | ③ | ④ |
|---|---|---|---|---|
| Ⓐ | | | | |
| Ⓑ | | | | |
| Ⓒ | | | | |
| Ⓓ | | | | |

Name _____    Date _____

# Explorer Calendar Journal

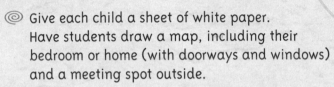

# Teacher Share

### SOCIAL STUDIES

## Mapping Fire Escape Routes

An important fire safety tip is planning escape routes. Tell students they should have at least two exits, in case one of the planned exits is blocked by fire. Have them map their routes to reinforce this safety tip.

◎ Give each child a sheet of white paper. Have students draw a map, including their bedroom or home (with doorways and windows) and a meeting spot outside.

◎ Have students create a miniature version of themselves on a small piece of construction paper and glue a length of yarn to it. Tape the yarn to one corner of the map. Let students practice their escape routes by guiding the miniature person through the map.

*Bonnie Webster and Mitzi Fehl*

### ART

## Smoke Detector Smarts

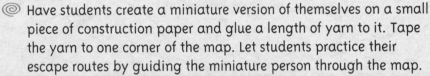

The United States Fire Administration lists the following tips about smoke alarms:

◎ Put smoke detectors in your home, especially near bedrooms and on each floor.

◎ Change old batteries in your smoke detector once a year. (SUGGESTION: Change batteries when you turn the clocks back in October.)

◎ Check smoke detectors monthly to make sure they are working properly.

◎ Keep smoke detectors dust-free.

Reinforce these tips by having your students make model smoke detectors. Start by showing students a real smoke detector. Point out where the batteries go, the red light that shows it is on, and other features. Give each student two dessert-size paper plates. Have them apply glue to the edges and then sandwich them together to make the detector. Students can add details like the red light and filter. Have them write their name on the rim to resemble a smoke detector manufacturer's name. Have them write smoke detector facts on the front.

LANGUAGE ARTS, SOCIAL STUDIES

# Fire Engine Collaborative Banner

Brainstorm with students what they have learned about fire safety. Record ideas on chart paper. Distribute copies of the banner activity page to each student. (See page 60.) Have students record a fire safety rule of their choice on the banner sheet. Tape the fire engines side to side to make an informational banner.

## Book Break

# Arthur's Fire Drill
### by Marc Brown (Random House, 2000)

"Always remember to first get out of your house quickly." In this easy-to-read sticker book, Arthur explains all the fire safety rules. Invite students to share their worries about school fire drills. Discussing these worries will alleviate future fears during a fire drill and ensure a safer fire drill.

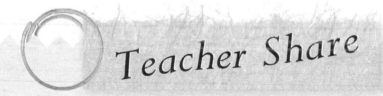

# Teacher Share

SOCIAL STUDIES, ART, TECHNOLOGY

## Spread the Word

Combine computer skills with fire safety by letting children use a program such as *Print Artist* or *Kid Pix* to create informational posters. Children can combine pictures and graphics with safety tips. Laminate posters and display them in school or around the community.

*Jim Kinkead*

**TIP**

Enrich your history lesson with this extra Ben Franklin connection. One of Ben's most important inventions protects homes and buildings from fires ignited by lightning—the *lightning rod*. It captures lightning bolts and sends them safely to the ground, so structures do not catch fire. The Empire State Building gets struck about 30 times per year. Without the lightning rod, this great building would be in danger.

**TIP**

Before starting the game, encourage students to estimate how many cups it will take to fill the bucket. If sand is not an option, use marbles, small blocks, or any other small object.

SOCIAL STUDIES, SCIENCE

# Ben Franklin's First Fire Company

Incorporate some history into your study of Fire Safety Week by introducing students to the fact that Ben Franklin started America's first volunteer fire department. Share with students the following facts:

◎ Living conditions in Colonial America were dangerous.

◎ Buildings were close together and usually made of wood.

Ask students to explain why Ben may have been so concerned about starting a fire department. Go further by comparing conditions of Colonial times to conditions of today.

MOVEMENT

# Don't Play With Fire!

This version of "Duck, Duck, Goose" lets students have fun while practicing the procedure of "Stop, Drop, and Roll." Have students sit in a circle. Ask one child to be the firefighter and walk around the circle patting heads and saying "Safe, Safe, Fire!" The student who has his/her head patted at the word "Fire" goes into the middle of the circle and demonstrates "Stop, Drop and Roll." This person becomes the next firefighter and repeats the procedure.

SOCIAL STUDIES, MOVEMENT

# Firefighter Relay

Long ago firefighters fought fires by passing buckets of water down a line. They needed to work as a team to quickly and safely put out the fire. Have students practice teamwork by trying the technique themselves. (You'll need a large open space, preferably outdoors.)

◎ Organize students into teams of four to six. Have each team stand in a line.

◎ Place a small bucket of sand at the head of each line and a small empty bucket at the end. (The sand takes the place of water in this activity.) Supply each team with a stack of cups.

◎ Have the first student in each group scoop up some sand in a cup and pass it down the line until it gets to the last student. Have the last student dump the sand into the other bucket. The first student goes to the end of the line and the procedure is repeated. This continues until all the sand has been transferred to the second bucket. The first team to do this has put out the fire!

**Book Break**

# No Dragons for Tea:
# Fire Safety for Kids and Dragons

### by Jean Pendziwol (Kids Can Press, 2008)

"Even when scared, you must never hide, And once you are out, don't go back inside." After reading this rhyming book, invite students to create dragon puppets out of brown paper lunch bags. Have them use their puppets to retell the story, sharing safety tips in their own words.

## SOCIAL STUDIES

# Dalmatian History

Learn about the famous fire department mascot—the Dalmatian! Discuss with students that long ago, when fire carriages were pulled by horses, Dalmatians helped to guide and protect firefighters through dark and busy streets. Today fire trucks do not need help, but Dalmatians are still many fire departments' mascots. (For a related activity, see Computer Connection, right.)

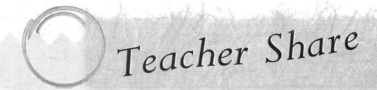

## *Teacher Share*

### MATH

# Dalmatian Dots

**W**hen we think of firefighters and dogs, most of us think of Dalmatians. These spotted dogs can help make practicing math facts fun! Give each child a copy of page 61. Ask children to write eight numbers between 2 and 12 on the dots (using each number only once), then have them pair up to play a game. To play, have students take turns rolling two dice and adding the two numbers together. If the answer matches one of the numbers on their dots, they color it in with a black crayon. The first student to color in all the spots is the winner.

*Teresa Cornell*

### C**o**m**P**ut**e**r
## Connection

Did you know that Benjamin Franklin, George Washington, and painter Pablo Picasso all had pet Dalmatians? Learn more amazing Dalmatian facts at the Sparky Web site.

*Sparky the Fire Dog*

www.sparky.org

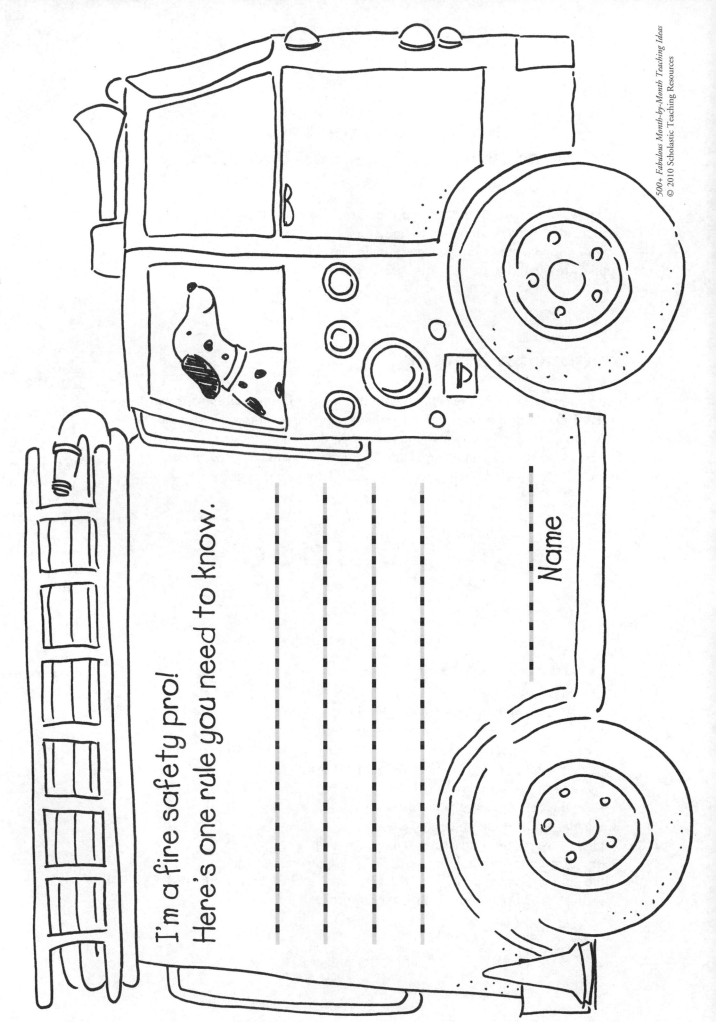

I'm a fire safety pro!
Here's one rule you need to know.

Name

Name _____ Date _____

Dalmatian
Dots

# Teacher Share

## Character Costumes

**P**lan a Halloween parade that doubles as a literature lesson. Ask students to create costumes that represent favorite book characters. These costumes do not have to be elaborate—for example, a child can dress up as Harry Potter with a pair of round, non-prescription glasses, a cape, and a broom. Have children hold the books that match their costumes as they parade through the halls. This parade will introduce students to new books and eliminate the problem of gory costumes that make some people uneasy about allowing costumes at school.

*Mark Klein*

**TIP**

Look for Halloween-related objects at a dollar store, and collect stuff lying around the house, to make this an easy and inexpensive addition to your writing program!

## Spill a Scary Story

Inspire creative writing in the classroom with this independent-writing activity. Fill tennis ball containers with small plastic toys that have a Halloween theme—such as ghosts, pumpkins, cats, spiders, skeletons, keys, fake teeth, and so on. Label the containers "Spill a Scary Story." Place the Spill a Scary Story containers at a center, along with writing paper and pencils. Have students take turns shaking the containers, then spilling some of the goodies and writing stories about the objects. The objects will help students write details and plot the events of their scary story.

### Book Break

## Miss Hildy's Missing Cape Caper
### by Lois Grambling (Random House, 2000)

This easy-reader mystery follows Miss Hildy as she sets out on Halloween night to find her stolen cape, cap, magnifying glass, and little black book. Children will laugh and be surprised by the ending, too!

## Teacher Share

# Mystery Math House

**S**tudents can make their own Halloween houses and practice math at the same time.

- Brainstorm a list of scary things one might see in a haunted house (bats, jack-o'-lanterns, spiders, skeletons, ghosts).

- Have each child make a haunted house picture with two windows and a door. Have them cut three sides of each window and the door to make flaps. Show students how to spread glue on the back of their house, then place it on another sheet of paper, glue side down.

- Invite students to choose three scary things. Have them draw a different number of these things in each opening—for example, 4 bats, 2 spiders, 1 ghost.

- Ask students to write a number sentence on the bottom of the page to match their drawings.

- Students can glue their haunted houses on larger construction paper and add spooky scenery to their pictures.

*Bobbi Williams*

# Ghostly Messages

Invite your students to send secret messages to classmates and learn a little chemistry at the same time. You'll need: Betadine® (iodine substitute), small jars, small bowls, an eyedropper, lemon juice, paintbrushes, and white paper.

- Have students dip a paintbrush into the lemon juice and write a secret message on white construction paper—for example: *Have a Spooky Halloween!* Set the papers aside to dry.

- While the papers are drying, put water into the jar and add a little bit of the Betadine® solution. (For safety reasons, this should be done by the teacher.)

- Have students choose one of the secret messages each, dip a paintbrush into the Betadine® mixture, and brush it over the paper. This will make the invisible writing appear white, while the rest of the paper will turn purple.

**TIP**

Your students will no doubt be curious as to what made the writing reappear. Paper has starch in it. When Betadine® (iodine) mixes with starch it turns purple. When students brush the paper with Betadine, the lemon juice stops the color change, so only the paper around it turns purple.

# Teacher Share

## Ghost Feet

**P**ractice measuring skills and create scary pictures, too. Invite students to trace one of their feet on white paper, then cut it out, and add eyes and a spooky mouth to make a ghost. Give students rulers and have them measure how long their ghosts (feet) are. Have students bring their ghosts to the front of the room. Ask questions such as: *Who has the biggest ghost? Who has the smallest?* Hold up a ghost at random and ask: *How many ghosts are larger than this one? smaller?*

*Kate Roach*

MATH

## Jack-o'-Lantern Math Story Mat

This math story mat activity allows students to create jack-o'-lanterns again and again while practicing math skills. Give each student 25 or more pumpkin seeds and a math story mat. (See page 66.) Read aloud a story problem. (See samples below.) Have students place the seeds on the story mats to show their answers.

 One jack-o'-lantern has five seeds for a mouth, two seeds for a nose and one seed for each eye. How many seeds are on that pumpkin's face?

 Three jack-o'-lanterns equally shared 21 seeds to make their faces. How many seeds are on each pumpkin's face?

 Jack the pumpkin has a seed for each eye, one seed for a nose, and six seeds for a mouth. Jack loses two teeth (seeds). How many seeds does he have left?

**Book Break**

## The Halloween House
### by Erica Silverman (Farrar, Straus & Giroux, 1997)

"In the Halloween house, above bent candlesticks, a papa ghost hovered with his little ones, six. 'Boooooo,' said the papa. 'We boooooo,' said the six. So they booooooed through the night above bent candlesticks." This book is full of fun counting rhymes (10 to 1) with friendly illustrations of spooky creatures.

**TIP**

Have children team up to play a game with the math story mats. Have players place seven pumpkin seeds inside one of the pumpkins on their mats. The first player rolls a die and adds or takes away that number of seeds. The goal is to have seven seeds on each pumpkin (one for each eye, a nose, and four for a mouth).

Camilla's Pumpkin Book

LANGUAGE ARTS

# Pumpkin Mini-Book

Get your students excited about poetry, writing, and pumpkin carving. With this mini-book activity, your students will also learn about feelings. First, introduce the poem at right:

To make the books, give each child a pumpkin pattern. Have children trace and cut out the pumpkins, then punch holes and tie them together with string or yarn. Have children follow these steps to complete each page:

◎ Draw a face on each pumpkin to show a feeling.

◎ Complete this sentence on each page: *This pumpkin feels ____ .*

## My Perfect Pumpkin

I love my perfect, plump pumpkin.
It's not too fat
And it's not too thin.
It's not too swollen
And it's not caved in.
So I'll carve him a smile
To make him grin!

—*by Kelly*

SNACK

# Pumpkin Face Bakery

Turn your classroom into a bakery for a fun and delicious follow-up to the Pumpkin Mini-Book activity (above). You'll need large gingersnap or sugar cookies, orange frosting, and candy corn. Have students spread orange frosting on their cookies, then use candy corn to create a face. Encourage experimentation with different expressions—for example, happy or surprised.

TIP

Check for food allergies before decorating and eating cookies.

## Book Break

# I Spy Spooky Nights

by Jean Marzollo (Scholastic, 2005)

This book of picture riddles will invite students back again and again as they try to find all sorts of ordinary objects used to create lots of spooky settings. The book will also provide students with plenty of inspiration as they create their own haunted houses. They'll discover how cotton can become smoke from a chimney, small branches can become shadowy trees, and more.

SOCIAL STUDIES

# Costume Time Line

Invite students to learn a little bit about themselves and their families by making Halloween time lines. Ask students to interview their parents, older siblings, or family friends about costumes they wore for Halloween. Some good stories will certainly come out of these interviews. Students can record the information to share in class. Follow up by having them make picture time lines of their past Halloween costumes.

Name _____

Date _____

# Jack-o'-Lantern
# Math Story Mat

# November
## Teaching Ideas

As a teacher, you know that the months of the year are highlighted by special topics. Harvest the teaching opportunities that naturally come with November with these great activities that will enrich your curriculum and engage students in meaningful learning.

November is divided into four sections, one for each of the following topics: HARVEST, NATIVE AMERICANS (the Wampanoag), CHILDREN'S BOOK WEEK, and THANKSGIVING. Within each section, you'll find a range of activities focusing on subjects that include math, social studies, science, language arts, art, movement, and music. Children will create a "Harvest Tree" banner (see page 71), discover why popcorn pops and how a book is made, and of course learn all about the Pilgrims' first Thanksgiving. (See "Squanto's Journey," page 80.) Use these terrific teaching ideas to make the most of November in your classroom—a month ripe with tradition and ready for the picking! Other activity highlights include:

- a reproducible send-home activity calendar
- literature links
- computer connections
- hands-on math and science activities
- an easy-cook snack
- an interactive mini-book
- a "piggyback" song
- ready-to-use reproducible activity pages
- an emergent reader mini-play
- a collaborative banner
- a math story mat
- and lots more!

Name _____

# November Activity Calendar

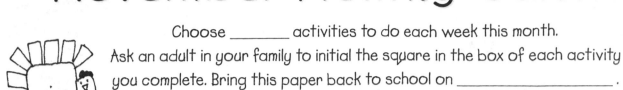

Choose _____ activities to do each week this month.
Ask an adult in your family to initial the square in the box of each activity
you complete. Bring this paper back to school on _____ .

| Monday | Tuesday | Wednesday | Thursday | Friday |
|---|---|---|---|---|
| Write the word *November* on a sheet of paper. Cut apart the letters. Make new words!  **No**  **Ben**  **me** | Look at a calendar. Count the days in November. How many other months have the same number of days? | Thanks + giving = Thanksgiving. List other words that are made by putting two words together. | The word *giving* comes from the word *give*. Make new words by adding -ing to these words: *make, bake, joke, poke.* | Look at the sentences on this page. Underline the sentences that are questions. |
| Go on a shape scavenger hunt. How many of these shapes can you find?  | Say the word *Thanksgiving*. Take turns with a family member saying more words that start with -th. | November is the eleventh month of the year. How many number sentences can you make that have 11 for an answer? | Go on a nature scavenger hunt in your home! How many things can you find that came from nature? | Celebrate Children's Book Week! Read a book each day this week with a family member. Take turns choosing the books. |
| Act out a scene from a favorite book. You can be more than one character. Just change your voice! | How many Thursdays are there in November? Are there more Mondays or fewer Mondays? | Author William Steig was born on November 14, 1907. How many years ago was that? Read one of his books. Try *Brave Irene.* | *T* is for *turkey*! What other animal names start with *t*? Take turns with someone in your family naming them. | Collect 20 small objects. Sort them into two groups. Sort them into three groups. What other ways can you sort them? |
| Look at the sky from a window. Draw a picture that has a sky like the one you see. | Tell a story about a turkey family's Thanksgiving. Give your turkeys names. Tell where your story happens. | Unscramble the words to find four harvest foods:  **qusahs**  **orcn**  **skinpmup**  **ppales** | Look at this turkey.   Find a matching turkey on this page. | Turn *November* into a tongue twister! Make up a sentence using as many words as you can that start with *n*. |

500+ Fabulous Month-by-Month Teaching Ideas © 2010 Scholastic Teaching Resources

# Harvest Game

Invite students to "harvest apples" with a game that strengthens counting skills. Give each pair of students a sheet of drawing paper, a low-number cube (such as 1–6), a small cup, and 20 small red objects (such as buttons, beans, or counters). Have children make their game boards by drawing a large tree on the paper. The tree can have leaves but no fruit. Invite children to place the 20 red objects (apples) on the tree. Each player takes a turn rolling the number cube. The number shown equals the number of "apples" to pick from the tree and place in a cup. If the number of apples remaining is fewer than the number shown, the player takes all those apples. The winner is the player who has the most apples in his or her cup.

**TIP**

This game goes quickly, so children can play several times.

## Book Break

## Radio Man/Don Radio
### by Arthur Dorros (Rayo, 1997)

Diego and David's families travel together as migrant farm workers. Wherever they go, Diego takes along his radio. When Diego's family moves on to the apple orchards of the Northwest, the friends have to say goodbye. Diego looks for David wherever they go, and when he calls a farm-workers radio show to say "Hello" to his friend, David is listening. Text appears in English and Spanish, and a glossary provides translations of Spanish phrases.

SCIENCE, ART, MATH

# "Harvest Tree" Collaborative Banner

Children explore foods that are harvested from trees with this collaborative banner. Brainstorm food items that grow on trees—for example, apples, peaches, pears, oranges, lemons, grapefruit, almonds, walnuts, avocados, and olives. Discuss how each food tastes and looks different, yet all come from trees. Give each student a copy of the reproducible activity sheet. (See page 76.) Have children draw one type of fruit or nut on their trees, then cut them out. Guide children in arranging their trees on a long sheet of craft paper to make a banner. Ask them to group similar trees together—for example, citrus fruits, nuts, and so on. Display the banner, then ask questions to make math connections and more—for example, ask:

@ How many citrus trees are in our banner?

@ How many more [name type of tree] are there than [name type of tree]?

@ Which tree has the most fruits or nuts on it?

@ Can you think of a tree that gives us food that is not part of our banner?

**Connection**

<u>Agriculture in the Classroom</u>

www.
agclassroom.org

Classroom-ready materials include lessons for helping students explore the life cycle of an apple, where their food comes from, what plants need to grow, and more.

SOCIAL STUDIES, MUSIC, MOVEMENT

# This Is the Way We Harvest Our Food

Invite students to experience the movements involved in harvesting crops with this fun song and movement activity. First, discuss how different crops are harvested in different ways. Farmers must reach high to pick apples, oranges, and pears from trees. Farmers must reach low to pick squash, carrots, and other garden vegetables. Farmers today use large machinery to harvest grains. But years ago they used *scythes*, or long, curved knives, to cut rice, wheat, and oats in the fields. Farmers made a sweeping motion with their arms when they used this tool. Model these motions for the children, then lead them in "harvesting" their own crops. Ask them to:

◎ reach high to pick from trees

◎ bend low to pick from their garden

◎ sweep arms back and forth to cut from the fields

Now that your students are warmed up, sing this song, incorporating harvest motions as indicated by the foods. (Fill in the blanks with a food from each category.)

## This Is the Way We Harvest Our Food

*(Sing to the tune of "Here We Go 'Round the Mulberry Bush")*

This is the way we harvest the _____,          (tree motion)
Harvest the _____, harvest the _____.
This is the way we harvest the _____,
So early in the morning.

This is the way we harvest the _____,          (garden motion)
Harvest the _____, harvest the _____.
This is the way we harvest the _____,
So early in the morning.

This is the way we harvest the _____,          (field motion)
Harvest the _____, harvest the _____.
This is the way we harvest the _____,
So early in the morning.

# Teacher Share

## Estimation Ear

**H**ave your students examine an ear of dried corn and record an estimate of how many kernels there are. Invite a volunteer to count the kernels in one row. Share this information with the class, then let students revise their estimates. Let another student count the number of rows of kernels on the ear. (Guide the student by marking the first row so he or she knows where to stop.) Again, let students revise their estimates. Finally, remove the kernels from the cob. Let children take turns counting them out in groups of ten. Count by tens to find the actual number of kernels and compare to estimates. Which of students' estimates (the first, second, or third try) was closest? Explain that estimates are reasonable guesses based on what we know about a situation. The more we know, and the more information we have, the more accurate our estimates become. This helps remove some of the misconceptions among younger kids that estimates are random or lucky guesses.

*Bob Krech*

## "Colors of the Harvest" Mini-Book

Practice color recognition while exploring the fruits and vegetables of the harvest. Display harvest fruits and vegetables in a variety of colors on a small table. Ask students what colors they see. List the colors and names of the fruits and vegetables on the chalkboard. Write this sentence frame on the board: *Red is _____*. Invite students to complete the sentence by filling in fruits and/or vegetables—for example, *Red is apples, cranberries, cherries,* or *strawberries*. Give children sheets of 8 1/2- by 11-inch paper cut in half. Have them staple the pages to make a book. Invite them to create a cover on the first page. On each inside page, have them copy the sentence frame (changing the color each time) and complete it by writing names of fruits and vegetables that go with each color. Students can illustrate their books, then take turns reading them aloud.

SCIENCE, LANGUAGE ARTS

# "It's Harvest Time!" Mini-Play

Your young readers star as pumpkins, cranberries, and sunflowers in a mini-play that introduces the way plants grow. Give each child a copy of the play. (See page 77.) Before performing the play, make a word wall that includes key vocabulary, including *cranberries, sunflowers, pumpkins, bushes, ground, stalks, vine, harvest, seeds,* and *pick.* Let children illustrate the words to provide visual clues. In preparation for performing the play, let children make simple props. Children who are cranberries can cut out and color small red circles and glue them to construction-paper bushes. Children playing the part of pumpkins can color paper-plate pumpkins (glue them to craft sticks) and hold them up at the appropriate times. Sunflowers can start out with tiny sprouts, then make bigger and bigger sunflowers to display.

SCIENCE

# Harvest Seed Surprise

Children play this fun game as they discover the kinds of plants that grow from different seeds.

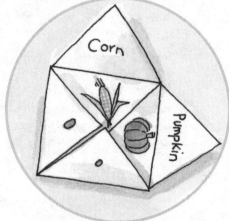

- Provide a variety of seeds such as watermelon seeds, corn kernels, and flower seeds.

- Give each student a copy of the activity sheet. (See page 78.) Show students where to glue four different seeds, where to draw a picture of what the seed becomes, and where to write the label. Follow the illustration (above) as a guide.

- Give children time to play a peekaboo game by trying to guess what one another's seeds will become. They can lift the flaps to check their answers. Some seeds are very surprising!

## Book Break

# Pumpkins
### by Ken Robbins (Square Fish, 2007)

Close-up color photos and straight-forward text follow the life-cycle of a pumpkin. Young readers can compare a pumpkin that would fit in the palm of their hand to one that weighs more than 1000 pounds.

Book Break

# Tops and Bottoms

### by Janet Stevens (Harcourt, 1995)

In this Caldecott Honor book, a lazy farmer bear with lots of money is tricked by a poor rabbit with lots of smarts. The rabbit makes a deal with the bear to farm his land. The rabbit lets the bear decide if he wants the "tops or the bottoms" of the harvest. When the bear picks the tops, the rabbit plants vegetables such as carrots, beets, and radishes, whose fruits lie underground. When the bear picks the bottoms, the rabbit plants lettuce, broccoli, and cabbage. In the end, tired of being tricked, the bear decides to stop being lazy and farm his own land.

## Teacher Share

SCIENCE, ART, LANGUAGE ARTS

## "Tops and Bottoms" Lift-the-Flap Book

Investigate which vegetables are harvested aboveground and which are gathered from below the ground. Make a T-chart labeled "Tops" and "Bottoms." Give each child a sheet of white construction paper. Have children fold the piece of paper down from the top to the middle of the paper and up from the bottom to the middle of the paper. Label the top flap "Tops" and the bottom flap "Bottoms." Have students draw appropriate vegetables under each flap. They can label their pictures, too.

*Juli Lowe*

Make an interactive bulletin board garden. Cover a display space with brown paper on the bottom and blue on top. Let children cut out pictures of vegetables and fruits. Laminate them and put Velcro® on the back of each. Put pieces of Velcro on the bulletin board, too, both on top and on the bottom. Place the pictures in an envelope and tack to a corner of the board. Let students take the pictures out of the envelope and stick them up where they belong—above or below ground.

**Harvest Tree Collaborative Banner**

My tree is full

of ----------- to eat.

Will they be sour, crunchy, or sweet?

Name -----------

# It's Harvest Time!

by Nancy I. Sanders

## Characters
(to be played by small groups of students)

Cranberries ✿ Sunflowers ✿ Pumpkins    **Setting:** A garden

**Cranberries:** We are baby cranberries,
Small and green and round.
We're growing
On green bushes
Planted in the ground.

*(crouched low to the ground)*

**Sunflowers:** We are baby sunflowers,
Small and green and round.
We're growing on
Green flower stalks
Planted in the ground.

*(crouched low to the ground)*

**Pumpkins:** We are baby pumpkins,
Small and green and round.
We're growing on
A long green vine
Planted in the ground.

**Cranberries:** We are growing cranberries.
We like the sun and rain.
We're growing riper every day,
But we still look the same.

*(starting to stand)*

**Sunflowers:** We are growing sunflowers.
We're having so much fun.
We're growing taller every day,
Climbing to the sun.

*(low to the ground)*

**Pumpkins:** We are growing pumpkins.
We're getting big and round.
We're growing fatter every day
Sitting on the ground.

**Cranberries:** We are bright red cranberries,
Small and sour, not sweet!
We're ready now.
It's harvest time!
Pick us all to eat.

*(standing tall)*

**Sunflowers:** We are yellow sunflowers.
Our cheerful faces say:
We're ready now.
It's harvest time!
Pick our seeds today.

**Pumpkins:** We are big orange pumpkins,
Just right for pies and fun.
We're ready now.
It's harvest time!
Pick us, one by one.

# Harvest Seed Surprise

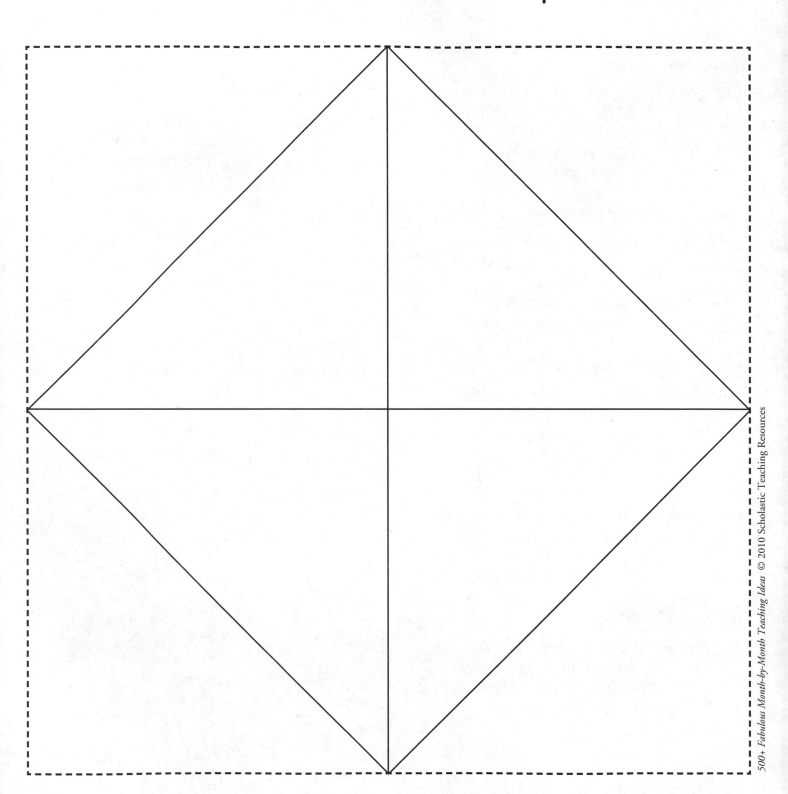

LANGUAGE ARTS, SOCIAL STUDIES

# Native American Picture Dictionary

Invite children to learn and understand Native American words while working together to create a classroom dictionary. List Wampanoag words and their meanings on the chalkboard. (See Wampanoag Word List, below.) Have each student choose one word to write and illustrate on a sheet of drawing paper. Collect the finished pictures and have students work together to arrange them in alphabetical order. Add sturdy front and back covers and bind them to make a book. (Brads or yarn ties work well.)

## Wampanoag Word List

**ahtomp:** bow

**kouhquodt:** arrow

**mishoon:** canoe

**noohkik:** parched corn

**petan:** quiver

**pniese:** war leader and advisor

**sachem:** leader or chief

**sobaheg:** stew

**tummock:** beaver

**Wampanoag:** The Eastern People

**wetu:** house

**wiaseck:** knife

SOURCES: *Tapenum's Day* by Kate Waters (Scholastic, 1996), *The Wampanoag* by Laurie Weinstein-Farson (Chelsea House, 1989), *From Abenaki to Zuni* by Evelyn Wolfson (Walker and Company, 1988).

## Book Break

# Tapenum's Day: A Wampanoag Indian Boy in Pilgrim Times
### by Kate Waters (Scholastic, 1996)

Through vibrant photographs of a Wampanoag family at Hobbamock's Homesite on Plimoth Plantation, students see what daily life was really like for a Wampanoag boy. After sharing the book, invite students to discuss and compare the details of Tapenum's day with their own daily routine. Other books in this series include *Sarah Morton's Day: A Day in the Life of a Pilgrim Girl* and *Samuel Eaton's Day: A Day in the Life of a Pilgrim Boy.*

## TIP

As you plan lessons about the Wampanoag Indians, keep these facts in mind:

◎ *Wampanoag* is pronounced (wampa NO og).

◎ The Wampanoag lived in the area we now call Massachusetts before the Pilgrims came.

◎ A Wampanoag leader is called a *sachem*, pronounced (SAY chum).

◎ A Wampanoag house is called a *wetu*, pronounced (WEE too).

◎ Today, many Wampanoag still live in Massachusetts and Rhode Island.

Name _____ Activity Page Date _____
Harvest Time Math Story Mat

MATH

# Harvest Time Math Story Mat

Children practice counting skills and following directions as they use a story mat that pictures harvest time in a Wampanoag village.

◎ Give each student a copy of the reproducible story mat on page 83. Provide counters or beans as manipulatives.

◎ Read the story (see below) aloud as children place their markers on the mat.

◎ Follow up by asking children to count the number of Wampanoag in their village. Compare results.

◎ Have children make up their own stories about the Wampanoag village. Let them take turns sharing their stories while the class uses their story mats to show the math.

## Read-Aloud Story

The Wampanoag are busy preparing for the harvest. Listen and use your markers to show what they are doing. One Wampanoag is in each wetu cooking stew for the harvest festival. Two Wampanoag are gathering reeds beside the river to weave new mats. Three Wampanoag are hunting squirrels near the forest trees. Four Wampanoag are fishing at the river. How many Wampanoag are in the village today?

### Computer Connection

Visit these Web sites to learn more about the Wampanoag.

Boston Children's Museum
tc.bostonkids.org/

Mashpee Wampanoag Indian Artist
www.realbodies.com/rpeters/

Plimoth Plantation
www.plimoth.org

## Book Break

# Squanto's Journey: The Story of the First Thanksgiving

by Joseph Bruchac (Voyager, 2007)

Though the story of Thanksgiving is familiar to many children, this one, told from Squanto's point of view, offers a different perspective on this time in history.

# Teacher Share

LANGUAGE ARTS

## Native American Similes

Give grammar a Native American twist. Introduce students to *similes* (using *like* or *as* to compare two objects). Give examples such as "fast as a cheetah" or "hot as the sun." Explain to students that Native Americans sometimes had names that described who they were or what they did by comparing themselves to something in nature—for example, "Runs Like the Wind" or "Wise as an Owl." Encourage students to think of three adjectives to describe themselves. Have them write these words on a sheet of paper. Next to each adjective, have students list something in nature that matches their word—for example, *tall/tree* or *busy/bee*. Copy the following sentence frames on the chalkboard: _____ *like a/an* _____, and _____ *as a/an* _____. Have children use their word pairs to complete one of the sentence frames, copying it on paper folded in half to make a name plate. They can decorate their name plates with crayons, markers, glitter, and other art supplies.

*Al Mandia*

SCIENCE

## Why Does Popcorn Pop?

Squanto helped the Pilgrims during that first hard year in America by teaching them how to plant corn. Though the Pilgrims did not have corn at their first Thanksgiving, it is part of many traditional Thanksgiving feasts. Try this tasty experiment with corn to get children thinking about science. Using a small microwave oven or hot-air popper, pop some popcorn. Ask: *Why do you think the kernels pop?* Record ideas on chart paper. Theories may range from scientific to silly. After the popcorn has popped, allow students to see how many kernels popped and how many did not. Explain that it is the moisture (water) within each kernel that makes it pop. When the kernel is heated, the moisture turns to steam and presses against the hard outer part of the kernel until POP…you've got popcorn. Ask students why they think some kernels did not pop. (*Kernels that did not pop did not contain enough moisture.*) Share *The Popcorn Book* by Tomie de Paola (Holiday House, 1984) while students enjoy eating their science experiment!

**TIP**

Share these fun facts about popcorn:

◎ Unpopped kernels are called "Old Maids."

◎ There is a Native American legend about a small demon that lives inside each kernel, and when he gets mad, he pops!

◎ Native Americans threw their kernels into an open fire and waited for the popped corn to shoot out.

Native Americans

**TIP**

Invite children to make a permanent "campfire" for the class powwows. Have them cut out different-sized triangles (flames) from yellow, red, and orange construction paper. After cutting, guide children in folding one side of the triangle about an inch to allow for a line of glue. Cut out a round piece of brown construction paper (wood base). Have children glue their triangles to the brown circle so they stand upright. Now they have a "campfire" to sit around!

CLASSROOM MANAGEMENT

# Powwow

In many Native American tribes, including the Wampanoag, difficult situations and important events were discussed when the chief called a *powwow*—meetings that take place around a campfire. Rename your November class meetings as *powwows*. The new name may add a more important feel to class meetings because children will know the importance of powwows to Native Americans.

RHYTHM AND MOVEMENT

# Pop, Pop, Popcorn!

This action rhyme is a fun way to add movement to a lesson about corn.

| | |
|---|---|
| Pop, pop, popcorn in a pan. | (Children crouch in a small ball.) |
| Warmer. Hotter. | (Children start to wiggle.) |
| Bam! Bam! Bam! | (Children jump to their feet.) |

Teacher Share

SOCIAL STUDIES

## Build a Wetu

Students work together to build a wetu that becomes a learning center for working on Native American projects. Here's how:

◎ Cut brown paper grocery bags into rectangular mats, punching holes all around the edges. Crumple the paper. Have students use yarn to sew the mats together in rows. Sew several rows together.

◎ Set up a card table for the frame of the wetu. Place a large mound of crumpled paper on top of the table to create a dome shape. Drape several layers of mats over the card table until it is completely covered and resembles a wetu.

◎ Stock the wetu with books and craft supplies. Invite children to imagine what they would have done inside a wetu to cook, sleep, and socialize.

*Judy Wetzel*

Name _____

Date _____

# Harvest Time Math Story Mat

MATH, LANGUAGE ARTS

# A-Book-a-Day Calendar

Children love to learn with calendars, especially if a surprise awaits them each new day. Here's how your students can make a calendar together that's filled with fun surprises and features a different book each day of the month. Follow the illustration (left) and the directions below to make the front of a lift-the-flap calendar for the month of November. Start this project a week or so in advance of the first day of the month so that your calendar is ready to display for November 1st.

◎ Create a calendar template as shown on a large sheet of heavyweight paper. Cut around three sides of each square to make flaps. Spread paste on the back of the calendar, being careful to place it along the outer edges and in between the rows.

◎ Place the calendar glue-side down on a sheet of posterboard. Let dry. Fill in the calendar by writing the month and days of the week across the top. Number each square.

◎ Have children take turns writing clues about a favorite classroom book, one book per flap. (See examples, at left.)

◎ Display your completed calendar in time for November 1st. Let a different child lift a flap each day to share the clue. Who knows the book?

LANGUAGE ARTS

# Prop Up a Good Book

Liven up your classroom library by pairing up props and books. Use ribbon to fasten an object like a magnifying glass to a mystery book, or a small teddy bear to a bear book. Other props to match with books include rubber insects, fake coins, and plastic foods. These props will encourage even the most reluctant readers to pick up and open a book!

## TIP

The following are examples of clues children might include on the calendar:

◎ What color is Harold's crayon? (Answer: purple; from *Harold and the Purple Crayon* by Crockett Johnson; HarperCollins, 1998)

◎ Who helps Strega Nona? (Answer: Big Anthony, from *Strega Nona* by Tomie de Paola; Simon & Schuster, 1975)

Book Break

# Good Books, Good Times!

Selected by Lee Bennett Hopkins (HarperCollins, 1990)

This delightful collection of poems celebrates the joy of reading books. After sharing the book, invite your students to write their own poems about the magic of reading.

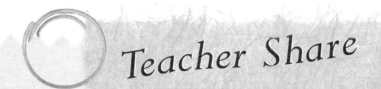

## Teacher Share

LANGUAGE ARTS

### New Arrivals

Just like the birth announcement of a new baby, excite your students by wheeling in new book arrivals in a baby carriage. Set the mood in your classroom by reminding the children to keep calm and quiet, like they would with a sleeping baby, while you introduce each new arrival by giving a quick book talk.

*Cheryll Black*

**TIP**

Children may be surprised to learn that the very first books were clay tablets with symbols carved into them!

ART

### Bookmark Gifts

Encourage reading by letting children make bookmarks to give as gifts. Make multiple copies of the bookmark template on page 89. Demonstrate how to cut out the pattern, spread glue on the back, then fold on the solid line. For an extra special touch, punch a hole at the top and thread with ribbon. Let students make and decorate bookmarks during free time. Encourage them to give the bookmarks to friends and family members. For durability, glue bookmarks to oaktag or laminate.

**COMPUTER**
**Connection**

Children's Book Council

**www.cbcbooks. org**

The Children's Book Council, sponsor of Children's Book Week, offers posters, kits, bookmarks, and other materials at its Web site.

### Book Break

### Bookworm
#### by Molly Coxe (Golden Books, 2000)

This easy reader tells the rhyming tale of Bookworm, who is too busy reading to get ready for the coming winter. After sharing the book, ask children to tell why we might call a person who reads a lot a "bookworm." Explain that the real definition of a bookworm is "a name for any insect that feeds on books." Some insects, such as beetles, love to eat starchy material like wood and paper! Beetle larvae actually look like worms; that's how the term "bookworm" came about. Make a connection between a real worm eating a book and a reader "eating up" a book with his or her eyes and mind.

LANGUAGE ARTS, MOVEMENT

# Musical Reading Chairs

Combine music and movement with reading by playing this variation of "Musical Chairs." Invite children to bring in one or two favorite books to place on their desks (or have children select favorites from the school or classroom libraries). Have a tape recorder or radio ready for playing. How to play:

◎ Have each student stand behind his or her desk with chairs pushed in. When the music begins, the students begin walking around the desks, looking at the books. When the music stops, students must sit down at the closest desk. (Unlike Musical Chairs, everyone gets a seat!)

◎ Invite students to open the book on their desk and quietly skim the book until the music begins again. (Allow approximately three to five minutes.)

◎ Continue the game for at least five rounds. When finished, gather to discuss the new books students want to read!

## Book Break

## Library Lil
### by Suzanne Williams (Dial, 1997)

Library Lil is someone to be reckoned with for her zany love of reading (even encyclopedias!) and her commitment to get everyone to read books.

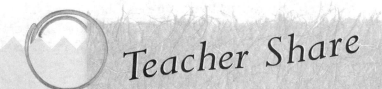

## Teacher Share

LANGUAGE ARTS

## Reading From A to Z

Challenge your class to read their way through the alphabet. Create a chart that has the letters from A to Z written down the left side, leaving room to write a few book titles next to each letter. Invite children to write the names of books they've finished next to the letter that matches the first letter of the title.

*Stacey Suter*

**TIP**

Here's another great title to celebrate Children's Book Week:

*Library Mouse* by Daniel Kirk (Abrams, 2007). Sam, a mouse, makes his home in the wall of a library's reference section. Sam loves to read and is inspired to write his own book, "Squeak! A Mouse's Life." Soon people want to meet the mysterious author.

LANGUAGE ARTS

# Scavenger Hunt

Use the poem below to introduce library research skills. First, read the poem aloud to students. Make a list of topics mentioned in the poem, such as *pirates*, *dragons*, *castles*, and *deserts*. Have children copy this list on a piece of paper. Then, go to the school library and have children find a book title for each topic on the list. Help them use the card catalog or book search subject index to locate these titles. Invite them to choose one book from their list to check out and read. When you get back to the classroom, compare the different titles children found for each topic.

## Treasures

Pirates who sail on the wind-tossed seas,
Dragons in faraway lands,
Castles with kings and beautiful queens,
Deserts with shimmering sands.
Lost boys, mermaids, and pixie dust,
Water from magical brooks,
Unicorns, giants, and leprechaun's gold.
Discover these treasures in books!

—by Nancy I. Sanders

## Teacher Share

LANGUAGE ARTS

## What Happens Next?

Entice your children into reading a chapter book by starting to read a selection (letting them think you intend to read the whole book), then stopping abruptly after a chapter or two. Children will clamor to get their hands on the book. Try to have a few copies of the book available, so more than one reader can find out what happens next.

**Cheryll Black**

## TIP

Copy the poem for children to take home and read with their families. Have children ask older members of their family to list titles of books that were their childhood treasures. If their family has a favorite book, encourage children to bring it to school to share.

## Computer Connection

Print out pictures of children's book covers from online bookstores, such as www.amazon.com.

Make sure these books are available in your library. Let children choose book covers (of books they haven't read) and write about what they think happens. After students read the books, have them compare what actually happened to what they thought would happen.

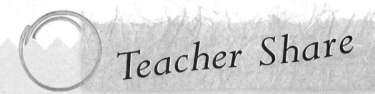

## Teacher Share

### LANGUAGE ARTS

## We're All Teachers!

**Y**our students become the teachers when they share favorite books with their classmates. Let children sign up to be "teachers." Have them select a favorite book, prepare to read it aloud, then create an activity based on the book. This might be a paper and pencil task (such as a word search based on characters), a class discussion (they can prepare a list of questions), a class retelling (recorded on chart paper), and so on. Children love both sides of this activity—having a classmate "teach" and taking a turn teaching. It encourages careful reading and listening, and gives children a chance to build leadership skills!

*Sue Lorey*

### TIP

How were the first books published? Johannes Gutenberg invented the mechanical printing press in the 1400s. Before that, books were written by hand and could sometimes take years to create!

### Book Break

## How a Book Is Made
### by Aliki (HarperCollins, 1986)

From idea to published book, Aliki describes in simple yet technical detail all the stages of writing and illustrating a children's book. Students will be fascinated by this inside look at the publishing world.

### LANGUAGE ARTS

## Books We Like

Students get to know their classmates' reading preferences with this activity. Teach children the word *genre* (a category of books). List various genres on the board, such as *mystery, biography, fantasy, realistic fiction, poetry, picture books, historical fiction, folklore,* and *science fiction*. Ask students which genres or topics are their favorites. Take a poll, then have students team up with a classmate who has the same favorite genre. Go to the library and have children select an example of that genre. Back in the classroom, let children take turns sharing their books and telling a little bit about why they like that genre.

# Bookmark Gifts

A gift to

_____

From

_____

A bookmark
is a special friend.
It marks my place
'till the story ends.

LANGUAGE ARTS

# Word Family Turkeys

Set up an interactive bulletin board to build phonics skills with word families. Follow the illustration and these directions as a guide:

◎ Make a large construction-paper turkey for each word family you want to reinforce. Cut out construction paper feathers but do not attach them to the turkeys. Display the turkey shapes on a bulletin board.

◎ Write words that belong to the target word families on the feathers— for example, *chick, click, kick, lick, pick*. Write each word family (phonogram) on the body of a turkey—for example, *-ick*.

◎ Place pieces of Velcro® on the back of each feather and around the outer edges of each turkey.

◎ Mix up the feathers and place them on a table near the center. Have students match feathers to turkeys, using the Velcro to attach them.

## Computer Connection

Billy Bear's Happy Thanksgiving

www. billybear4kids.com Invite students to print out the harvest stationery at this site and write Thanksgiving notes to special people in their lives.

## Book Break

# Thanksgiving at the Templetons'
by Eileen Spinelli (HarperCollins, 2004)

Originally published in 1982, this re-illustrated edition features a family of wolves in place of people.

MATH

# Shopping for a Turkey Dinner

Invite your children to "shop" for a Thanksgiving feast and practice addition at the same time. Provide students with photocopies of grocery store advertisements. Guide children in searching for favorite foods while also planning a balanced feast. After selecting their items, have children list and add up the prices. Combine students' totals for a grand total.

**Book Break**

# Thanksgiving
### by Laura Alden (Children's Press, 1993)

This cheerful book shows a family's tradition at Thanksgiving of choosing fun and helpful activities to do during holiday preparations. After sharing the book, you can make a classroom version of the "Take Your Turn" game. Write suggestions on slips of paper such as "Choose a song for the class to sing" or "Clean our desks." Children may then take turns choosing these slips of paper from a basket for the whole class to enjoy doing together.

MATH

# Favorite Foods Graph

*Yum! Yum!* Give children copies of the turkey templates on page 96. Ask students to write down four of their favorite Thanksgiving Day foods, once on each turkey. Form groups of about five students each. Have children take turns sharing their choices, making a list of foods in the

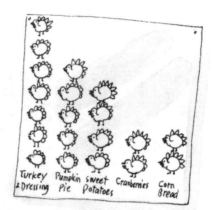

process. Encourage children to double check the lists to make sure all foods are included. Bring students together to share their lists. Use the information to set up a graph of all the foods students mentioned. Let children take turns taping their turkey graph markers to the graph to show which Thanksgiving foods are their favorites. Encourage children to "dress up" the graph with colorful drawings of each food! Discuss the completed graph, asking questions such as: *Which are the top three favorite Thanksgiving foods?*

**Book Break**

# Let's Celebrate Thanksgiving
### by Peter and Connie Roop (The Millbrook Press, 1999)

Share this informational book and laugh together over the clever riddles. Discover anew what happened at the first Thanksgiving. After sharing the book, hold foot races and jumping contests.

## COmPUTer Connection

*Plimoth Plantation*

**www.plimoth.org**

Investigate the harvest celebration of 1621 ("The First Thanksgiving") with this comprehensive set of materials, designed to have students take on the role of historians as they separate fact from fiction, analyze primary sources, consider different points of view, and more.

**TIP**

Invite other classrooms to join your class for a Thanksgiving Field Day of races and outdoor games. For directions to authentic games Pilgrims played, see *Pilgrims* by Susan Moger (Scholastic, 1995).

# Teacher Share

MATH, SOCIAL STUDIES

## Mayflower Number Line

*How many days did the Pilgrims sail across the ocean on the Mayflower?* Let your students count out the days on a number line while they share ideas about how the Pilgrims might have spent time on board the ship.

◎ Make a number line from a narrow strip of paper for the 66 days they traveled, from September 16, 1620 to November 21, 1620. Mount this on the wall.

◎ Make a small paper ship to represent the Mayflower. Pin or clip the Mayflower to the first number.

◎ Each day have a volunteer take turns rolling a die and moving the Mayflower accordingly on the number line.

◎ Write number sentences on the chalkboard for what happens—for example, Day 29. Roll a 6. Write 29 + 6 = 35. Encourage students to share ideas about what the Pilgrims might have done during those days. (See "Lift-the-Flap Mayflower," page 94, for resources.) Make predictions about how long they think it will take the classroom Mayflower to get to the end of the number line. Continue this activity until reaching the end of the number line.

*Sharon Thompson*

**TIP**

Thanksgiving as a national holiday has a presidential history. In 1789, George Washington proclaimed November 26 as a day of thanksgiving. For many years, though, the country had no regular national Thanksgiving. But in 1863, Abe Lincoln made it official. After a woman named Sarah Hale wrote articles and sent letters to Lincoln, he proclaimed the last Thursday in November as the official holiday. In 1939, Franklin D. Roosevelt made it one week earlier to make the holiday shopping season longer. Finally, in 1941, Congress made it a law that Thanksgiving would be a regular national holiday on the fourth Thursday in November.

Book Break

## The Pilgrims at Plymouth

by Lucille Recht Penner (Random House for Young Readers, 2002)

This informational book is packed with fun facts and colorful pictures about the Pilgrims and their new life in America. After sharing the book, ask children what they learned about Pilgrims that was different from what they thought before.

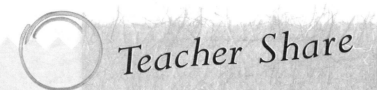

## Teacher Share

SOCIAL STUDIES

### A Mayflower Meal

Dining on the Mayflower was not a yummy experience. Many foods spoiled, so the choices were limited. Invite children to experience some of these foods by offering their closest substitutes. For example, bring in dried beef, cheese, and stale crackers (as "hardtack"). After children taste these items, they will surely become thirsty. This is an excellent opportunity to share the fact that water was not readily available because it was too dirty. But, unlike the Pilgrims, your students may take a trip to the water fountain!

*Stacey Suter*

Check for food allergies before serving the Mayflower meal.

## Book Break

### Thanksgiving Is

by Gail Gibbons (Holiday House, 2005)

With colorful illustrations and a manageable amount of text, this book provides young readers with information about the history of Thanksgiving and other harvest festivals throughout time. After reading, make a Venn diagram to compare and contrast Thanksgiving long ago and now.

SCIENCE

## Plant Parts Chart

Take apart a Thanksgiving feast to learn more about the parts of a plant. Invite children to cut out pictures of Thanksgiving fruits and vegetables. Arrange them on a table and gather children around. Ask: *Which food is a seed? a stem? a root? a leaf? a fruit? a flower?* For example, broccoli and cauliflower are flowers. Corn and peas are seeds. Celery and asparagus are stems. Potatoes, onions, and carrots are roots. Lettuce and cabbage are leaves. Pumpkins and apples are fruits. Let children spend some time exploring the foods and grouping them. Then use the pictures to make a chart. Write the words for plant parts on sentence strips and trim. Tack these up on a bulletin board. Let children take turns placing the pictures where they go. Discuss other foods that belong in each group.

For more Thanksgiving teaching activities, see *The Thanksgiving Activity Book* by Deborah Schecter (Scholastic, 2000). This book includes a reproducible Mayflower board game, a Thanksgiving Memories mini-book, riddles, art activities, poems, songs, a pocket-chart poetry poster, and more.

**TIP**

November and the upcoming months are filled with holidays. This is a good time to invite children's relatives into the classroom to share how different holidays are celebrated in their homes.

**TIP**

Invite children to pair up and create word problems using the items in their Lift-the-Flap boats. Have children share with another student pair.

**Book Break**

# A Time to Keep: The Tasha Tudor Books of Holidays

by Tasha Tudor (Simon & Schuster, 1996)

With simple text describing holiday celebrations through the year, this book will spark discussions about family holiday traditions. After sharing the book, let children talk about ways their families celebrate Thanksgiving and other holidays.

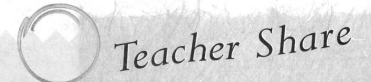

## *Teacher Share*

SOCIAL STUDIES

## Lift-the-Flap Mayflower

Children learn about provisions brought on the Mayflower with this project. For background information share the books *If You Sailed on the Mayflower in 1620* by Ann McGovern (Scholastic, 1993) and *On the Mayflower: Voyage of the Ship's Apprentice & a Passenger Girl* by Kate Waters (Scholastic, 1999).

- Have children cut a large boat shape from brown construction paper.
- Guide them in drawing four squares on the boats, then cutting around three sides of each square, as shown, to make four flaps.
- Have children glue their boats to white construction paper, being careful not to glue down the flaps.
- Have children cut out three masts, glue them to their boats, then add tissue paper sails.
- Together, make a list of provisions Pilgrims brought on the Mayflower—for example, cheese, lemons, clothes, tools, furniture, seeds, mirrors, and knives. Have students draw several items under the four flaps.
- Display the boats, letting children peek under one another's flaps to see some things the Pilgrims brought to America.

*Barbara Gauker*

# 'Twas the Night Before Thanksgiving
## by Dav Pilkey (Orchard Books, 1990)

Children will laugh out loud when you share this adaptation of the classic tale "'Twas the Night Before Christmas." A class field trip to a turkey farm changes the holiday plans for all the turkeys. After sharing the book, spark a class discussion by asking: What differences did you notice between *'Twas the Night Before Thanksgiving* and *'Twas the Night Before Christmas?*

## Teacher Share

### SCIENCE AND NUTRITION

## Thanksgiving Food Pyramid

**S**tudents enjoy sharing family traditions as they help build a food pyramid representing their Thanksgiving feasts. Draw a large triangle on posterboard. Divide it into four sections to represent the food pyramid. Label the pyramid: Breads and Cereals, Fruits and Vegetables, Dairy and Proteins, and Extras. Invite children to cut out or draw pictures of three foods they'd like to eat for Thanksgiving. Newspaper or magazine ads, grocery coupons, junk mail, and food labels are good sources of pictures. Let children take turns gluing their pictures to the pyramid. Together, plan an assortment of healthy Thanksgiving meals!

*Denise Pettinger*

 **TIP**

To help build the home-school connection, try using the reproducible send-home letters in *Instant Send-Home Letters* by Joan Novelli (Scholastic, 2000). Send-home letters to support your Thanksgiving lessons include "Celebrating Special Days," "Ask Me About Science," and "Getting Along."

## Favorite Foods Graph
## Turkey Markers

# December

# December
## Teaching Ideas

*I*t's a rare child (or adult) who is not excited when December rolls around. There's Christmas, Hanukkah, Kwanzaa, snow, starry nights, colorful winter birds, decorations, presents, songs, games, and more—all combined with the spirit of peace, giving, and brotherhood that our December holiday traditions symbolize. There may be no more special time of year.

The teaching ideas for December include activities, books, songs, and poems to help you channel children's natural enthusiasm, excitement, and motivation to create great opportunities for fun and learning. You'll find four engaging themes: HOLIDAYS will involve your class in books, traditions, and activities related to Christmas, Hanukkah, and Kwanzaa as well as the ever present (and always popular) holiday cookies and candy. (See "Hurray for Holidays! Class Book," page 101.) STARS capitalizes on the incredible beauty and mystery of the night sky, its scientific aspects as well as the fantasy and imagination it captures and inspires. Children will love the stellar activities like "Creative Constellations" (page 109) and "One-Snip Star" (page 111). ANIMALS IN WINTER will be a favorite with children—inviting them to explore how animals keep warm in winter, where they go, and what they do. The JAN BRETT AUTHOR STUDY is perfect for December, with many stories featuring memorable animal and human characters, wintry settings, holidays, and wonderful, warm themes brought to life with detailed and compelling text and illustrations. Other December delights you'll find include:

☆ a send-home activity calendar

☆ hands-on math and science activities

☆ a fun and easy no-cook recipe

☆ ready-to-use reproducible pages—including a mini-play, a starry word wheel, and more

☆ an easy-to-learn song children will love to sing again and again

☆ literature links from old favorites to new classics

☆ an holiday class book for children to make and share

☆ and many more activities for planning a dazzling December!

Name _____

# December Activity Calendar

Choose _____ activities to do each week this month.
Ask an adult in your family to initial the square in the box of each activity
you complete. Bring this paper back to school on _____ .

| Monday | Tuesday | Wednesday | Thursday | Friday |
|---|---|---|---|---|
| Write the word *December* on a sheet of paper. Cut apart the letters. Make new words! **bed** **be** **red** | Happy birthday, Jan Brett! (December 1) Have you read her book *The Mitten*? Find more Jan Brett books to read. | December is the twelfth month. Draw pictures of things that come in groups of 12. | Fill in the blank: $6 + \underline{\phantom{xx}} = 12$ Write new number sentences that have 12 as an answer. | Draw a picture that shows how you dress for cold weather. Label the things you wear. |
| Tell someone in your family about a favorite holiday activity. Ask that person to tell you about one, too. | Count the points on this star. Find a star on this page that looks the same. | Look at the words on this page. Find two that rhyme with *took*. | Look at a calendar. Find the first day of winter. How many weeks until spring? | How many -e's in *December*? Which other month has the same number of -e's? |
| What two words make *snowflake*? What new words can you make by putting the words here together? **fire, house, truck, dog, fly** | What is winter like where you live? Describe what the other seasons are like, too. | Put one ice cube on a plate and one in an empty jar. Which do you think will melt first? Find out! | Draw a snowflake on every fifth day of a December calendar. Count the days by fives. | How many days are in December? How many fewer days are in November? |
| Pretend you're a weather reporter. Give someone in your family the report for today. Make a prediction for tomorrow. | What are the last two letters in the word *December*? Name three other months with the same two letters at the end. | Think of a gift you can give someone special that doesn't cost any money. Give it to that person! | What year is it now? What year will it be when January starts? | Turn *December* into a tongue twister! Make up a sentence using as many words as you can that start with d. |

500+ Fabulous Month-by-Month Teaching Ideas © 2010 Scholastic Teaching Resources

# Teacher Share

LANGUAGE ARTS, ART

## Hurray for Holidays! Class Book

Students celebrate many different holidays and even the same holidays in many different ways. Help students share these experiences with each other by creating a class book about holiday traditions. Send each student home with a sheet of drawing paper. Attach a note asking families to help write about a family holiday tradition and illustrate it. Once all of these are returned, create a cover, then bind the pages to make a class book. Let children take turns taking the book home to share with their families.

*Judy Meagher*

## Book Break

## Night Tree

### by Eve Bunting (Harcourt Brace, 1991)

The family in this story has a tradition of going into the woods each year on Christmas Eve and decorating a pine tree with popcorn, cranberries, and other goodies for the animals who live in the woods there. After reading the book you may want to find a tree near your school to adopt as your own "class tree." You can string popcorn, cranberries, and raisins on the branches of your tree and watch for friendly winter visitors.

MATH

# Calendar Activity: How Many More Days?

Use your class calendar and students' anticipation for the holidays to focus on math concepts. Staple a large, blank December calendar on a bulletin board. Write the numbers from 1–31 in their respective boxes and mark the month's holidays. Have students routinely estimate and then count how many more days there are until a given December holiday. To check answers, have students count backwards from the holiday to the day they started on. A good way to help with this sort of counting is to let students apply sticker dots or tacks to each day as they count. This provides an easy method for going back and checking the count and helps students visualize the difference between one given date and another.

*Teacher Share*

MATH, ART

## Geome-Trees

This holiday tree-inspired project helps students practice shape recognition and patterning while providing a decorative display space.

◎ Give each child a 12- by 18-inch piece of green construction paper, a pencil, scissors, and glue. Have students cut a triangle-shaped tree from the paper. (See sample, right.)

◎ Give students construction paper, foil, tissue paper, and recycled gift wrap. Have them cut shapes from the supplies and glue them on the "trees" to create patterned rows. Each row should contain a different, consistent pattern.

◎ Have students glue their trees to 12- by 18-inch paper and display them on a bulletin board. Gather students around to identify all the different shapes and patterns they see.

*Judy Wetzel*

**TIP**

You may want to have a few shape templates or shape pieces, such as attribute blocks or pattern blocks, available as students cut out their shapes.

*Teacher Share*

## Adopt an Angel

Instead of having a class holiday gift exchange, you may want to get everyone involved in the spirit of the season by "adopting an angel." Contact local service agencies and ask to be matched with a family that has a child or children close in age to your students. You may also choose to "adopt" a local agency that provides assistance for families in need—for example, a food shelf or a shelter for homeless families.

Together, plan a gift to donate to the family or agency. Start planning well in advance so that you have time to raise money or make something. Students might donate money they earn at home by doing extra chores, or money from a school recycling drive. Your students will have other ideas for getting a gift together. For example, they might bring in a toy or book in good condition that they no longer play with. They can work together to clean up the items, then donate them to an agency that works with children. Or, your students might each sew a square for a quilt, and donate it to a family with a new baby. Wrap the gifts in handmade gift wrap (students' hand stamps on craft paper makes lovely wrapping paper) and deliver them to the agency on behalf of your class.

*Charlotte Sassman*

Book Break

# Hershel and the Hanukkah Goblins
### by Eric Kimmel (Scholastic, 1990)

This has got to be the most exciting Hanukkah story of all time! On the first night of Hanukkah, Hershel arrives in a little village plagued by goblins who prevent the people of the town from celebrating Hanukkah. Hershel outwits the goblins, including the dreaded King of the Goblins, and restores Hanukkah to the town. This is a good way to introduce Hanukkah traditions in a very motivating context.

SCIENCE, SOCIAL STUDIES

# Light Science

Many holidays, such as Hanukkah, Christmas, Las Posadas, and Kwanzaa, include candles and lights in their celebrations. The story of Hanukkah also includes specific references to lighting oil lamps. Let students observe some dramatic changes of matter with a "holiday light" experiment. Put some lamp oil in a small jar. Set a cotton wick in it. Place the oil in the jar on one side of a bucket balance scale. On the other side place an equal amount of weight.

Light the wick and ask students to watch what happens. As the oil burns off, the balance scale will tip. Students can watch as the liquid matter turns to a gas due to heat. Discuss how other substances change their state of matter due to temperature—for example, water turning to ice or ice melting to water. Have students summarize these ideas by writing or drawing a science equation to record a change of matter they have seen—for example, *oil + heat = gas* or *ice + heat = water*.

**Book Break**

# K Is for Kwanzaa:
# A Kwanzaa Alphabet Book
### by Juwanda G. Ford (Scholastic, 1997)

Colorful illustrations and enlightening explanations fill this fun, age-appropriate alphabet book. Use the book as an inspiration for a class holiday alphabet book. Talk about the December holidays your students celebrate. Ask students to suggest holiday ideas for each letter of the alphabet. Have students write and illustrate individual pages of the book. Put them together for your own holiday alphabet book.

LANGUAGE ARTS, SOCIAL STUDIES

# "Holiday Lights" Mini-Play

Learn more about the role of light in various holidays with the mini-play on page 107. Begin by learning a little about each holiday—for example, when it is celebrated, by whom, and how. Give each child a copy of the play. Divide the class into four groups—one for each holiday. Have children practice their lines, paying attention to the rhythm of the language. Give students time to make simple props—for example, they might color flames on sheets of paper to hold above their heads. (See illustration, left.) Bring students together for a reading, then take your show on the road!

MATH

# Candy Counter

In December the stores are filled with bags of hard candy. These sweets make bright, inexpensive, and very motivating manipulatives. Fill a large, clear container like a glass pitcher or kitchen canister to the brim with an assortment of candies. Give each student a piece of lined paper. Have students fold the paper in thirds vertically. Ask students to estimate how many candies they think are in the container and write these estimates in the first section of the paper. Remove about one fourth of the candy from the container. Have students count this candy and then return it to the container. With this new information, ask students if they would like to revise their estimates. Have students record revised estimates in the second section of their papers. Remove one half of the candy in the container. Have students count this candy and then return it to the container. Allow for a third estimate. Compare estimates, do a final count, and discuss students' thinking.

**TIP**

Check for food allergies before letting children sample the candies.

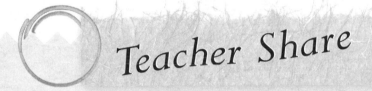

_Teacher Share_

MATH

## Cookie Shop Math

Cookies and holidays seem to go hand in hand. To enjoy this situation, and provide some practical consumer math experience, bring in a class supply of three or four different kinds of cookies. Arrange the cookies on separate plates (one type per plate). Place a different price tag next to each plate. Pair up children and let them take turns being "shopkeeper" and "shopper." Give the shopper a target amount of money you want them to work with, in play money or real coins, and a copy of the order form on page 108. Have the shopper first complete the order form that tells how many of each cookie he or she will be buying and what the total cost will be. This is given to the shopkeeper, who checks it and then "fills the order." When this is complete and correct, students switch places. When everyone has had a turn, let students enjoy their "purchases"!

_Bobbie Williams_

## Teacher Share

MATH

## No-Cook Recipe: Peppermint Fudge

### Peppermint Fudge

several candy canes
3 one-gallon reclosable bags
rolling pin
1 pound powdered sugar

1 stick margarine
1/2 cup baking cocoa
1 teaspoon vanilla extract

◎ Place the candy canes in a reclosable bag. Use a rolling pin to crush them.

◎ Place the remaining ingredients in a second bag, add the crushed candy, and zip it. For extra protection, double-bag the ingredients by placing the zipped bag inside the third bag.

◎ Pass the bag around and have each child squeeze and knead until the ingredients are thoroughly mixed and pull away from the sides of the bag. Spread the mixture in an 8-inch-square pan, refrigerate until cool, then use a cookie cutter or knife to cut into pieces.

There are plenty of candy canes around in December. Often, too many! Here's a simple no-cook recipe that can help your class use up those candy canes while making some tasty fudge together. Use the experience to discuss fractions, measuring, and other math skills.

*Ann Flagg*

MUSIC, MATH, LANGUAGE ARTS

## Our Twelve Days

Our Twelve Days of December
1 a monkey in a coconut tree
2 little parakeets
3 cups of hot cocoa
4 chocolate cakes
5 computer games
6 pieces of bubble gum
7 candy bars
8 little puppies
9 stuffed animals
10 goldfish
11 comic books
12 bottles of soda

Learn and sing the traditional holiday song "The Twelve Days of Christmas." Two good versions to share with children are *The Twelve Days of Christmas*, illustrated by Joanna Isles (Hyperion, 1992), and *The Twelve Days of Christmas*, illustrated by Jan Brett (Putnam, 1986). After reading the book aloud, list the numbers 1 through 12 on chart paper. Next to each number write the corresponding word—for example, next to 3, write "French hens."

Now, tell students they are going to help you rewrite the song. You can make it "The Twelve Days of"…Christmas, Hanukkah, Kwanzaa or December! Begin a new chart with the numbers 1 through 12. Ask students to suggest new gifts for each day. Record suggestions next to the numbers. When the chart is complete, sing the new version together. (You may have to sing it numerous times to try out each idea.) For a little math aside, it is interesting to add up the total number of gifts given over the 12 days.

# Holiday Lights Mini-Play

## Characters

Christmas candles ☆ Hanukkah candles ☆ Las Posadas candles ☆ Kwanzaa candles

**All:** We are all candles.
Look at our light.
Each of us helps
To make holidays bright.

**Christmas Candles:** We sit on branches
Making Christmas trees shine.

**Hanukkah Candles:** In Hanukkah menorahs
We stand eight in a line.

**Las Posadas Candles:** At Las Posadas
We're carried at night.

**Kwanzaa Candles:** In a Kwanzaa kinara,
Just look at our light.

**All:** We are all candles
Now here we go.
We helped make each
Of our holidays glow.

*(stage direction: candles "go out," kids duck down, house lights go out)*

Name _____  Date _____

# Cookie Shop Math

## Order Form

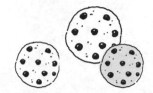

| Cookie Type | Price Each | How Many | Total Cost |
| --- | --- | --- | --- |
|  |  |  |  |
|  |  |  |  |
|  |  |  |  |
|  |  |  |  |
|  |  |  |  |

# Teacher Share

## Creative Constellations

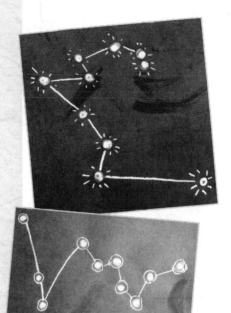

**D**ecember skies are great for spotting stars and constellations. They're fun to see, but even more fun to make. Give each student a sheet of 11- by 17-inch black construction paper. Provide students with small containers of white glue and pieces of popcorn or cereal. Have students put their papers on the floor, then carefully dip a piece of cereal or popcorn into the glue and drop the piece on the paper. Have them do this with ten pieces. While the papers are drying, ask students to imagine that their pictures are really a scattering of stars in space. Ask: *What does your pattern of stars remind you of?* Have them decide, then create constellations by connecting the "stars" with chalk lines.

*Jackie Clarke*

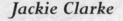

## Book Break

# National Audubon Society First Field Guides: Night Sky

(Scholastic, 1999)

Detailed descriptions, photographs, and sky maps will teach your young sky-watchers about the wonders of the world above them. Build science vocabulary with the glossary, which includes dozens of words from *alignment* to *zodiac*.

## Stellar Students

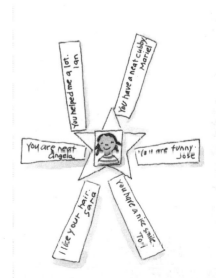

It's always good to create opportunities for developing and bolstering self-concept. Each week designate one of your students as "Star of the Week." Ask students to write compliments about the Star of the Week on sentence strips and sign their name. In the center of a bulletin board, place a star with the student's name and/or picture. Tack up the compliment sentence strips so that they appear as rays of light emanating from that center star.

SOCIAL STUDIES, LANGUAGE ARTS

# When You Wish Upon a Star

In many traditional stories, stars are for wishing—particularly on the first star of the evening or a shooting star. Use this tradition as a story starter for your class. Ask students: *If you were to see a wishing star, and could have only one wish, what would you wish for?* Have students share their wishes. Follow up by having students write about what a character from a book might wish for—for example, in *Curious George Takes a Job* by H. A. Rey (Houghton Mifflin, 1947), George might wish he was not quite so curious. (Students will have lots of fun recalling all of the reasons why.)

ART, SCIENCE

# Night Sky Scratchboard

Scratchboard is a beautiful technique that children can use to create artistic interpretations of the night sky. You can buy prepared scratchboards, but it's also fun to make them.

◎ Give each student a piece of oaktag. Have students press hard with light-colored crayons to completely cover the paper with a thick layer of color. (Yellows, whites, oranges, reds, and light blues work well.)

◎ Have children paint over the crayon with black tempera paint or india ink. Let dry for a day, then give students toothpicks and have them use these as they would pencils to make night sky designs on their scratchboards. The toothpick scratching will remove the top coat of ink or paint to reveal colorful designs below—in this case, a night sky full of shining stars.

MATH

# Shapely Stars

A star is an interesting shape and can provide a good jumping-off point for some geometry exploration. Begin by asking students what a star shape looks like. Have volunteers come to the chalkboard to draw various possibilities—for example, a five-pointed star, Star of David, asterisk-type star, and so on. Discuss the attributes of these stars and what makes each unique. Now, provide students with a good supply of pattern and/or attribute blocks. Ask: *How many different ways can you make a star using these?* Have students combine shape pieces to make as many different stars as they can from their shapes, and display these on their desks. At the end of the session, have students tour the desks to see the different ways their classmates combined various shapes to create stars.

# Teacher Share

LANGUAGE ARTS

## Starry Word Wheel

**H**elp students practice words in the *-ar* word family with a star-shaped word wheel. Give children copies of page 114, and have them cut out and color the circle and the star. Help students use a sharp pencil to poke a hole through the circle and star at the black dot. Have them place the star on top of the circle and attach at the center with a brad, then turn the wheel and read the words. Students can use this word wheel as a pattern for making more word wheels. What new words can they make?

*Natalie Vaughan*

MATH

## One-Snip Star

Try this magical technique to make five-pointed stars with a few simple folds and one snip of the scissors.

◎ Give each child a square sheet of paper.

◎ Guide students in following the directions (right) to fold and cut their papers. Count the points on the stars together: *Do they all have five points?*

◎ Give children assorted paper to make more stars on their own. Foils and fluorescent papers add a sparkly touch.

◎ Let children hang their stars from thread. Dangle from the ceiling to create a sparkling night sky in the classroom.

Adapted from *Science Tricks and Magic for Young People* by George Barr (Dover, 1968)

Step 1.
Fold square in half.

Step 2.
Fold X to Y.    Step 2 completed.

Step 3.      Step 3 completed.
Fold b to a

Step 4.      Step 4 completed.
Fold C to D.

Step 5.      Step 5 completed.
Cut right through
on this line.

Open to see star.

## Teacher Share

LANGUAGE ARTS

### Free Verse Star Poem

After having done some work in the unit on stars, have students complete this free verse poem either individually or as a class.

*Natalie Vaughan*

**Stars**

*by* _____

Stars _____.        *(complete with present*
Stars _____.        *tense verbs)*
Stars _____.
Stars _____.

_____ stars.        *(complete with -ing words)*
_____ stars.
_____ stars.
_____ stars.

Stars are _____.        *(complete with adjectives)*
Stars are _____.
Stars are _____.
Stars are _____.

## Book Break

### Stargazers
by Gail Gibbons (Holiday House, 1992)

This book covers history, astronomers, constellations, rotation, and everything a young scientist needs to know about stars in an easy-to-understand format. Invite each student to choose a fact from the book to share with the class. Using the One-Snip Star technique (see page 111), have each student make a star from white construction paper. Let students write their facts on the stars, then use them to create a display. Give the display a name, such as "A Galaxy of Star Facts."

# Teacher Share

## Star Watch

As your class learns about stars, hang a large sheet of black paper on a bulletin board surface. Stock a nearby table with books and other resources on space and stars, as well as felt pens, scissors, metallic paper, glitter, glitter crayons, white chalk, glue sticks, silver and gold pens, and other art materials.

Create a schedule, assigning three or four students to look at the sky each night. Have them report on what they saw the following day by responding to this chant (done in a definitive rap-type beat):

> Late at night when the moon is high
> The stars come out and light up the sky.
>
> (Ryan, Ryan) tell us what you saw.
> What do you think that you might draw?

Have students use the materials to add a record of their observations to the Star Watch display.

*Judy Meagher*

MOVEMENT

## Star Catchers

Here's a fun and easy game that provides everyone with a good run around. Divide the class into two groups: "stars" (one third of the students) and "catchers" (two thirds). Mark off two boundaries, about 20 feet apart. Have the stars stand together at one end and the catchers stand in the middle, between the two ends. The catchers start the game by chanting, "Star light, star bright, how many stars are out tonight?" Stars respond with "More than you can catch!" Stars then run as fast as they can to the opposite end, trying to avoid being tagged by a catcher. Stars who are caught become catchers, and the game continues until all stars are caught.

Adapted from *A Year of Hands-on Science* by Lynne Kepler (Scholastic, 2008)

**Cut out**

**ar**

## Starry Word Wheel

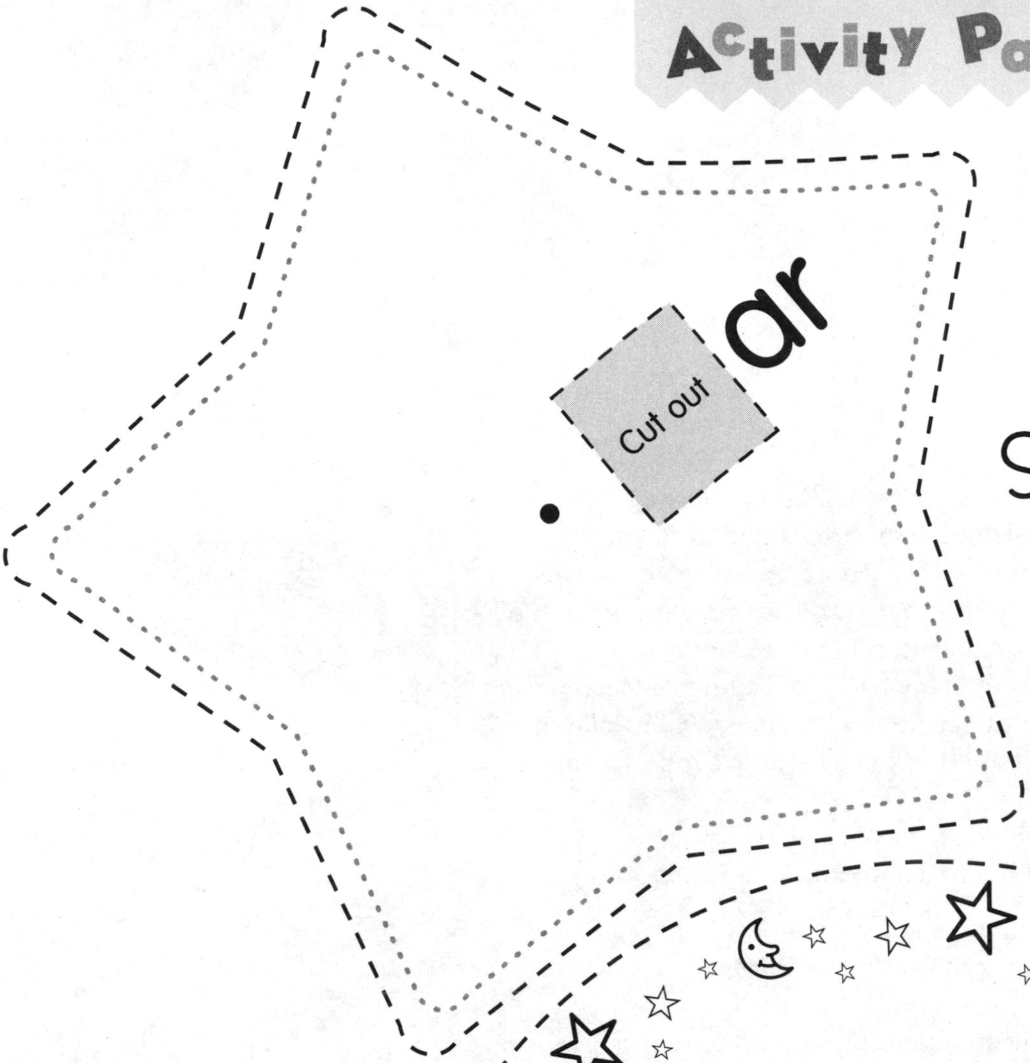

st

qs

q

c

f

## Book Break

# Hibernation

(Patterns in Nature series)

by Margaret Hall (Capstone, 2008)

The close-up photograph on the book's cover of a bear settling in for a winter nap, with inset photos of a bear eating grass and catching a fish, will draw young readers right in to learn more about the science of hibernation. Like other titles in the series, this book provides children with opportunities to practice using features of nonfiction, including a table of contents, chapter headings, photos and diagrams, a glossary, and an index.

SCIENCE

# Winter Habitats Mural

Where do bears and other animals go in winter? Help children understand with this project that animals have different ways of dealing with cold weather. Start by introducing the terms *active* (an active animal continues to be up and around in winter), *dormant* (the animal's body slows down and it "sleeps" for part of the winter), and *hibernate* (the animal goes into a deep sleep for the winter; the heartbeat slows down; the body temperature drops).

Then have children work together to create a mural that shows a range of habitats including a pond, woods (include roots and evergreen trees), fields, caves, and hollowed-out trees. Have them include snow on the ground, and an underground area. Copy a set of the animal cards on page 118 and cut them apart. Give each child (or pair of children) a card. Have children color in their animals, then help them research how the animals spend their winters. For example, a child with the woodchuck card will discover that these animals hibernate underground in burrows. Ask children to write a fact on their cards about where their animals go in winter, then place them in the correct places on the mural. When the mural is complete, discuss the many homes animals have in winter. Let children identify which ones are active or dormant, and which ones hibernate.

Adapted from *Hands-On Nature* by Jenepher Lingelbach (Vermont Institute of Natural Science, 1986)

### TIP

Here's where the animals pictured on the Animal Habitat cards go in winter:

- ◎ **Little Brown Bat** (hibernates): cave
- ◎ **Black Bear** (dormant): cave or under fallen tree
- ◎ **Beaver** (active): pond, below ice
- ◎ **Woodchuck** (hibernates): in burrow
- ◎ **White-Tailed Deer** (active): woods
- ◎ **Cottontail Rabbit** (active): brush
- ◎ **Raccoon** (dormant): hollow trees
- ◎ **Squirrel** (active): trees
- ◎ **Meadow Mouse** (active): tunnels in snow
- ◎ **Coyote** (active): fields, woods
- ◎ **Snowshoe Hare** (active): woods
- ◎ **Chipmunk** (dormant): tunnels in snow

After students have successfully answered the questions in the stories, invite them to place a number of bears of their choosing in the park scene. Then tell them to send some of the bears to the cave. How many bears are left outside of the cave? Invite students to tell a partner a new story while the partner manipulates the pieces to match the story.

MATH, SCIENCE

# Bears at Home Math Story Mat

Math story mats are a fun way for students to practice math skills with manipulatives in an engaging story context. After exploring what bears do in winter, use the reproducible story mat (see page 119) and the manipulative patterns (see page 120) to have children "act out" the two math activities below. Have children color and cut out the manipulatives first. Ask them to color three large and three small bears black, and three large and three small bears brown. (They will need multiple copies of the manipulatives.) Then read the story through once while children listen. Read it a second time and have children use the manipulatives and story mat to act out the story as it unfolds.

## Wake-Up Time

The sun comes up and the bears are starting to wake up. A large black bear goes to sit on a ledge. Two small black bears join him. Then a large brown bear climbs the tree and sits on a rock to warm himself. *How many bears are out this morning? How many are black?*

## Time for Bed

Night is falling. The bears are going to sleep. A large brown bear goes into the cave first. Two little brown bears follow. A black bear still sits on the ledge. *How many bears are in the cave? How many bears are still in the woods?*

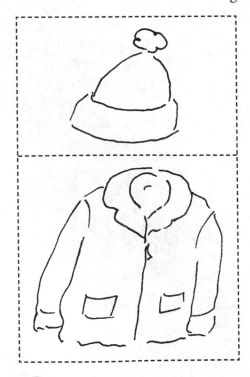

MATH

# Clothing Combinations

Use hats and coats to help students explore the concept of *combinations*. Give each child multiple copies of the patterns at right. (Enlarge first.) Ask children to color each hat and each coat a different color and/or pattern and cut them out. Now have children make as many combinations of hats and coats as they can. For example, a blue hat and a green coat, a blue hat and a red coat, a blue hat and an orange coat are three possible combinations. Simplify the activity by beginning with just two hats and one coat. Have students record all the possible combinations and report to you on them. Add one item at a time until students are working with all three hats and coats. Have them record results carefully and see if they can discover any patterns or make any predictions. Let them make and add more coats and hats to test their predictions.

# Teacher Share

## Fun Hat Day

t's not just animals that have to stay warm in winter. We do, too. One of the best ways, of course, is with a hat. Ask: *How can wearing a hat help keep you warm?* (Explain that hats help keep heat from escaping from their bodies, the same way mittens help hold the heat in their hands.) To have some fun and creativity with this, designate a Fun Hat Day. Set up for this day by having students help collect hat-making materials—paper grocery bags, fabric scraps, foil pie plates, whatever. Give students time to create hats, adding decorative embellishments with ribbon, glitter, and other supplies. Don't forget the camera!

*Rita Galloway*

SCIENCE

## Design a Nose Warmer

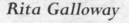

Investigate ways of staying warm with an activity that challenges children to invent ways to keep their noses warm. Provide an assortment of materials to make nose warmers—for example, pipe cleaners (good for attaching to nose warmers and hooking around ears like eyeglasses), yarn, fabric scraps, cotton balls, gauze bandages, wool. Direct children to use the materials to make nose warmers that:

◎ stay on their noses (no hands)

◎ let them breathe

◎ keep their noses warm when they hold an ice cube to it for one minute

Have children make their nose warmers, then test them: Each child places an ice cube in a reclosable sandwich bag and holds it to his or her nose for a minute. Talk about how well the warmers work. Encourage children to suggest ways of making nose warmers that work better.

# Activity Page

## Little Brown Bat

Here's how
I spend winter:

_____
_____
_____

## Black Bear

Here's how
I spend winter:

_____
_____
_____

## Beaver

Here's how
I spend winter:

_____
_____
_____

## Woodchuck

Here's how
I spend winter:

_____
_____
_____

## White-Tailed Deer

Here's how
I spend winter:

_____
_____
_____

## Cottontail Rabbit

Here's how
I spend winter:

_____
_____
_____

## Raccoon

Here's how
I spend winter:

_____
_____
_____

## Squirrel

Here's how
I spend winter:

_____
_____
_____

## Meadow Mouse

Here's how
I spend winter:

_____
_____
_____

## Coyote

Here's how
I spend winter:

_____
_____
_____

## Snowshoe Hare

Here's how
I spend winter:

_____
_____
_____

## Chipmunk

Here's how
I spend winter:

_____
_____
_____

Name _____

Date _____

# Bears at Home Math Story Mat

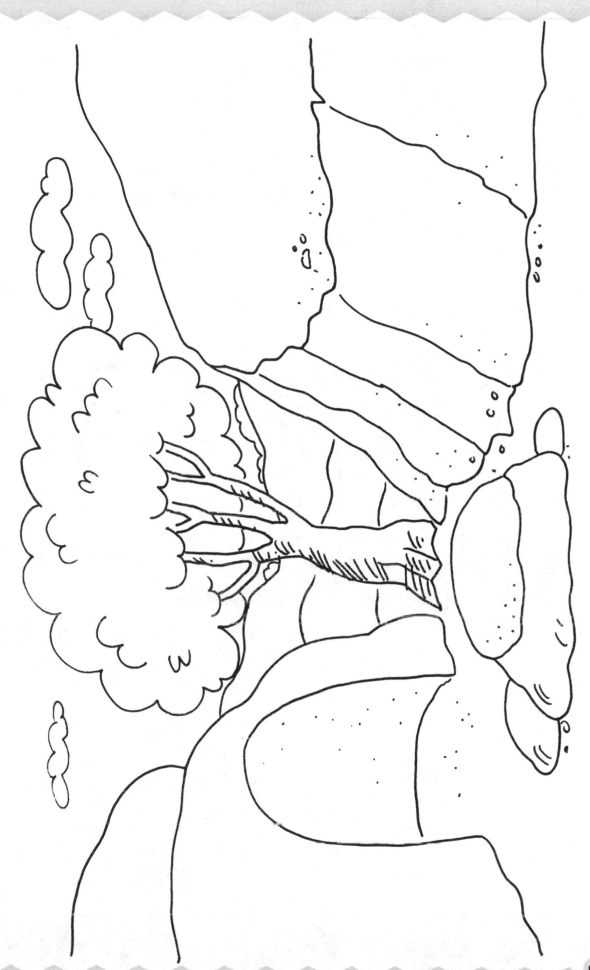

500+ Fabulous Month-by-Month Teaching Ideas © 2010 Scholastic Teaching Resources

# Bears at Home
# Math Story Mat

500+ Fabulous Month-by-Month Teaching Ideas © 2010 Scholastic Teaching Resources

LANGUAGE ARTS

# All About Jan Brett

Jan Brett has been writing and illustrating books for children since 1978. She is well known for her bright, detailed, realistic illustration style and her many memorable animal characters. Jan not only illustrates but writes many of her books as well. Her themes and settings cover a wide range of ideas, characters, and settings. Involve children in researching information about Jan Brett. Have them record facts about the author on mitten-shaped cards (in honor of her well-known book, *The Mitten*), and display them near a collection of her books. Some facts to get students started follow.

◎ Jan Brett lives in Massachusetts.

◎ She has a real hedgehog, Buffy, and a Siberian husky, Perky Pumpkin.

◎ Jan likes to travel to new places all over the United States and even around the world for inspiration, settings, and sketching.

◎ Jan was born on December 1st, (another great reason to plan a December Jan Brett author study).

LANGUAGE ARTS

# Progressive Bulletin Board

As you and your students share books by Jan Brett, build an interactive bulletin board. The more students read, the more it grows!

◎ Have students draw a new book cover for Jan Brett books they read. Have them write a brief summary on an index card.

◎ Display book covers on a bulletin board, with a library card pocket tacked under each. Place completed index cards in a large manila envelope at the bottom of the display.

◎ Let students visit the display, matching index cards to the books and placing them in the appropriate pockets.

◎ Continue adding books and index cards to the display as students read them.

Books by Jan Brett include the following:

◎ *Gingerbread Friends* (Putnam, 2008)

◎ *The Three Snow Bears* (Putnam, 2007)

◎ *Hedgie Blasts Off!* (Putnam, 2006)

◎ *Honey...Honey...Lion!* (Putnam, 2005)

◎ *The Umbrella* (Putnam, 2004)

◎ *Daisy Comes Home* (Putnam, 2002)

◎ *Hedgie's Surprise* (Putnam, 2002)

◎ *Gingerbread Baby* (Putnam, 1999)

◎ *The First Dog* (Harcourt, 1998)

◎ *The Hat* (Putnam, 1997)

◎ *Comet's Nine Lives* (Putnam, 1997)

◎ *Armadillo Rodeo* (Putnam, 1995)

◎ *Town Mouse, Country Mouse* (Putnam, 1994)

◎ *Trouble With Trolls* (Putnam, 1992)

◎ *Berlioz the Bear* (Putnam, 1991)

◎ *The Mitten* (Putnam, 1989)

◎ *Annie and the Wild Animals* (Houghton Mifflin, 1985)

◎ *Fritz and the Beautiful Horses* (Houghton Mifflin, 1981)

## Teacher Share

# A Mini Mitten Unit

In *The Mitten* (Putnam, 1989), assorted animals put a child's lost mitten to good use—burrowing inside to keep warm. Use the story as a springboard for a variety of activities, all of which use mittens!

◎ Cut out and number 100 tagboard mittens. Let children color them, then laminate for durability. Place the mittens in a pocket chart in random order. Let children arrange the mittens in order. Start small. Begin with mittens 1–20. Gradually add another 10 to 20 mittens for students to work with. For a change of pace, have students place mittens in the pocket chart by twos, fives, or tens.

◎ Have students pretend they lost a mitten and an animal crept inside to keep warm. Have them draw a picture of their mittens and the animals inside.

◎ Play a mitten game. Have children trace their hands (fingers together) to make mitten shapes. Have them cut out the mittens and color them, creating any pattern they like to make matching mittens. Collect the mittens, mix them up, and tack them to a display. Let children take turns matching mittens.

*Mary Rosenberg*

**TIP**

Students can use their book report borders as a guide for oral retellings of the stories.

# Book Report Borders Banner

A distinctive feature of Jan Brett's style is her use of border artwork. Not only are the borders decorative, detailed, and beautiful, but they often tell a part of the story. Invite students to give this same technique a try as a way of retelling the stories they read. Give students copies of the template on page 126. Have them use the center area to draw a picture from the book. Have them weave characters, events, and other elements into the borders, then complete the information at the bottom. Tape students' book report borders together side to side to make a Jan Brett banner.

MATH

# Comet's Target Numbers

In *Comet's Nine Lives* (Putnam, 1996), Comet the cat goes through eight of his nine lives in a series of mishaps on Nantucket Island. All's well that ends well, of course. Number nine is never used up, but *nine* is an important number in the story. After reading about Comet ask students to assemble a collection of nine similar items on their desks. This could be nine crayons, nine erasers, nine books, or any other items commonly found in the room. Now change the target number, say to *seven*, and have students change their set of objects accordingly. Have students describe how they have changed their sets. For example, if they start with nine, and you ask them to show a set of seven, they may tell you that they have taken away two. Ask how this might be written in a number sentence form, and record it on the chalkboard or have them record it at their desks on paper or mini white-boards. Try this with a variety of target numbers, and add or subtract objects accordingly based on your group's readiness.

LANGUAGE ARTS

# Collaborative Book Retelling

Jan Brett has written many original books, but she also has done a number of retellings of famous stories and supplied them with new illustrations. Take a look with your class at a few of these retellings:

@ *Goldilocks and the Three Bears* (Putnam, 1987)

@ *Beauty and the Beast* (Clarion, 1989)

@ *The Mitten* (Putnam, 1989)

@ *Town Mouse, Country Mouse* (Putnam, 1994)

@ *Gingerbread Baby* (Putnam, 1999)

Choose a well-known fairy tale, or even a Jan Brett book, and read it aloud to your class. Follow up by having students recall major events from the story. Record each on an index card. Have students team up with partners to write more about and illustrate each event. (Give each pair of students one index card to turn into a page of the book.) Students' pages should include an illustration and at least two sentences describing what is happening. When all pages are completed, have children work together to put the pages in order and number them. Make a front and back cover, bind, and let students take turns reading aloud their retellings.

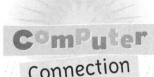
MUSIC, SCIENCE

# Animal Inspiration

Animals can be the inspiration for stories, poems, art, and music. In *Berlioz the Bear* (Putnam, 1991), a bee saves the day and Berlioz plays "The Flight of the Bumblebee" by N. Rimsky-Korsakov as a dedication to the bee. Listen to this piece of music, and ask the class if it reminds them of a bee and why. Divide the class into groups of four or five students. Ask each group to choose an animal (and keep its identity from the rest of the class), then think about the sounds it makes, how it moves, and what its personality seems to be like. Give each group some rhythm instruments. Have students work together to create a one-minute presentation of music, dance, and sound that will represent their animal. One thing, though—no words! Have students take turns sharing their presentations. Have students in the audience try to guess each group's animal.

MATH

# Animal Search and Sort

Have students list as many animals as they can find in Jan Brett books. Draw a Venn diagram on the chalkboard with two overlapping circles. In one circle write "Wild," in the other "Farm/Domesticated." Ask partners to tell which animals they found in their books. List these on the board next to the diagram. Then have students take turns at the board, writing an animal's name on the Venn diagram and explaining their decision about where it belongs. As you do this, consider that some animals might belong in both areas. For example, there are domesticated dogs and there are wild dogs. If this is the case, show students how the intersecting area between the circles includes both.

LANGUAGE ARTS

# Character Clouds

Hedgie, the hedgehog; Bo, the armadillo; Comet, the cat. All are fun and interesting animal characters from various Jan Brett books. Have each student pick a favorite character. Give everyone two large sheets of white construction paper. With the paper placed one sheet on top of the other, have children draw a cloud shape and cut it out. On one cloud shape, have children draw a picture of the character. On the other, have them write the name of the character, the book title, and three words that describe the character. Show students how to staple the two papers together almost all the way around the edges. Have them stuff their clouds with scrap paper or packing materials. Finish stapling the clouds closed, then punch two holes at the top of each cloud and display from the ceiling with yarn.

# Teacher Share

MATH

## Measuring Up

Jan Brett books include many different types of animals. Two that feature horses are *Fritz and the Beautiful Horses* (Houghton Mifflin, 1981) and *Armadillo Rodeo* (Putnam, 1995). Horses are big animals, and they are traditionally measured in a unique way—by "hands." A "hand" (abbreviation = hh) is the width across the human hand, usually four inches or 10 centimeters. The height of a horse is measured in hands from the ground up to the *withers* (the highest point on a horse's shoulder). Have students use their hands to measure the height of a horse, using these averages:

◎ heavy breeds of horses: between 16 and 17 hands

◎ ponies: under 14 hands.

Next, have students measure a partner from the ground up to the shoulder and record it in hands. *Who's taller than a pony? Who's shorter than a heavy breed of horse?*

**Theresa Marie**

**TIP**

Students may like to work out conversions in standard or metric equivalences.

SOCIAL STUDIES, MOVEMENT

## Reindeer Run

Teeka, a young girl, has a terrible time trying to get all the reindeer to cooperate in *The Wild Christmas Reindeer* (Putnam, 1990). She eventually finds that understanding works better than heavy-handed tactics. Try this game with your students to help bring home the same point.

◎ Designate a starting line and finish line about 50 yards apart. Divide the class into groups of five. Have members of each group hold hands and form a circle, then stand at the starting line.

◎ When you say *Go*, have the groups race to the finish line without breaking the circle. If anyone drops a hand, or the circle breaks for any reason, they must go back to the starting line and begin again. Students will discover that cooperation becomes as important as individual speed in this race.

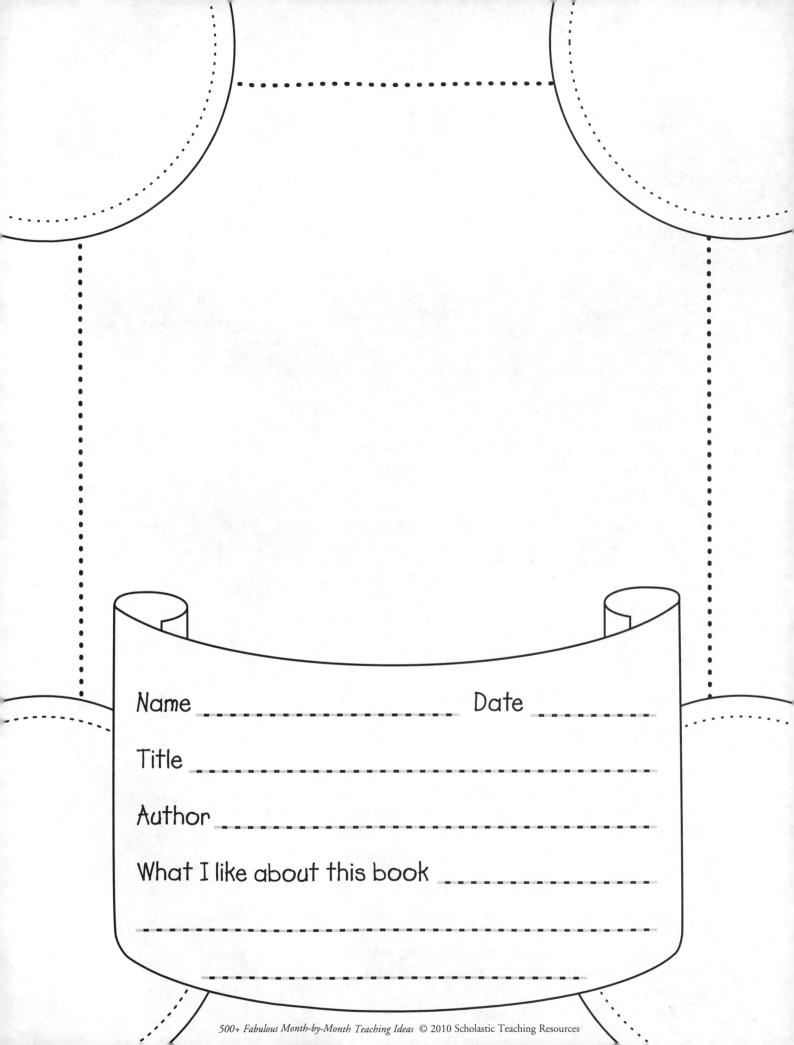

Name _____ Date _____

Title _____

Author _____

What I like about this book _____

_____

_____

# January

# January
## Teaching Ideas

It's January. Children have just come back to school from the holiday break. Teachers, too, are returning to work. In many areas, the weather is icy cold. It's the "Post-Holiday Slump," a time in which children need to be reacclimated to the classroom and, consequently, more effort may be required on the part of teachers to engage them in meaningful learning experiences. Teachers, these activities were made for you!

Make January an exciting month, full of celebration and renewal. The ideas and activities this month were specifically designed to help you "stump the slump"—quickly and easily! The topics fit naturally into the month of January: MARTIN LUTHER KING, JR.; NEW YEARS AROUND THE WORLD; ICE AND SNOW; and POLAR ANIMALS. Within each topic you'll find ideas to build skills in math, science, language and literacy, movement and dramatic play, music, social studies and history, arts and crafts, and poetry. Most of the activities naturally incorporate several content areas at once. For an art activity that incorporates social studies and history, try "Get on the Bus." (See page 131.) For a movement activity infused with science learning, try "Penguin Egg-Pass." (See page 150.) Other January highlights include:

- a reproducible send-home activity calendar
- an interactive mini-book for children to create
- terrific literature links
- an interactive math story mat
- reproducible activity sheets
- easy-to-make recipes that teach concepts and tickle taste buds
- an easy pattern for an inspirational social studies banner
- a collaborative calendar activity
- and many more winter wonders!

Name _____

# January Activity Calendar

Choose _____ activities to do each week this month.
Ask an adult in your family to initial the square in the box of each activity
you complete. Bring this paper back to school on _____ .

| Monday | Tuesday | Wednesday | Thursday | Friday |
|---|---|---|---|---|
| Write the word *January* on a sheet of paper. Cut apart the letters. Make new words!  **Jay** **ran** | Happy New Year! Write the number for the new year in two different ways. | Think of something that starts with *j*. Let someone in your family ask *yes* and *no* questions to guess what it is. | Ask an adult to help you make a snow cone: Crush ice and put it in a cup. Pour on some juice. Yum! | Look at a calendar. Find another month that has four of the same letters as *January*. |
| *Brrr! Cold!* How many other words for *cold* can you think of? | Check a calendar for the date today. Write the number two different ways. | List things you love about winter. Write them on paper, one word on each line. You've made a list poem! Give it a title. | Look at this snowflake. Find a matching snowflake on this page. | Be your family's weather reporter. Look out the window. Tell about the weather. Use lots of details. |
| We honor Martin Luther King, Jr. on the third Monday of January. How can you help make your world a more peaceful place? | Describe a dream that you have for yourself or a friend. What can you do to help make it happen? | Make a chart to show sunny, rainy, snowy, and cloudy days this week. | Cut out ten pictures from a magazine. Put them in a bag. Take them out one at a time to tell a story. | Look at the words on this calendar. Can you find two that rhyme with *ran?* |
| Plan a mini "Winter Olympics" with your family. Think of fun events, like a snowball toss. Take turns trying them! | Try an experiment: Place a plain ice cube on one plate and one sprinkled with salt on another. Which will melt fastest? | Guess the temperature outdoors. Find out what it is. Is it warmer or colder indoors? How much? | Happy Birthday, Bill Peet! (January 29) Celebrate with a Bill Peet book fest. Try *Big Bad Bruce*. | Turn *January* into a tongue twister! Make up a sentence using as many words as you can that start with *j*. |

500+ Fabulous Month-by-Month Teaching Ideas © 2010 Scholastic Teaching Resources

# Teacher Share

LANGUAGE ARTS, SOCIAL STUDIES

## Take the Pledge!

The celebration of Martin Luther King, Jr. Day on the third Monday in January is not just a celebration of the man himself, but of the values he held and inspired. Give children the opportunity to demonstrate and notice those values daily by taking a pledge. You can write the pledge yourself or have children help you create it. An example might be: "I promise to do my best to be fair and kind, to share equally, and to treat others as I would like to be treated." Write the pledge on sentence strips and tack it to the top of a bulletin board. Write children's names on sentence strips, and add them to the display along with their photos. Have children stand in front of the board, raise their right hands, and take the pledge!

*Rita Galloway*

### TIP

Cut stars out of construction paper. Place the stars in a basket near the bulletin board, and invite children to write things they notice classmates doing that are in line with the pledge—for example, "Jose helped me clean up even though he didn't make the mess." Place the stars next to the appropriate children's names or pictures.

SOCIAL STUDIES, ART

## Get on the Bus

Explain to children that in certain parts of the country in the time of Martin Luther King, Jr., African American people were made to sit in the back when they rode a bus. Only those with white skin could sit in front. But Martin Luther King, Jr. and his supporters, including Rosa Parks, helped to change all that. Today, everyone can sit on the bus together, no matter what their differences.

Discuss the concept of fairness, then give each child a copy of the bus template on page 135. Let children cut the window flaps on three sides as indicated, and fold them back. Next, have them glue a piece of paper to the back of the bus, making sure it covers the window openings. Let children place people of all colors, sizes, and shapes in the windows. They can cut out faces of people from magazines or draw them. Have children cut out and display their buses. Children can lift the flaps and see who's on the bus!

### TIP

If children are drawing their pictures, you may want to provide multicultural crayons (available at art and school-supply stores). These crayons come in a range of skin colors to represent diversity.

# Martin's Big Words: The Life of Dr. Martin Luther King, Jr.

### by Doreen Rappaport (Hyperion, 2001)

This Caldecott Honor-winning picture-book biography combines the author's own words with original text and quotes from Dr. King's writings and speeches to tell the remarkable story of this great civil rights leader's life and work. A timeline and additional resources invite readers to learn more.

## Teacher Share

ART, SOCIAL STUDIES

## Diversity Portraits

One of the best ways for children to discover the diversity in their classroom is by making self-portraits. Have each child create a self-portrait. Display portraits side by side along with a sheet of chart paper. When children notice diversity in the portraits (different hair, eye, or skin color; different genders; different clothing; different hairstyles), have them record it on the chart. As children's observations accumulate, discuss them with the group. *Did the portraits help them notice things they hadn't thought of before?*

*Catherine Wenglowski*

**TIP**

Learn more about the life and work of Martin Luther King, Jr. with the activities, literature links, and primary source materials in *Famous Americans: Martin Luther King, Jr.* by Maria Fleming (Scholastic, 1995).

# If You Lived at the Time of Martin Luther King

### by Ellen Levine (Scholastic, 1990)

This book brings the Civil Rights Movement alive for children. Its question-and-answer format helps children imagine what it would be like to be a part of the Montgomery Bus Boycott, the March on Washington, and more.

# Teacher Share

ART, SOCIAL STUDIES

## Feelings About Fairness

Make puppets to explore fairness. Have children cut two same-size circles out of paper, then place the end of a craft stick between them and glue them together. Have them draw a happy face on one side and a sad face on the other, then use their puppets to respond to situations such as the ones below. After each experience, be sure every child eventually gets a sticker, a drink of water, and so on.

@ Give half the children a sticker. Have them use their puppets to show how they feel. Ask children who did not get a sticker to do the same.

@ Say, "Boys can get up and get a drink of water. Girls, remain seated." Have children show their feelings with the puppets.

At first, children who get preferential treatment will probably show the happy side of the puppet, and those who don't will probably show the sad side. As you continue, you might find that children realize that what's happening isn't fair. Use the experience to introduce the concept of discrimination. Discuss ways Martin Luther King, Jr. fought against it.

*Mary Jane Banta*

## Computer Connection

The King Center
www.thekingcenter.org
Audio excerpts let visitors to this site listen to Dr. Martin Luther King, Jr. speak. A biography and timeline are also available.

MUSIC, SOCIAL STUDIES

## Sing About Dr. King

Write the lyrics to "Harmony and Peace" (see below) on chart paper and sing it together to the tune of "B-I-N-G-O." Follow up by inviting children to share ways they help create harmony and peace in the classroom. Go further by asking how they can promote harmony and peace at home. Talk about ways people work together for peace in your community and in the world.

**"Harmony and Peace"** *(to the tune of "B-I-N-G-O")*

Dr. King taught us to live
In harmony and peace—
P-E-A-C-E,
P-E-A-C-E,
P-E-A-C-E,
In harmony and peace.

He taught us not to fight or quarrel,
But love one another.
L-O-V-E, love!
L-O-V-E, love!
L-O-V-E, love!
He said to love one another.

That's not fair.

Let's talk about it.

TIP

To encourage children to think more deeply (and to gently steer them away from more "material" dreams, such as a new bicycle), you may want to use question prompts—for example, *What would you change in our neighborhood to make it a better place to live? What are some things you'd like to do for others? Is there anything you'd like to learn, or learn to do better, in the future?*

SOCIAL STUDIES

# Peaceful Solutions

Martin Luther King, Jr. believed that problems in the world, such as prejudice, could be solved without violence. Have chart paper and a marker ready, and ask children to think of conflicts that may occur in their lives—for example, an argument over the rules of a game, a problem on the playground, trouble sharing a toy, and so on. Record suggestions on chart paper. Let children take turns role-playing the situations to show how conflicts can be resolved peacefully.

LANGUAGE ARTS

# "I Have a Dream" Collaborative Banner

One of Martin Luther King, Jr.'s most famous speeches is known as the "I Have a Dream" speech. His dream was that people of all races and cultures would learn to respect and get along with one another. Talk with children about *dreams*: a dream can be a hope, a wish, or a goal you would like to reach.

Make copies of the dream cloud activity sheet on page 136. Ask children to tell you about Dr. King's dream. Record their ideas in a dream cloud. Copy a picture of Dr. King and tape it in the space provided. Now let children fill out their own dream sheets. Display a sheet of craft paper, trimmed to 12 inches high, and long enough to accommodate a banner page for each child plus a few extra. Glue Dr. King's dream cloud to the craft paper, then have children add theirs. Soon you will have a Martin Luther King, Jr. "I Have a Dream" banner circling your classroom for discussion and inspiration.

I have a dream. My dream is:
to have world peace

I can help my dream come true by:
helping my family and my friends

Name Kamil

Book Break

# Happy Birthday, Martin Luther King
### by Jean Marzollo (Scholastic, 1993)

The beautiful illustrations and simple text in this book make it ideal for teaching young children Martin Luther King, Jr.'s life story and the Civil Rights Movement. After reading the book, ask: *What would you give Dr. King for his birthday? What would you thank him for?*

# Get on the Bus

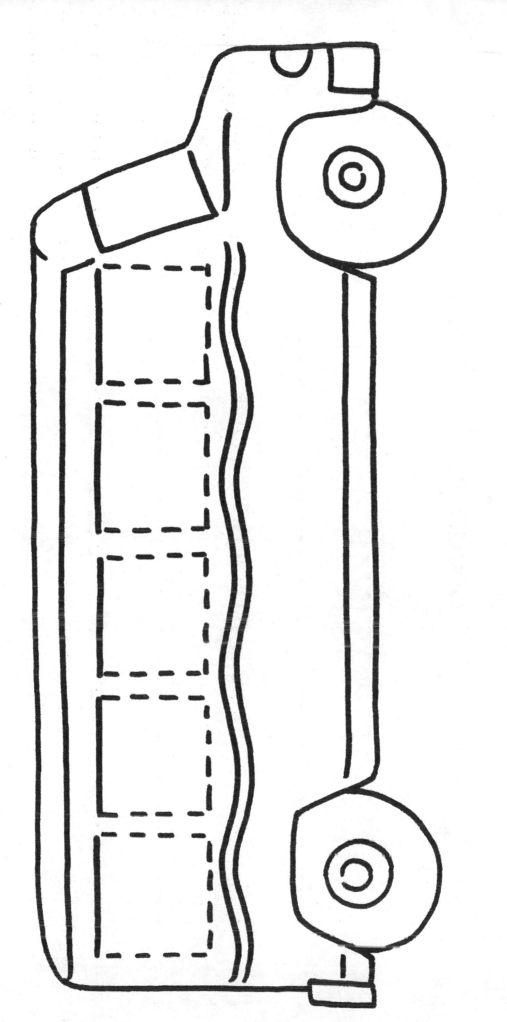

Name _____

"I Have a Dream"
Collaborative
Banner

I have a dream. My dream is:

I can help my dream come true by:

Draw a picture of yourself. Glue it here.

Name

LANGUAGE ARTS, SOCIAL STUDIES

# Happy New Year! Mini-Book

People all over the world celebrate the new year, but not always at the same time. The Chinese New Year falls between January and February. (The date varies from year to year.) Tet, the Vietnamese New Year, happens in February. The Jewish New Year falls between September and October. (The date varies from year to year.) And in Iran, the New Year is celebrated in springtime! But no matter when the new year begins, people all over the world have one thing in common: They all have celebrations and say "Happy New Year!"

   Make copies of the mini-book activity sheets on pages 142 and 143. Write the names of the following places on chart paper in random order: *Argentina, China, France, Greece, Hawaii, Israel, Italy, Japan, Portugal, Sweden.* Have children cut out the pages and staple them to make a mini-book. On page 1, have them write their names. On the following pages, have them fill in the names of the places using the words on the chart paper. If children need help you can reveal the answers: page 2 = Argentina, 3 = China, 4 = France, 5 = Greece, 6 = Hawaii, 7 = Israel, 8 = Italy, 9 = Japan, 10 = Portugal, 11 = Sweden. On the last page, let children write what we say in America: *Happy New Year!*

## Teacher Share

MATH

## Safe Fireworks

Celebrate the New Year with a dazzling "fireworks" display in your classroom, and practice counting backward at the same time!

◎ Get a roll of bubble wrap (available in many stationery, packaging and postal stores) and cut it into large squares, one for each child.

◎ Invite parents and caregivers to the classroom for the fireworks celebration.

◎ Position adults around the room and provide them with confetti.

◎ Let children gently step onto their squares. Together, shout "Ten, nine, eight, seven, six, five, four, three, two, one—Happy New Year!" Let children jump on the bubble wrap as the adults toss the confetti in the air. The loud, crackling noises and shower of color will create the effect of fireworks right in your classroom!

*Megan Banta*

TIP

Make hats and noisemakers for your celebration. (See "New Year's Hats and Shakers," page 141)

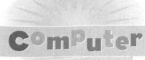
## Connection

To find out more about Chinese year signs and what they mean, check out the following Web sites:

www.new-year.
co.uk/chinese/
calendar.htm

www.holymtn.
com/astrology/
year.htm

holidays.kaboose.
com/chinese-
new-year/
chinese_new_
year.html

SOCIAL STUDIES, MATH

# What's Your Chinese Animal Sign?

Explain to children that the Chinese New Year takes place sometime in January or February. Chinese years run on a lunar cycle, so the date changes from year to year. Each year is represented by a different animal. The animals run in a cycle of 12, always in the same order: rat, ox, tiger, rabbit, dragon, snake, horse, sheep, monkey, rooster, dog, and pig. After 12 years, the cycle starts all over again.

Copy the chart below on chart paper. Have children record their birthdates, then use the chart to figure out what Chinese year they were born in and draw a picture of the animal. Display children's work and discuss how they arrived at their answers.

| American Year | Chinese Year | Animal |
|---|---|---|
| 1998 | January 28, 1998 — February 15, 1999 | Tiger |
| 1999 | February 16, 1999 — February 4, 2000 | Rabbit |
| 2000 | February 5, 2000 — January 23, 2001 | Dragon |
| 2001 | January 24, 2001 — February 11, 2002 | Snake |
| 2002 | February 12, 2002 — January 31, 2003 | Horse |
| 2003 | February 1, 2003 — January 21, 2004 | Sheep |
| 2004 | January 22, 2004 — February 8, 2005 | Monkey |
| 2005 | February 9, 2005 — January 28, 2006 | Rooster |
| 2006 | January 29, 2006 — February 17, 2007 | Dog |
| 2007 | February 18, 2007 — February 6, 2008 | Pig |
| 2008 | February 7, 2008 — January 25, 2009 | Rat |
| 2009 | January 26, 2009 — February 10, 2010 | Ox |

## Book Break

# Lion Dancer: Ernie Wan's Chinese New Year
## by Kate Waters (Scholastic, 1991)

Follow Ernie Wong as he prepares for Chinese New Year in New York City's Chinatown. Let children perform a lion dance of their own!

# Teacher Share

## SOCIAL STUDIES

## Celebrate With Grapes

It is a New Year tradition in many Spanish-speaking countries to celebrate the coming of midnight by eating grapes. When the clock begins to strike 12, people eat a grape for every gong of the bell. Bring a bell and some grapes to school to celebrate the New Year as the Spanish do! (Check for allergies before serving the grapes.) To avoid possible choking, you can let children do the activity in teams: Line children up and have each eat a grape for a separate ring of the bell. Or, wait between rings to make sure children have swallowed. After the last ring (and grape), wish one another "Feliz año nuevo!"

*Bob Krech*

## SOCIAL STUDIES

## Celebratory Snack

Jewish people in Israel and all over the world celebrate their New Year, *Rosh Hashanah*, in September or October. (The date varies from year to year.) Rosh Hashanah (Hebrew for "Head of the Year") is celebrated for two days. One holiday tradition is to eat apples dipped in honey. Try having it for snack one day.

◎ Slice several apples into wedges. Pour honey into a bowl and set the bowl on a plate. Arrange the apple slices around the bowl. As you prepare the snack, discuss what this tradition might mean. (*The apples and honey symbolize hope for a "sweet year."*)

◎ Let children dip the apple wedges into honey. As children pass this traditional snack to their friends, they might even like to wish them a "Shanah Tovah" (a good year)!

If you will be slicing the apples to be eaten at a later time, try brushing them with a little lemon juice. This will help keep them from turning too brown. Check for allergies before serving.

Book Break

## The World's Birthday:
## A Rosh Hashanah Story

### by Barbara Diamond Goldin (Harcourt, 1995)

Join Daniel as he celebrates the Jewish New Year with his family. After reading, discuss some of the traditions mentioned in the book. You might want to stop by a bakery and pick up a loaf of challah for snack one day.

SOCIAL STUDIES, ART

## Surprises for Tet

The Vietnamese celebrate their New Year in February: The holiday is called *Tet*. Children traditionally receive special red envelopes on this day with money inside. Try this version of the tradition in class. Assign children secret "Tet partners" (no telling!). Give each child an envelope to color red. Have children create a special gift for their recipient: a drawing, special message, or a "coupon" for a special favor. Have children sign their names to the gifts and place them in the envelopes. Mark the names of recipients lightly on the envelopes. After children go home, put the envelopes in their cubbies. The next morning, they'll have two surprises: They will receive a special gift and find out who gave it to them!

Book Break

## Ten Mice for Tet

### by Pegi Deitz Shea (Chronicle, 2003)

This counting book introduces readers to the Vietnamese New Year. Endnotes provide additional background information about the holiday. Pronunciation is provided for Vietnamese words.

# Teacher Share

ART

## New Year's Hats and Shakers

Noisemakers and funny party hats are part of New Year celebrations everywhere. Follow these steps to make hats.

- Let each child choose a sheet of construction paper (11- by 14-inch). Wrap the paper around the top of each child's head to make a cylindrical hat, and mark the spot where it will be stapled or taped together to fit.

- Let children cut the paper about one inch beyond the mark you made.

- Provide children with markers, paint, glitter, glue, feathers, beads, and other collage materials. Have children decorate their hats and write their names on them.

- Again, wrap children's papers around their heads and tape the ends together to fit. For a more secure attachment, staple (when hats are off children's heads).

Follow these steps to make shakers.

- Provide children with empty toilet-paper tubes or clean juice cans. (Make sure the edges are smooth to prevent injury.)

- Let children wrap construction paper around their tubes or cans and tape in place. Have them fill the tubes or cans with a handful of dried beans, and close off the other end by taping construction paper over it and securing with a rubber band.

- Let children decorate their shakers with markers, paint, and collage materials.

Have a New Year celebration in the classroom (see "Safe Fireworks," page 137), and let children wear and shake their creations!

*Jennifer Boss*

**Happy New Year!**

By _____

①

In _____ ,

we say
¡Feliz Año Nuevo!

②

In _____ ,

we say
Gong Xi Fa Cai!

③

In _____ ,

we say
Bonne Année!

④

In _____ ,

we say
Eftihismenos
O Kenourios Hronos!

⑤

In _____ ,

we say
Hau'oli Makahiki Hou!

⑥

In _____ ,
we say
Shanah Tovah!

⑦

In _____ ,
we say
Felice Anno Nuovo!

⑧

In _____ ,
we say
Akemashite Omedeto!

⑨

In _____ ,
we say
Prospero Ano Novo!

⑩

In _____ ,
we say
Gott Nytt År!

⑪

In America, we say

_____

_____ !

⑫

SCIENCE, MATH, SOCIAL STUDIES

# Track the Snow Calendar Activity

Explore winter weather with a calendar activity. Start by creating a simple wall calendar. Place a large piece of tagboard horizontally and write the month across the top. Underneath, write the days of the week. Make gridlines and write the date in each square. On a smaller piece of tagboard, write *Our Estimates* and create four columns labeled "Estimated Snow Days," "Actual Snow Days," "Estimated Inches," "Actual Inches." Divide the columns into four rows labeled Week 1, Week 2, Week 3, Week 4.

Gather children together and ask: *How many days do you think we will have snow this week? How many inches of snow will have fallen by the end of the week?* (If you live in an area where it is unlikely to snow, you can choose to track a different area of the country.) Write children's guesses on the chart. Each day, keep track of the weather through observation, local newspapers, television, radio, even the Internet! (See Computer Connection, left.) Let children take turns marking the calendar each day, drawing a snowflake for days it snows, and a snowflake with a slash mark through it for no-snow days. As the month goes on, encourage children to continually reevaluate their estimations, depending on how the weather has been so far. As their estimates change, write the new ones on the chart. At the end of each week, compare total snow days and inches with children's estimates. How close did they come?

For an extension to this activity, hang a U.S. or world map in the classroom. Let children place white pushpins in the areas they think there will be snow. Keep track through web sites and other media.

LANGUAGE ARTS

# "The Living Snowmen" Mini-Play

Explore rhyming words and give children a chance to express their dramatic flair with the mini-play on page 148. Introduce the play by writing words from the play on the chalkboard, such as *place, face; dive, alive.* Invite children to find the rhyming pairs. Give children time to practice their parts in groups, then bring children together for a rehearsal. Children can create simple props, such as snowmen, penguins, and polar bears cut out of cardboard.

# Teacher Share

## Easy-Cook Snowball Treats

If there's one thing children love about winter, it's making snowballs. Here is an easy recipe for snowballs they can make—and eat! Gather the following ingredients: 3 tablespoons margarine or butter, 1 package (10 ounces, about 40) regular marshmallows, 6 cups crisped rice cereal, and about 2 cups confectioners' sugar.

◎ In a large saucepan, melt margarine or butter over low heat. Add marshmallows and stir until melted completely. Remove from heat. Add cereal and stir until well coated. Let cool.

◎ Let children roll handfuls of the mixture into balls.

◎ Pour about 2 cups confectioners' sugar into a large zip-close bag. Have children take turns putting their snowballs into the bag, zipping it closed, and shaking. Place the sugar-coated "snowballs" on waxed paper to cool completely.

◎ Enjoy your edible snowballs! (Check for food allergies first.)

**Variations:** You can also use a microwave oven to create these treats. Microwave the butter and marshmallows on high 2 minutes in a microwave-safe mixing bowl. Stir to combine. Microwave on high 1 minute longer and stir until smooth. Continue as directed above. Microwave cooking times may vary.

*Jennifer Boss*

## Book Break

## The Black Snowman
by Phil Mendez (Scholastic, 1991)

A black snowman comes to life and tells young Jacob about the amazing history of his ancestors. After reading the book, talk about why it was important for Jacob to meet a snowman that looked like him. Ask: *What would you look like as a snowman?* Have children draw their interpretations.

MATH

# Snowman Math Story Mat

Give each child a copy of the snowman story mat on page 149. Ask: *How many children are dancing around the snowman?* Give children sticky-notes, or anything else that will cover up the dancing children one at a time. Read aloud the counting rhyme that follows and have children use the manipulatives to act it out.

> A snowman stood on the snowy ground,
> Five little children danced around,
> One fell down on the snowy ground—
> How many left to dance around? Four!

As children cover up the dancers, pause after the line, "How many left to dance around?" Let children count and call out the number. Repeat until there are no children left. Then recite the last verse. (Children can invent their own ways of acting it out—for example, by covering up the snowman with their hands.)

> A snowman stood on the snowy ground,
> The sun came out and it shone around,
> It shone and shone and it shone all day,
> The snowman melted all away.

SCIENCE

# How to Make an Ice Cube Fly

Use this activity to teach children about the ways matter can go through physical changes. Talk about the different forms water can take: liquid (*water*), solid (*ice*), and gas (*steam*). Place a few ice cubes in a portable plug-in teapot. (You can also use a regular teapot and a hot plate. In either case, watch children closely for safety.) Tell children to take a good look at the ice cubes because you are going to make them fly. (This is usually met with "No way!") Plug in the teapot or hot plate. When the ice melts, it turns into water, which comes out of the teapot as steam. You made the ice cubes fly!

*Deborah Rovin-Murphy*

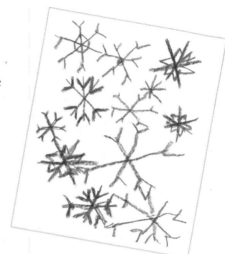

SCIENCE, ART

# Observing Frost Crystals

It's amazing how much students can get out of this quick and easy activity. Give children glasses or glass jars (supervise closely for safety), and let them dip them quickly into a sink or bowl filled with water. Place the glasses and jars in the freezer immediately. Wait until the glasses become frosty. Let children observe the frost through magnifiers and draw the patterns they see. Frost—made up of crystals of frozen water—can create beautiful and amazing patterns. When children have finished drawing, let them compare patterns with one another.

MATH, SCIENCE

# Make Your Own Ice Cream!

This activity is a terrific way to show children the wonders of ice, and how freezing can change things. Before you start, divide the class into small groups. Gather the following items for each group: 4 cups crushed ice, 1/2 cup rock salt, 1 quart-size zip-close bag, 1 sandwich-size zip-close bag, 1/4 cup milk, 1/4 cup heavy cream, 2 tablespoons sugar, 1/2 teaspoon vanilla, scissors, small bowls, and spoons. Guide children in following these steps:

◎ Put 2 cups of crushed ice and 1/4 cup of rock salt into the quart-size zip-close bag. Pour the milk, heavy cream, sugar, and vanilla into the sandwich-size bag. Seal this bag tightly.

◎ Place the smaller bag inside the larger bag. Gently squeeze out the air and seal it carefully. Pass around the bag and take turns gently squeezing it for about 5 minutes total. *What is happening inside the bag?*

◎ Drain the water from the larger bag, and add remaining ice and salt. Seal and squeeze until the mixture is very thick.

◎ Remove the small bag from the ice and dry the outside of the bag. With scissors, cut one of the bottom corners off the small bag and squeeze the contents into small bowls. Enjoy your icy treat! (Check for food allergies first.)

Book Break

## Ice Cream Bear
### by Jez Alborough (Walker, 1999)

"It's twice as nice as snow or ice; it's Bear's idea of paradise." Children will enjoy the rhyming verse in this whimsical story about a polar bear that dreams of ice cream! After a few readings, you might try placing sticky-notes on the pages of the book to cover the rhyming words. When you come to the end of a line, ask children to guess the hidden word. Pull off the note to reveal the answer!

# The Living Snowmen

by Pamela Chanko

## Characters
(to be played by small groups of students)

Children ❄ Snowmen ❄ Polar Bears ❄ Penguins

**Children:** Snow is falling down
On our little town.
Snow falls again—
Let's make snowmen!

**Snowmen:** Winter is here!
Winter is here!
We are alive
Again this year!

**Polar Bears:** Why do you stay
In one place
And wear a carrot
On your face?

**Snowmen:** Winter is here!
Winter is here!
We are alive
Again this year!

**Penguins:** You cannot swim,
You cannot dive.
How can you say
You are alive?

**Snowmen:** Winter is here!
Winter is here!
We are alive
Again this year!

**Polar Bears
& Penguins:** They cannot move,
They cannot dive.
How can they prove
They are alive?

**Children:** Animals, animals,
Why the fuss?
In winter
Snowmen come alive—
Because they're alive to us.

*500+ Fabulous Month-by-Month Teaching Ideas* © 2010 Scholastic Teaching Resources

# Snowman Math Story Mat

500+ Fabulous Month-by-Month Teaching Ideas
© 2010 Scholastic Teaching Resources

**TIP**

Since children will be taking their shoes off, it is probably best to do this activity in a carpeted area. Check the area carefully for possible hazards, especially if children are doing the activity barefooted. Add a math dimension to this game by setting up a tally sheet. Write "Try #1," "Try #2," and so on down the left side. In the space following each number, children can make tally marks to track how many people passed the egg before it dropped. Look for improvement over time!

SCIENCE, MOVEMENT

# Penguin Egg-Pass

Penguins are very unusual animals! They are birds, but they cannot fly. And while in most bird families it is the mother bird that sits on her eggs to keep them warm, in penguin families it is the father who does this important job. Male penguins have a special pouch under their bellies to keep eggs warm in the cold environment of the Antarctic. After the mother penguin releases an egg, she passes it to the father; he protects the egg while the mother swims off to hunt for food.

But how does one penguin pass an egg to another? They certainly can't use their flippers—so they use their feet! The penguins stand very close together with their feet touching and pass the egg without letting it drop. Invite children to play a penguin egg-passing game to see what this is like. Have children take off their shoes. (The activity works best with bare feet.) Provide them with a plastic egg or a tennis ball, and have them line up in a row, very close together. Have children pass the "egg" to one another using only their feet. How far can they go without letting it drop? Children will enjoy playing this game in small groups during free-play time, too.

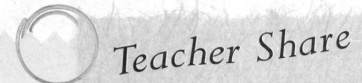

# Teacher Share

MATH

## Penguin Problems

Use penguins as characters in problem-solving activities. Give children paper, pencils, and markers or crayons. Pose a problem to children: *There are eight penguins. Some are playing on the icebergs, some are swimming in the water, and some are in the rookery. Create a picture to illustrate your penguins. Write a number sentence to match.* You can extend this into a writing activity: Have children create stories that go along with their individual penguin problems, and display them next to their pictures. Create a penguin-problem class book with children's work. Children will be proud to have you share their story problems with the class for math practice!

*Mitzi Fehl*

$2+2+4=8$

SCIENCE

# Animal Adaptations

How do animals keep warm in the cold, cold environment of the polar regions? Many of them have a layer of fat under their skin called *blubber*. To find out how blubber works, try this experiment. You will need the following materials: 4 zip-close sandwich bags, 1 cup of solid shortening, and a big bowl of ice water. Have children work in groups. Guide them in following these steps:

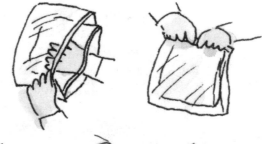

◎ Make a plain plastic mitten by turning one of the bags inside out and placing it inside another bag. Zip the tops of the bags together. Try not to let too much air get between the two bags.

◎ Now make a fat-filled plastic mitten. Place the shortening in a bag. Turn another bag inside out and carefully place it in the first bag. Zip the tops of the bags together as before. Move the shortening around with your hands to spread it evenly between the two bags. Make sure the shortening spreads all the way around both sides of the mitten.

◎ Place the plain plastic mitten over your hand, and put your hand in the ice water. *How does it feel?*

◎ Place the fat-filled mitten over your hand, and put your hand in the ice water. *How does it feel now?*

◎ *Which bag kept your hand warmer? Why do you think so?*

## Book Break

# Antarctica

by Helen Cowcher (Farrar, Straus & Giroux, 1991)

This book describes the environment of the Antarctic and the amazing animals that make it their home. After reading the book, talk with children about the effects of people on animals and nature. Sometimes it is positive, sometimes not. Ask: *What can people do to help protect the animals and environment of the Antarctic?* Record suggestions on chart paper. You might consider following up by writing a class letter to a conservation society or federal agency.

# Penguin Feathers

For this activity you will need large-size crayons, drawing paper, markers, scissors, an eyedropper, and a cup of water. First, let children draw a penguin, using the crayons. Help them to make sure that every part of the penguin is completely covered with a thick coat of crayon—even the white parts! (Children can use white crayons for this.) On a different sheet of paper, let children draw any polar mammal they choose, using markers. Have them cut out each animal. Now let children fill the eyedropper with water and sprinkle drops over both animals. Do they see a difference? (*The water will bead up on the penguin; it will soak through the other animal.*) Explain that penguins have waxy feathers, similar to the crayon surface. Their feathers repel water, just as the crayons did. Can children figure out the reason for a penguin's waxy feathers? (*They help penguins glide more quickly through the water, and help them to dry off much faster when they go on land.*)

### SCIENCE

# Polar Animal Dominoes

Children will have fun playing this polar animal domino game in small groups. To prepare the game, make several copies of the domino activity sheets on pages 153 and 154 for each group. Let children cut out the dominoes, making sure to cut on the dashed lines only. They can also color in the animals if they like. To play, have children in a group divide the dominoes evenly, then follow these steps.

◎ One child sets out any domino to start.

◎ The next child tries to find a matching animal on one of his or her dominoes and places it next to the matching square.

◎ Children continue taking turns and making matches until all the dominoes are gone or there are no more possible matches.

**TIP**

As children learn more about polar animals, they can vary the rules a little bit—for example, making matches according to animals that live on land, animals that live in the water, and animals that live both places. They might also try playing according to species (mammal or bird) and habitat (Arctic and Antarctica).

**Book Break**

# Face to Face With Polar Bears

(Face to Face With Animals Series)
by Norbert Rosing (National Geographic, 2007)

Striking photographs take readers into the habitat of these marine mammals to explore their habits, physical characteristics, and environment. Sidebars provide additional details (and acquaint young readers with a feature of nonfiction).

# Activity Page

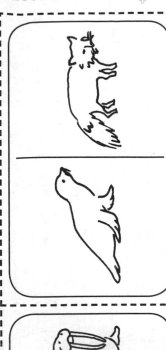

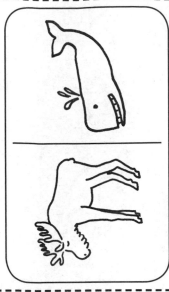

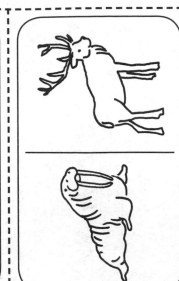

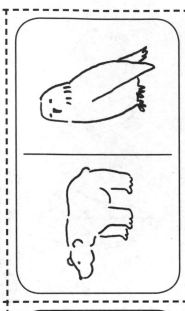

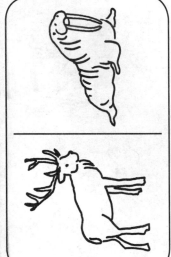

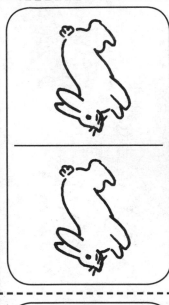

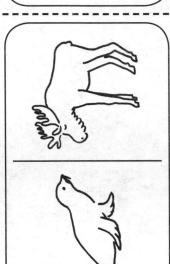

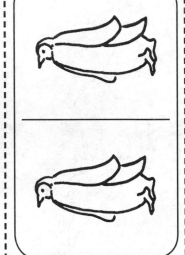

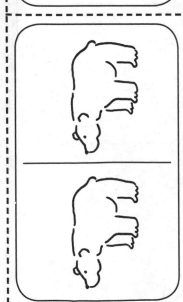

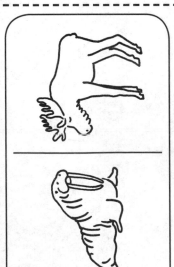

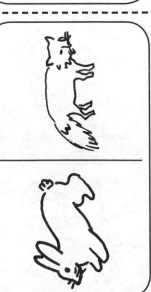

# February

## Groundhog Day, Shadows

## Valentine's Day

## Presidents

## Teeth

# February
## Teaching Ideas

The month of February may bring more winter to many of us—but it also comes with a wealth of teaching opportunities. February 2nd invites stories of groundhogs forecasting the weather—and explorations into whatever weather is happening around you. Children's excitement for Valentine's Day starts building long before February 14th rolls around, and, of course, everyone looks forward to Presidents' Day—a time to celebrate our nation's leaders (and for many to have a day off!). February is also Dental Health Month, making it a great time to investigate teeth—a topic full of interdisciplinary connections.

These February activities and ideas will make it easy for you to integrate these topics into your teaching. There are four sections—one for each topic (GROUNDHOG DAY/SHADOWS, VALENTINE'S DAY, PRESIDENTS, and TEETH). Activities for each topic connect every corner of your curriculum—from reading and writing to science, movement, music, and art. Many of the activities naturally integrate several disciplines. For example, "Rock-a-Bye Shadow" brings science and music together in an easy-to-learn song about light and shadows. (See page 161.) "Counting on Presidents" combines math and history as children learn about money and the presidents whose pictures appear on it. (See page 171.) "What Big Teeth!" combines math and science as children discover surprising facts about animal friends. (See page 180.) Other special features for February include:

♡ a reproducible send-home activity calendar
♡ computer connections
♡ hands-on math and science activities
♡ literature connections
♡ collaborative bookmaking projects
♡ an easy-to-learn "piggyback" song
♡ a reproducible mini-book to make
♡ no-cook snacks to make and enjoy
♡ a reproducible mini-play
♡ a rhyming collaborative banner
♡ ready-to-use reproducible activity pages
♡ and much more February fun!

Name _____

# February Activity Calendar

Choose _____ activities to do each week this month.
Ask an adult in your family to initial the square in the box of each activity
you complete. Bring this paper back to school on _____ .

| Monday | Tuesday | Wednesday | Thursday | Friday |
|---|---|---|---|---|
| Write the word *February* on a sheet of paper. Cut apart the letters. Make new words! **are  bear  far** | Look at a calendar. Count the days in February. Are there any other months with the same number of days? | Look at this heart.  Find a matching heart on this page. | Find Presidents' Day on a calendar. How many days in February come before Presidents' Day? after? | Look at some coins. Which coins have pictures of President Lincoln and President Washington on them? |
| Who is the president of our country? Tell what you know about this person. | Tell five things you'd like the president to do to make this country better. What can you do to help your country? | How many pennies in a quarter? Which is worth more: 75 pennies or 4 quarters? | Look at a calendar. Find a month that has four of the same letters as February. | *Be mine.* List as many words as you can that have the word *be* in them. **belong  because  maybe** |
| Unscramble these words to make a Valentine message: **Valentine  you  mine  be  will** | What is red? Make a list of things that are red. You've made a list poem! Give your poem a title. | Go outside with an adult in your family. Can you make your shadows hold hands even when you're not? | Use a flashlight to make shadows of objects. What's the tallest shadow you can make? shortest? widest? | Look at pictures in a newspaper with a family member. Tell a story about what you see. |
| It's Dental Health Month! Make a blank calendar. Give yourself a star each time you brush your teeth. | Listen to the ending sound of the word *teeth.* Take turns with a family member naming words that begin with or end in *th.* | Some sharks can grow 2,000 teeth in one year! Count your teeth. How many more does a shark have? | Put water in two plastic cups. Sprinkle salt in one. Put the cups in the freezer. Which do you think will freeze first? | Turn *February* into a tongue twister! Make up a sentence using as many words as you can that start with *f.* |

## Light and Shadow

(Scholastic, 1996)

This *I Can Read About Science* book uses poems to introduce concepts related to the sun, rainbows, shadows, and more.

# Teacher Share

MOVEMENT, SCIENCE

## What Do You See, Groundhog?

Celebrate Groundhog Day and introduce an investigation of shadows with this movement activity. Make a simple groundhog mask by taping ears to a construction-paper headband. Invite a volunteer to be the "groundhog" and put on the ears. Have the other children line up front to back with legs apart to make a tunnel or "burrow." Give the first child in line a flashlight. Have the groundhog go to the back of the burrow and crawl through. When the groundhog sticks his or her head out, what will it see? The first child can choose whether or not to shine the light on the groundhog to make a shadow. Have the groundhog go back in the burrow if he or she sees its shadow, or crawl all the way out if there's no shadow. Play again, letting children take turns being the groundhog.

*Nicole Vig*

**TIP**

What is another name for a groundhog? Challenge children to find out! (woodchuck)

## Groundhog Day!

by Gail Gibbons (Holiday House, 2007)

As a groundhog peers out from its burrow, text explains the legend of Groundhog Day, which falls on February 2, and what this event forecasts about the arrival of spring. Facts about groundhogs' diet, habitat, and offspring provide young readers with background information, and a two-page spread takes them into an underground burrow.

TIP

For this and other
partner activities, try
using a "Partner Can."
Write each student's
name on a piece of
tagboard. Place the
names in an empty can.
(Check to make sure
the edges are smooth.)
Whenever students
need to pair up, shake
the can and take out
two names at a time to
partner up.

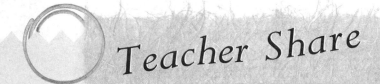

# Teacher Share

LANGUAGE ARTS

## Groundhogs and Other Ways to Predict Weather

After letting children discuss the possibility of a groundhog predicting weather, share other examples of weather lore—for example, *When sheep gather in a huddle, we'll soon have a puddle.* Write these sayings on chart paper, then let children pair up for some weather-forecasting fun. Have them either copy and illustrate one of the sayings on the chart paper, or come up with an original bit of weather lore. For children who want to write their own, the *Scholastic Rhyming Dictionary* by Sue Young will come in handy. These illustrated examples of weather lore make an interesting display that will spark lots of discussions.

*Lori Vig*

When cows all sit down it will rain.
When cows all stand up it won't rain.
Teal A.

SCIENCE, LANGUAGE ARTS

## Groundhog Shadow Play

Explore light and shadow with the groundhog puppets on page 163. Let each child choose a groundhog pattern to color and cut out. (Glue to tagboard first.) Have children glue their groundhogs to craft sticks. Darken the room and give each pair of students a flashlight. Have them work together to make shadows. Can children with small groundhogs make shadows that are bigger than those of the large groundhogs? To do this, they will have to experiment with the placement of their groundhog and the light. (*Moving the groundhog closer to the light makes it bigger. Moving it away makes it smaller.*) Follow up by letting children share their findings. This is a good opportunity for science journal writing.

SCIENCE, ART

# Silhouette Shows

Many students are familiar with the standard silhouette—a framed profile of someone in shadow. To make a silhouette, light is projected on a person's profile, and the resulting shadow on the wall is traced on dark paper. This shape is cut out and mounted on light-colored paper. Demonstrate the procedure for children, then invite them to create silhouette shows in small groups. Have students plan their cast of characters, then draw and cut out outlines of each. Have them tape their cutouts to craft sticks or straws, then practice their shows. To create shadows (or silhouettes), they'll need to project light on a wall and hold their puppets in between the light and the wall. For Silhouette Show ideas, see Tip, right.

**TIP**

Suggestions for silhouette shows include:

◎ Dramatize a favorite children's book. (Make silhouettes of the characters and related props.)

◎ Act out a groundhog popping out of its tunnel on Groundhog Day: What does it see? What happens?

◎ Act out an original story.

# Teacher Share

MUSIC, SCIENCE

## Rock-a-Bye Shadow

Introduce and explore concepts of light and shadow with this gentle rhyming song, sung to the familiar tune of "Rock-a-Bye Baby." After singing the song several times, try these activities to learn more.

◎ Use a flashlight to simulate the sun, making tall and short shadows by changing the position of the "sun" in the sky.

◎ Look for rhyming words in the song—such as *small*, *tall*, *wall*. Use them to reinforce word families.

◎ Listen for opposites in the song—for example, *big/small*, *higher/shorter*, and *far/near*. Invite children to suggest other opposites. Record them on sentence strips, mix them up, and place in a pocket chart. Let children move the words around to match opposites.

*Peg Arcadi*

### Rock-a-Bye Shadow

I make a shadow, big or small.
When the day starts, my shadow is tall.
The higher the sun, the shorter it gets.
My shadow is gone, when the sun sets.

I make a shadow on the wall.
When the light's far, my shadow is tall.
When the light's near, my shadow grows long.
And when the light's off, my shadow is gone.

# I Spy Mystery: A Book of Picture Riddles
### by Jean Marzollo (Scholastic, 2005)

Display the picture on pages 12 and 13 of this popular picture riddle book. Ask: *What direction do you think the light is coming from to make these shadows?* Let children experiment with a flashlight and objects in the classroom to discover the answer. Go on to look for peculiar things in the picture. For example, are there shadows that don't have objects with them? What might be making them? Find the monster face shadow. What objects were used to make it? Experiment with objects in the classroom to make other funny shadow faces.

# Teacher Share

MATH, SCIENCE

## Standing in My Footsteps

Explore the relationship of the sun's position to shadow size with this "foots-on" activity.

◎ Take children outside on a sunny day to a safe, empty paved area. Have them partner up to trace one another's feet on the pavement. (Provide chalk.) Have them stand in their footprints while their partners trace their shadows. Do this early in the day, if possible. Note the position of the sun. (Remind children not to look directly at the sun.)

◎ Take children outside to the same spot several more times during the day. Have them stand in their footsteps while their partners trace their shadows. (You might provide different-colored chalk each time.) Note the position of the sun each time.

◎ At the end of the day, compare the length of the different shadows. Guide children in making a connection between the time of day, the sun's position, and the length of their shadows. Ask: *Where was the sun when your shadow was longest? shortest? What time tomorrow do you think you would see the longest shadow or the shortest?*

*Natalie Vaughan*

# Groundhog Shadow Play

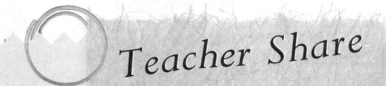

## Teacher Share

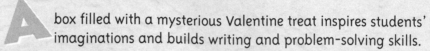

LANGUAGE ARTS

# Valentine Treasure Box

**A** box filled with a mysterious Valentine treat inspires students' imaginations and builds writing and problem-solving skills.

◎ Wrap a box and lid with Valentine paper. (The size of the box should be just big enough to hold what's going inside.)

◎ Place a Valentine treat, or a coupon with clues that lead to the treat, inside the box. For example, if you're sharing heart-shaped cookies, you might provide directions students can follow to find the cookies. Pin the box to a bulletin board.

◎ Before Valentine's Day, invite children to write about what they think is inside the box and why. Encourage them to think about the size of the box as they make their guesses.

◎ Collect all guesses before February 14th. Reveal the contents on Valentine's Day and enjoy the surprise!

*Mary Modoono*

LANGUAGE ARTS, MATH

# "Your Half, My Half" Mini-Play

Students form two groups to perform a mini-play with a surprise ending! Divide the class into two groups: A and B. Instruct children in group A to cut out and decorate hearts, one for every two students. Have them write a Valentine message on the hearts, then cut them in half to make puzzles. Make sure children in both groups practice their lines, then get ready to perform the play. Give children in group A one half of each heart. Place the other half of each heart in a book. When children in group B get to the part where they look for the missing half of each heart, let them search (with children in group A giving clues), then put the hearts they find together to read the messages. Children in group B can keep the hearts or present them to members of the audience. Switch the groups around (A is B, B is A) for a repeat performance so that everyone gets to make and receive a special valentine. Use the play to explore fractions: *How many halves in a whole?*

LANGUAGE ARTS

# "Be Mine" Valentine Puzzles

Looking for little words in big words is a strategy that helps young children read and write new words. Use a familiar Valentine message—*be mine*—as a springboard for strengthening this strategy. Share a conversation candy heart that says *be mine*. Read it with children and write the word *be* on the chalkboard. Spell it together, then ask children to listen for that sound in this word: *belong*. Ask them how they might spell the first part of that word (*be*). Write the word *belong* on the chalkboard so that children can see that the letters are the same. Now say three words—for example, *butter, behave,* and *bandage*—and ask children to identify the one that they think starts with the letters *be*. Follow up by giving children blank paper hearts. Have them write words that start with *be* on their hearts (such as *believe, before, begin, between, belong, beneath, beside, because,* and *beautiful*). Show students how to cut their hearts in half to make puzzles to share with one another.

**TIP**

You can easily adapt this activity to make a festive Valentine word wall. Cut out a large heart shape and write the words "Be mine" on it. Display this on a wall. Cut out smaller hearts in pinks and reds. Have children write words that start with the letters be on the hearts and add them to the display.

## Teacher Share

LANGUAGE ARTS, ART

## Message in a Puzzle

These easy-to-make valentines are fun to put together and read. Write each child's name on separate slips of paper. Place the names in a bag. Let each child draw a name from the bag. Provide heart-shaped templates (big enough to write a message on). Have children trace and cut out a heart, then write a friendly message to their valentines. After decorating the hearts, have children cut them into puzzle pieces and place them in an envelope labeled with their valentine's name. Let children exchange these puzzles on Valentine's Day. What a great surprise when they put their puzzles together!

*Lori Viq*

**TIP**

Valentine puzzles make nice, quick gifts for your students' special area teachers. Cut out giant puzzles for more fun, and have each child write a message on it.

## TIP

To turn friendship rings into mini-books, remove staples, then place the strips one on top of another and staple along the left side to bind.

# Teacher Share

## Friendship Rings

These friendship rings grow each day as children write positive messages to each of their classmates. The rings are easily transformed into friendship books that children will cherish. (See tip, left.)

◎ Cut uniform strips of colored paper (about 12 by 3 inches). Give one to each child. Have children write their names on the strips and glue a small photo (or photocopy of a photo) next to their names.

◎ Show students how to staple the two ends together to form a ring (with the name and photo on the outside). String a clothesline across a wall and have children pin up their rings.

◎ Give each child a class list and a set of blank strips (one for each classmate). Beginning with the name that follows theirs on the class list, have children write a friendly message to each classmate, mentioning something positive about that child. Encourage them to be specific—for example, "I like the funny stories you tell about your dog." Have children sign their names, then locate the child's ring on the line, thread the strip through, and staple it to make a ring. Children will be excited to watch their friendship rings grow, until at last they can take them down and read them.

*Sue Lorey*

## Book Break

## Saint Valentine
by Robert Sabuda (Atheneum, 1992)

Surprise! While we might associate roses with Valentine's Day, the *crocus* is actually the "official" flower of this holiday. Learn more about the history of this favorite February holiday with this exquisitely illustrated book.

MATH

# Estimation Experts

A jar full of conversation hearts is just the thing to motivate a math lesson on estimation and counting skills.

◎ Fill a clear jar with candy hearts. Give each child a record sheet. (See sample, right.) Ask children to estimate how many hearts are in the jar and to record their guess in the first space.

◎ Take out about 1/4 of the candies (leaving the jar about 3/4 full) and count them with children. Put the candy back in the jar and let children revise their estimates if they wish.

◎ Repeat this procedure two more times. The last time, you will be removing about 3/4 of the candy hearts, counting them, and putting them back in.

◎ Conclude by counting all of the hearts in the jar. Let children compare each of their estimates with the actual number of hearts. *Which was their best? How close were they?* Encourage children to explain how they revised their estimates. Help them understand that estimates are not just random guesses. The more information they have about something, the better their estimates can be.

---

**Name _____ Date _____**

## Estimation Experts

**Estimate 1: _____** hearts

**Estimate 2: _____** hearts

**Estimate 3: _____** hearts

**Estimate 4: _____** hearts

Estimate

**1   2   3   4**

was my best!
(circle one)

I guessed _____ hearts
too many/too few.

---

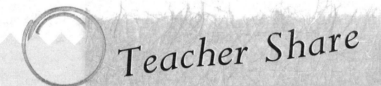

# Teacher Share

SOCIAL STUDIES, LANGUAGE ARTS

## Compliment Hearts

**E**xplore concepts of friendship by making collaborative cards that children will read again and again.

◎ Let children each use a heart template to trace and cut out a large heart. Ask children to write their names in the center of the heart.

◎ Have children place their hearts on their desks, along with a few markers or colored pencils. Let children rotate to each classmate's desk and write a compliment on that child's heart.

By the end of this activity, each child will have a heart full of compliments—and a big boost in self-esteem!

*Deirdre Parkhurst*

# Teacher Share

## Have a Heart

**A**ddition and subtraction practice is fun with an activity that lets children move around the room as they solve problems.

◎ Make a set of heart-shaped cards. Write an addition or subtraction problem on one side of each heart. Write the answer or solution on the back of each heart. Label each heart (A, B, C, etc.).

◎ Make a grid, with boxes labeled A, B, C, and so on to match the hearts. Give a copy to each child.

◎ Place a heart on each child's desk. Have children start with that heart, solving the problem, then recording the answer on their grid and turning over the heart to self-check.

◎ At a designated signal, have children rotate to the next desk, solving that problem. Continue in this way until children have solved all of the problems.

*Deirdre Parkhurst*

SCIENCE, MATH, FITNESS

# "A Big Heart" Calendar Activity

Ask children what they think it means to have a "big heart." (*to be especially kind, caring, and giving*) Ask children if they know how big their hearts are. Let them guess, then reveal that their hearts are about the size of their fists. Explain that the heart is a muscle and that, like other muscles in our bodies, we need to work at keeping it strong. Reinforce heart-healthy habits with this calendar activity.

◎ Give each child a heart-shaped card (with the fold at the top), sized to fit on a calendar square.

◎ On the inside of their hearts, have children write an exercise they can lead the class in. It can be silly or serious—for example, "Flap your arms like a bird for one minute." or "Do 20 jumping jacks, counting by twos." Have children sign their names to the outside of their hearts.

◎ Use a bit of removable wall adhesive to stick each heart to a calendar square. Write the date on each. When it's calendar time, let the designated child lift the flap and lead the class in a fitness activity!

# Your Half, My Half

## ❤A Fraction Valentine Play❤

**Characters**  Group A ♡ Group B

(A)  Will you be my valentine?

(B)  Yes, I think that would be fine!

(A)  Then here's a heart for you
to wear.

(B)  But only half of it is here!

(A)  Where can the other half be?

(B)  Let's take a look around
and see.

(A)  What do we need?
Where should we start?

(B)  We need another half
To make a whole heart.

(A)  Is it underneath that chair?

*(they search)*

(B)  No  It isn't anywhere!

(A)  Let's look for it out in the hall.

*(they look)*

(B)  It isn't anywhere at all.

(A)  Could this square be
the right part?

*(finds and holds up a piece of paper)*

(B)  No, it wouldn't make a heart.

(A)  Hey look!

(B)  The pieces are hidden
in that book!

*(Hearts are in book. Children tape
halves together.)*

(A&B) Two halves make a whole.
That's the end of our play.
Have a happy Valentine's Day!

*500+ Fabulous Month by Month Teaching Ideas* © 2010 Scholastic Teaching Resources

**TIP**

As a variation, have children list as many things as they can that contain a particular president's name—for example, post chart paper labeled "Thinkin' Lincoln." Have children record places (Lincoln, Nebraska; the Lincoln Memorial), things (Lincoln Logs), and so on that share Abraham Lincoln's name.

# *Teacher Share*

## Presidential Places Scavenger Hunt

Strengthen map-reading skills and geography concepts, and spark students' interest in our country's leaders, with this ongoing activity. Display a large, detailed U.S. map at children's eye level. Post chart paper nearby and a list of all the presidents. Challenge children to locate and list as many places as they can that bear the name of a president. Have them record their findings on the chart paper and mark the spots on the map with small sticky-notes. (They can sign their names to the notes.)

*Sue Lorey*

MATH, SOCIAL STUDIES

## What Big Feet!

What do your students know about George Washington? They may know that he was the first president and that his picture is on a coin. But when they imagine him, do they see a man who was 6 feet 2 inches tall with size 13 feet? Bring in a pair of size 13 shoes. Let children trace around them, then take off their own shoes and step inside. Ask: *How long do you think Washington's feet were?* Measure them to find out. Then have children trace and measure their own feet. *How much bigger were Washington's?*

SOCIAL STUDIES, LANGUAGE ARTS

## Mystery History

Spark students' interest in presidential history by posing a "Mystery History" challenge each day. Set up an eye-catching display area to post the challenge. Provide assorted resources for locating information, and a box for children to place their answers in. Sample Mystery History challenges include:

◎ Who was the tallest president?

◎ Which president was closest to your height?

◎ Name a president who was born in the state of [   ].

◎ What is the most common first name for a president?

MATH, SOCIAL STUDIES

# Counting on Presidents

Strengthen math skills with a math mat activity that connects money and presidents.

◎ Glue a picture of Abraham Lincoln to a paper plate and label it 1¢. Glue a picture of George Washington to a paper plate and label it 25¢.

◎ Place a quarter and a jar of pennies (more than 25) at a center along with the paper plates. Let children visit the center, inviting them to count out the number of pennies it takes to equal 25 cents and place them on the paper plate with Lincoln's picture.

◎ To vary the activity, cut out pictures of small toys or other items. Label the pictures with prices, such as 10¢, 15¢, and so on. Let children select pictures and count out the corresponding number of pennies. Or, have them count out pennies to make change from a quarter. Follow up by investigating other coins: *Whose picture is on a nickel? a half dollar? a dollar?*

Teacher Share

MATH

## What Coin Am I?

Children find it interesting that different presidents are on U.S. coins. Let them learn more about presidents and money by making these self-checking riddle boards.

◎ Give pairs of children two sheets of 4- by 4-inch posterboard and two of the same coin. Have children examine their coins closely, noting as many details as they can.

◎ Have children write their facts in the form of clues on one sheet of posterboard, ending with "What coin am I?" Have them tape their coins—one heads-up, one tails-up—to the other sheet.

◎ Show children how to place the clues on top of the coins and then tape the top edges together. (The clues can then be lifted then to reveal the coins inside.)

◎ Display the riddles. Let students read the clues for different coins, guess what they are, and lift the flaps to see if they're right.

*Bob Krech*

Connection

National Park Service
www.nps.gov
Take a virtual tour of President Lincoln's home in Springfield, Illinois, and view historic photos of the home over the years. Lesson plans for teaching with historic places, including Lincoln's home, are also available.

SOCIAL STUDIES, LANGUAGE ARTS

## Abe and I Mini-Book

Abraham Lincoln's life was full of big changes—including going from living in a log cabin as a boy to living in the White House as president! What are some of the ways students' lives are different from Abe's life as a boy? Use pages 175 and 176 to make mini-books that compare everyday life then and now. Have students complete each mini-book page, then add a cover and bind.

Students can make new pages to compare other parts of everyday life, such as communication. (Messages were sent by stagecoach when Lincoln was a boy. Children today have many options for communicating, including e-mail!)

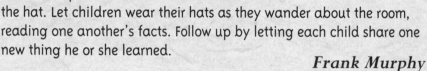

Teacher Share

SOCIAL STUDIES, LANGUAGE ARTS

### Stovepipe Hats

Surprise! Abe Lincoln kept notes stuffed in his stovepipe hat to remind him about important dates (and so he wouldn't lose the notes). Let children make their own stovepipe hats out of black construction paper. Have students tape notes about Abe to the outside of the hat. Let children wear their hats as they wander about the room, reading one another's facts. Follow up by letting each child share one new thing he or she learned.

*Frank Murphy*

### Book Break

## Mr. Lincoln's Whiskers
### by Karen Winnick (Boyds Mills Press, 1999)

Read about a young girl who wrote Lincoln to convince him to grow a beard. (He did!) After sharing this true story with students, you may find that they are inspired to make their own requests of the current President. (See Computer Connection, page 173.) For more on the sixteenth president, share the anecdote-rich *Abe Lincoln's Hat* by Martha Brenner (Random House, 1994).

Book Break

## The Legend of the Teddy Bear
### by Frank Murphy (Sleeping Bear Press, 2000)

Did you know that one of our nation's presidents helped to give one of our country's most popular toys its name? Share this story to trace the history of the teddy bear and to discover more about Teddy Roosevelt, including his many pets (kangaroo rats, birds, dogs, squirrels, kittens, even a pony!).

*Teacher Share*

MATH, SOCIAL STUDIES

## Design Your Own White House

Start by asking children if they know what the "White House" is. Share a picture of it and ask: *Why do you think it is called the White House?* Share a few more facts about this famous home—for example, some of the rooms are named after colors: There is a Green Room, Blue Room, and Red Room. One room is named after a shape: the Oval Office. Two bedrooms are named after people: the Lincoln Bedroom and the Queen's Bedroom. Let children design their own versions of the White House. Encourage them to show both interior and exterior views of the house and its rooms, and be sure they write or dictate labels for them. When finished, gather as a group and let children share their new visions for 1600 Pennsylvania Avenue!

*Rita Galloway*

### CoMPuter Connection

Take an online tour of the White House and e-mail the President! www. whitehouse.gov

comments@ whitehouse.gov

Address regular mail to:
The White House
1600 Pennsylvania Avenue NW Washington, DC 20500

Book Break

## Lives of the Presidents: Fame, Shame (and What the Neighbors Thought)
### by Kathleen Krull (Harcourt, 1998)

Which president enjoyed quilting? Which one weighed only 100 pounds? Who had two pet goats? Learn what the presidents were like in their everyday lives—what they ate, what they did for fun, and more.

SNACK, SOCIAL STUDIES

# Eat Like a President!

Plan a no-cook buffet to let children sample favorite foods of the presidents. Begin by asking: *What foods do you think a president might eat?* Some surprising presidential preferences have included turtle (Theodore Roosevelt), egg sandwiches (Franklin D. Roosevelt), and prune whip (Dwight D. Eisenhower). For no-cook presidential foods your students can help prepare, see the list that follows. (To learn more about presidents' favorite foods—and other things about their everyday lives—see Book Break, page 21, *Lives of the Presidents*.)

◎ Ulysses S. Grant liked cucumbers in vinegar for breakfast.

◎ Lyndon B. Johnson loved chipped beef and bread for breakfast.

◎ John Adams enjoyed cider.

◎ Richard Nixon was partial to pineapple rings with cottage cheese.

◎ Gerald R. Ford favored strawberries.

◎ Ronald Reagan's usual breakfast was bran cereal. He also enjoyed popcorn and, of course, jelly beans.

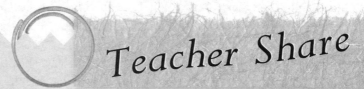

*Teacher Share*

MATH, SOCIAL STUDIES

## Graphing Presidents

fter learning about presidents and their families, graph information to help students make comparisons and draw conclusions. (The type of graph you use will depend on the data gathered.) Ideas for graphing include:

◎ How many children did each president have?

◎ How many presidents were married when they were elected?

◎ How many presidents had a cat for a pet? How many had a dog?

◎ How many presidents went to college?

◎ Which states were the presidents born in?

*Jan Armstrong Freitag*

# Activity Page

Abe lived in a log cabin with a dirt floor. It didn't have windows or running water.

(1)

I live in _____

_____

_____ .

Abe wore shirts made from a rough cloth called linsey-woolsey. He wore buckskin pants and a coonskin cap.

(2)

I wear _____

_____

_____ .

500+ Fabulous Month-by-Month Teaching Ideas © 2010 Scholastic Teaching Resources

Abe's mother cooked over a fireplace. His family grew vegetables. They went hunting for animals to eat. They made bread from cornmeal.

③

I eat food cooked _ _ _ _ _

_ _ _ _ _ _ _ _ _ _ _ .

My food comes from _ _ _ _

_ _ _ _ _ _ _ _ _ _ _ .

Abe helped his family by chopping wood for fires. He picked berries, nuts, and grapes to eat. He helped his father plant the garden.

④

I help my family by _ _ _ _

_ _ _ _ _ _ _ _ _ _ _ _

_ _ _ _ _ _ _ _ _ _ _ _

*500+ Fabulous Month-by-Month Teaching Ideas* © 2010 Scholastic Teaching Resources

SCIENCE, HEALTH

# Brush, Brush, Brush Your Teeth

February is Dental Health Month. And since it's also the month when children may be enjoying more sweets than usual in honor of Valentine's Day, why not plan a unit on teeth? Get started with an activity that will quickly and clearly demonstrate the benefits of brushing.

◎ Ask children why they think it's important to brush their teeth. Many will know that it's to prevent cavities. Ask: *Do you know how cavities can form in your teeth?* Explain that bacteria in our mouths change sugars in foods to acids. This causes a sticky substance called *plaque* to form on our teeth. Acids in the plaque attack tooth enamel (the outer layer of teeth), creating cavities. (Help children understand that lots of foods—not just candy—have sugars in them.)

◎ Fill two jars partway with vinegar. Tell children that the vinegar is like the acid in their mouths that can cause cavities. Place a raw egg in each jar. Explain that the eggshells are like their teeth.

◎ Remove one egg from the vinegar a few minutes after putting it in. Provide a toothbrush and toothpaste. Let children take turns gently brushing the egg and rinsing it. Set this egg on a paper towel. Explain that you will leave the other egg in the vinegar overnight. Ask: *What do you think we will see when we look at each egg tomorrow?* (The egg that was brushed and rinsed should be fine. The egg left in the vinegar will be pitted—like the cavities that form on teeth.)

## Book Break

# Grandpa's Teeth
### by Rod Clement (HarperCollins, 1999)

Everyone's a suspect in this funny story about Grandpa and his missing false teeth. Follow up with a class "teeth hunt." Hide a handful of dried white beans (the teeth) around the classroom. Challenge children to find them all.

**TIP**

This is a good time to talk about flossing, too. Ask: How do you think flossing helps prevent cavities? (It helps remove food from between our teeth, preventing plaque from forming.)

**Computer Connection**

American Dental Association
www.ada.org

Select "Smile Smarts Oral Heath Curriculum" for lessons plans, demonstrations, and activity sheets.

Kids Health
www.kidshealth.org

Kids take a "tooth tour" to learn what makes teeth work, how to take care of teeth, find out what "by the skin of your teeth" means, test their knowledge with a quiz, and much more.

## TIP

Primary teeth usually start to be replaced by permanent teeth by about six years of age. The front teeth are usually first to go. Primary teeth continue to be replaced by permanent teeth through about 13 years of age, at which time the 28 permanent teeth are usually in place.

## Computer Connection

Track how many teeth children around the world lose with the Internet Schoolhouse:

www.internet schoolhouse.com

MATH

# Tracking Teeth

*How many teeth have your students lost? How do they think this compares to the number of teeth lost by another class in the same grade? by a class of younger students? older students?* Conduct a survey to find out. Make copies of the tooth pattern here to gather data. Copy the pattern in a different color for each class that is participating in the survey. Have children write their names on the teeth and tell how many teeth they've lost. Use the markers to make a graph. Place the markers for each participating class side by side (above the number of teeth lost) to assist students in making comparisons. Use the graphs to guide a class discussion:

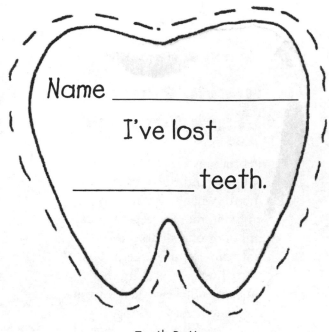

Tooth Pattern

Name _____

I've lost

_____ teeth.

- How many children in our class have lost only one tooth? more than one tooth? no teeth?

- Have more children in our class lost at least one tooth or not lost any teeth?

- How does our class compare to the class of older students? younger students?

- About how many teeth do you think the average child your age has lost by now?

- How do you think this data might change at the end of the year?

Book Break

# My Tooth Is About to Fall Out

### by Grace Maccarone (Scholastic, 1995)

A young girl worries about where she will be when her first tooth falls out. Follow up by letting children write or dictate stories about where they were when their first tooth fell out (or where they think they might be when it happens). Give students tooth-shaped papers to write their final copies on.

# Teacher Share

SCIENCE

## Testing Teeth

**TIP**

Check for food allergies before having children test their teeth as tools for grinding carrots.

**H**elp children discover the strength of their teeth with a hands-on investigation. Divide the class into small groups. Give each group the following materials: a hammer; a rolling pin; a block of wood; four carrot sticks plus an extra carrot stick for each child in the group. Give each child a copy of the record sheet on page 181. Have children test the tools listed on the record sheet in order to see how well each works to grind up a carrot stick. Have them conclude the investigation by testing their own teeth as tools. Guide children in using the record sheet to rate the tools from one to five (five being the highest rating). Discuss what makes teeth such good tools for biting and chewing—for example, they're hard, sharp, and so on.

*Natalie Vaughan*

**TIP**

Number of teeth on top, bottom, and in total follows (from left to right):

- fruit bat (12, 12, 24)
- hedgehog (20, 16, 36)
- guinea pig (10, 10, 20)
- kangaroo (18, 14, 32)
- giraffe (12, 20, 32)
- elephant (14, 12, 26)
- tiger (16, 14, 30)
- toucan (0, 0, 0)
- beaver (10, 10, 20)
- crocodile (30, 30, 60)
- hippopotamus (20, 18, 38)
- dog (20, 22, 42)

LANGUAGE ARTS, ART, MATH

## Collaborative Lift-the-Flap Banner

Give each child a copy of the banner template on page 182. Have them complete the rhyme for the animal of their choice, telling how many teeth the animal has on top, on the bottom, and in all. (Use the chart, right, for information.) Guide children in making the flap, cutting on the dashed lines and gluing the paper to another sheet of paper, being careful not to place glue on the flap or the area underneath. Have children draw and label a picture of their animal under the flap. Arrange papers side by side and tape together.

**TIP**

For more ideas and activities about teeth, see *Fresh & Fun: Teeth* by Jacqueline Clarke (Scholastic, 2000).

**TIP**

As a variation, let children play the part of the child and the Tooth Fairy. Tell them how many of each coin the Tooth Fairy is leaving. Have them place those coins under their pillows, then count them for a total.

**Book Break**

# Throw Your Tooth on the Roof: Tooth Traditions From Around the World
by Selby B. Beeler (Houghton Mifflin, 1998)

What tooth traditions are your students familiar with? Many may know the Tooth Fairy. Invite them to share their stories, then read this book to introduce tooth traditions around the world. Follow up with "What Will the Tooth Fairy Leave?" (See below).

MATH

## What Will the Tooth Fairy Leave? Math Story Mat

Invite the Tooth Fairy to visit your classroom with this math story mat activity. Give each child a copy of pages 183 and 184. Have children color the story mat, then color and cut out the child, pillow, Tooth Fairy, teeth, and coins. Share the following story problem. Have children use the manipulatives to act it out and find an answer. Continue sharing other stories, varying the number of teeth under the pillow and the coins the Tooth Fairy leaves.

How exciting! You just lost a tooth! It's time for bed. Be sure to place the tooth under your pillow before you go to sleep. (*Children place the tooth at the head of the bed, place the pillow on top, then put the cutout child into bed.*) What will the Tooth Fairy bring? Go to sleep or she won't come! (*Have children close their eyes. Visit each child's desk. Replace the tooth with coins, the same amount for each child.*) Wake up—it's morning! Time to look under your pillows. What did the Tooth Fairy bring? (*Have children look under their pillows and count the coins.*)

SCIENCE, MATH

## What Big Teeth!

"What big teeth you have!" The story of Little Red Riding Hood has made an indelible impression on most of us as to the feeding habits of wolves. Are a wolf's teeth really as big and scary as this favorite fairy tale might have us believe? What animal does have the biggest teeth? Challenge children to find out. (They may be surprised to learn that an elephant's tusks are teeth (incisors), which make this animal's teeth the biggest of all—up to 10 1/2 feet long.) Build in more math by comparing the size of teeth. *How much bigger are an elephant's teeth than a child's teeth?*

Name _____    Date _____

# Testing Teeth

How well did each tool grind up the carrot?
Rate the tools by circling a number from one to five.

<--- Hard to Grind                    Easy to Grind --->

| | | | | | |
|---|---|---|---|---|---|
| Hammer | 1 | 2 | 3 | 4 | 5 |
| Wood | 1 | 2 | 3 | 4 | 5 |
| Fingers | 1 | 2 | 3 | 4 | 5 |
| Rolling Pin | 1 | 2 | 3 | 4 | 5 |
| Teeth | 1 | 2 | 3 | 4 | 5 |

◎ Which tool was most like your teeth? _____

◎ Name other foods that you can grind with your teeth.

_____

_____

Name _____ Date _____

# Collaborative Lift-the-Flap Banner

What animal am I
with _____ teeth?
That's _____ on top
and _____ underneath!

Lift the flap
and you will see.
Who has more—
you or me?

*500+ Fabulous Month-by-Month Teaching Ideas* © 2010 Scholastic Teaching Resources

What Will the Tooth
Fairy Leave?
Math Story Mat

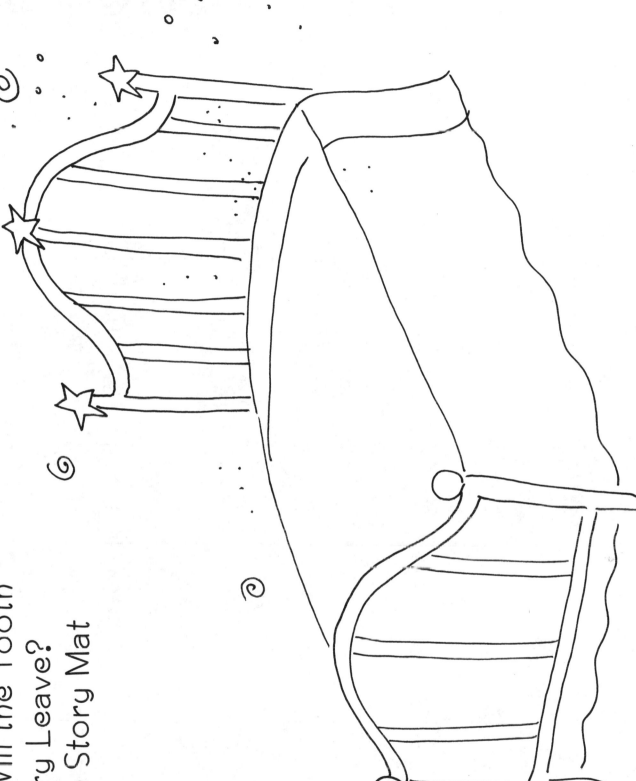

What Will the Tooth Fairy Leave?
Math Story Mat

Teeth

500+ Fabulous Month-by-Month Teaching Ideas © 2010 Scholastic Teaching Resources

# March

# March
## Teaching Ideas

*I* love the calendar year! With each new month, I anticipate the seasonal changes and celebrations that lie ahead. In March, there are plenty of reasons to celebrate! Women's History Month provides an opportunity to pay tribute to women who have made a difference. For example, children will learn about Elizabeth Cady Stanton and women's suffrage (see "The Right to Vote," page 190). National Nutrition Month encourages us to examine and learn more about our eating habits. The "windy weather" of March is food for our senses, and with the first day of spring falling somewhere around the twentieth, we begin to think about seeds and planting, with fun activities, such as "Lift-the-Flap Seed Houses" (page 206) and "Mystery Garden" (page 208).

Here, you'll find activities for each of the above topics to help you welcome March into your classroom. The activities are organized by curriculum area, but most integrate more than one subject. Here's a glimpse of just some of the other March ideas and activities you'll find:

- a reproducible send-home activity calendar
- a math story mat
- an easy-to-learn "piggyback" song
- literature links
- computer connections
- pocket chart poetry
- a reproducible mini-book
- hands-on math and science activities
- a no-cook recipe that celebrates spring
- interactive reproducibles
- collaborative books to make and share
- a collaborative banner
- and more spring fun!

Name _____

# March Activity Calendar

Choose _____ activities to do each week this month.
Ask an adult in your family to initial the square in the box of each activity
you complete. Bring this paper back to school on _____.

| Monday | Tuesday | Wednesday | Thursday | Friday |
|---|---|---|---|---|
| Write the word *March* on a sheet of paper. Cut apart the letters. Make new words. | Say the word *March*. What sound does it end in? List more words that end in this sound (*ch*). | Tell someone in your family what you think this means: *March comes in like a lion and goes out like a lamb.* | Happy Birthday to Peggy Rathman. (March 4) Look for safety tips in her book *Officer Buckle and Gloria*. Tell one you know. | Look at a newspaper. Find a number. Find a headline. Find a picture. What does each tell you? |
| March is the third month of the year. Name the second month. Name the fourth month. | Look at this shamrock. Find a matching shamrock on this page. | Look out a window. What are some ways you see wind at work? | Find today's date on a calendar. How many more days until April Fool's Day? | Celebrate Women's History Month! Look in books, newspapers, or on the Internet for stories about what women do. |
| Play a guessing game. Give clues about someone you and your family knows. Who can guess this person's identity? | Look at the sky. Draw a picture that has a sky like the one you see. | What is another meaning for the word *March*? Act out this meaning for someone in your family. | Start a plant indoors from a pit. Try an orange or lemon pit. Plant the pit in soil, place it in a sunny spot, and keep it moist. | Look at a calendar. Find the first day of spring. How many days until summer? |
| Look at a food label. Find a picture. Find some numbers. What do they tell you? | Listen for birds singing and calling. Try to make the sounds you hear. | A chickadee makes a sound like its name. Pretend you're a chickadee. What sound do you make? | March 30 is Vincent Van Gogh's birthday. This artist painted a picture called "Sunflowers." Make a painting of your favorite flower. | Turn *March* into a tongue twister! Make up a sentence using as many words as you can that start with *m*. |

# Teacher Share

LANGUAGE ARTS, SOCIAL STUDIES

## Bag-It Book Reports

**H**ere's a great alternative to the traditional "book report." Students choose a famous woman in history to read about. Then they prepare an oral presentation by gathering props that in some way relate to the woman's life. (See Book Break, below, for a way to model this.) Students place the props in a grocery bag decorated with pictures, symbols, and words that reveal more about the person. Let them take turns presenting their "bag-it" book reports during the month of March. Provide time for questions following each presentation. This is a great way for students to take the lead in learning about many different women.

*Natalie Vaughan*

· · · · · · · · · · **Book Break** · · · · · · · · · ·

## George Washington's Mother
### by Jean Fritz (Gosset & Dunlap, 1992)

Mary Washington smoked a pipe, hated dress-up clothes, and didn't believe what she read in the newspapers. Learn more interesting facts about this fascinating woman in this colorful biography.

Before sharing the book with students, pique their interest with this guessing game. Place the following items in a bag: newspaper, gingerbread pan, money, rock, pipe, a piece of dress-up clothing, and a picture of George Washington. Show them to students one at a time. Ask: *What do all these items have in common?* The answer: *George Washington's mother.* Read the book aloud and let students figure out how each item relates to Mary Washington.

SOCIAL STUDIES, MATH

# The Right to Vote

Students will be able to empathize with historical women such as Elizabeth Cady Stanton when they are left out of a classroom vote. Choose something to vote on that affects all members of the class, such as which book to read, or what equipment to bring to the playground. Create a ballot box by cutting a slit in the top of a shoebox. Explain to students that for now, only the boys will be allowed to vote. Distribute a slip of paper to each boy, and ask him to cast his vote by placing it in the ballot box. Withdraw the slips and record the votes on a graph. Ask the girls how it made them feel to be left out of the vote. Repeat the activity, letting only the girls vote this time. Ask the boys to share their feelings. Record the combined results from the first two graphs on a third one. Discuss how the results of the vote were different when both boys and girls had their say.

## Book Break

# You Forgot Your Skirt, Amelia Bloomer
### by Shana Corey (Scholastic, 2000)

Amelia Bloomer lived in the nineteenth century, when "proper women" wore heavy hoop skirts and tight corsets. Tired of being uncomfortable, Amelia dared to dress differently. Your students will enjoy learning about the trend she started and how she impacted women's rights. Use this book to introduce the activity "Fashion Heavyweights." (See below.)

SOCIAL STUDIES, MATH

# Fashion Heavyweights

In the 1800s, women wore clothing that weighed between 20 and 40 pounds. Let your students experience how difficult it was to move carrying all that weight. Place a large book-bag on a bathroom scale. Let students take turns adding books, one at a time, until the scale reads 20 pounds. Give each child an opportunity to lift the bag and walk around the classroom. Ask them to imagine wearing all that weight every day! Ask: *How much do you think pants and a shirt weigh?* Take out a child's shirt and pants (bring them to school in advance), and place them on the scale. Compare the weight of the pants and shirt to the weight of women's clothing in the 1800s.

Book Break

## Girls Think of Everything: Stories of Ingenious Inventions by Women

### by Catherine Thimmesh (Houghton Mifflin, 2000)

*Who invented the fire escape, pastry fork, and electric hot water heater?* Women, of course! Your students will enjoy hearing these stories of legendary females who have impacted our lives by turning their dreams into realities. They'll find out what inspired these inventors, what obstacles they encountered, and what it took to follow through.

SCIENCE, SOCIAL STUDIES

## Mystery History

*What do windshield wipers, alphabet blocks, and underwater telescopes have in common?* They were all invented by women! Play this guessing game so students can see that many objects still used today were the product of a woman's ingenuity. Gather the following objects: chocolate chip cookie, ice cream cone, paper bag, disposable diaper, signal flare, medical syringe, and interlocking block. Each day, place a different item inside a box. Give three clues about the object, and let students try to guess its identity. As you reveal each object, share the following information:

- ◎ chocolate chip cookie invented by Ruth Wakefield in 1930
- ◎ ice cream cone invented by an anonymous woman in 1904
- ◎ paper bags invented by Margaret E. Knight in 1870
- ◎ disposable diaper invented by Marion Donovan in 1951
- ◎ signal flares invented by Martha Hunt Coston in 1850
- ◎ medical syringe invented by Letitia Geer in 1899
- ◎ interlocking blocks invented by Mary Nolan in 1877

Book Break

## The Ballot Box Battle

### by Emily Arnold McCully (Knopf, 1996)

As the fictional neighbor of Elizabeth Cady Stanton, young Cordelia learns of this woman's fight for suffrage and how she once longed to "be as good as any boy" to please her father. Although more interested in horses than in voting, Cordelia goes to the polls with Mrs. Stanton. This experience leads to a turning point in Cordelia's life.

## Computer Connection

### National Women's Hall of Fame

www. greatwomen.org

Looking for a list of famous women in history? This site is a great place to start and includes a biography for all "Women of the Hall."

## Teacher Share

SOCIAL STUDIES, ART

### History-Maker Masks

In this activity, students will enjoy being interviewed as if they were famous women in history. To prepare for the interviews, let students choose a well-known woman to research and study. Supply a list of names (see Computer Connection, left) and make sure no two students choose the same woman. Encourage students to find out about the woman's birthplace, family, schooling, contributions to society, and so on, using the reproducible activity sheet to record information. (See page 193.)

To help students get into "character" for their interview, let them make masks from paper plates. They can decorate the plate using markers, fabric scraps, and yarn to look like the woman they studied. Attach a paint stick (available at paint and hardware stores) with glue or tape to make a handle.

During the month of March, set aside time for children to take turns being interviewed by a partner or the rest of the class. Wearing their mask, they should answer questions as that famous woman. *Who can guess the famous woman's identity?*

*Judy Wetzel*

Activity Page

Name Dylan            Date March 10

History-Maker Interview

I am going to learn about
Grace McCance

Birthplace: Missouri

Birthdate: 1882

Family: Harry, Margaret (mother), Stella (sister), Poppie (father) (baby sisters) Florence → Stella, Maud → the baby, sister → Nellie (baby sister #5)

Schooling: Country School

Made history by: being a pioneer girl in Nebraska

More facts about her: Quiltmaker herded cattle

## Book Break

# Girls Who Rocked the World: Heroines From Sacagawea to Sheryl Swoopes
## by Amelia Welden (Beyond Words Publishing, 1998)

Read about 33 real girls from around the globe—including Joan of Arc, Helen Keller, Wilma Rudolph, Mary Anning, Anne Frank—who made their mark on history before reaching their twenties.

Name _____ Date _____

# History-Maker Interview

## I am going to learn about

----------------------------------------- .

Birthplace: ----------------------------------------

Birthdate: ----------------------------------------

Family: ----------------------------------------

----------------------------------------

Schooling: ----------------------------------------

----------------------------------------

Made history by: ----------------------------------------

----------------------------------------

More facts about her: ----------------------------------------

----------------------------------------

----------------------------------------

# The Wind Blew
by Pat Hutchins (Aladdin, 1993)

Umbrellas, balloons, hats, and kites are just a few of the items claimed by the wind. As the owners scramble to catch their belongings, the wind mixes them all up and finally sends them back down.

LANGUAGE ARTS

## One Blustery Day...

The wind can be a mischievous fellow! In this pocket chart activity, children will enjoy reading and rereading a rhyme about objects taken away by the wind.

Write the following frame on sentence strips and place them in the pocket chart:

> I went for a walk,
> On a blustery day,
> And that terrible wind
> Blew my _____ away.

Ask each child to draw a picture of an object that the wind might "snatch." Let them take turns coming up to the pocket chart and placing their pictures in the blank space. With each new object, invite students to read the rhyme along with you. Go further by writing words for each object on cards. Students can substitute these for the pictures to complete line four.

---

**TIP**

Turn the pocket chart activity into an interactive chart by drawing a big gust of wind on a sheet of posterboard and gluing the sentence strips in the center. Laminate the chart and the objects that children create. Place a piece of Velcro® in the blank space in the rhyme and on the back of each object. Store the objects in a resealable bag and staple it to the back of the posterboard. Children can choose objects to fill the blank and practice reading the rhyme.

---

## One Windy Wednesday
by Phyllis Root (Candlewick Press, 1997)

On Bonnie Bumble's farm, a strong wind blows and mixes everything up. It blows the quack right out the duck, the moo right out of the cow, and the oink right out of the pig. Extend the book by doing a mini rewrite. Write the following on a sentence strip and place it in a pocket chart: *The wind blew the _____ out of the _____ .* Let students think of other ideas to fill in the blanks—for example, *the ink out of the pen* or *the milk out of the cup.*

# Teacher Share

SCIENCE

## March Weather Research

**D**oes March really come in like a lion and go out like a lamb? Present this research question on the last day of February, and let students collect weather data to find the answer.

Make copies of the lion and lamb calendar pieces (see page 197), and let students color and cut them out. Ask students to tell what they think "lion weather" is like. (*wild and ferocious*) "Lamb weather"? (*gentle and mild*) Each morning, choose one child to put a lion or a lamb on the calendar to symbolize the nature of the weather for that day. (Use removable adhesive.)

At the end of the month, restate the research question. Let students look at the data collected on the calendar to determine the answer. Remove the calendar pieces and use them to create a graph to find out whether there were more "lion" or "lamb" days in the month of March.

*Judy Meagher*

MATH

## Moved by the Wind

*Can the wind move any object?* This experiment helps students realize that the size and shape of an object, as well as the strength of the wind, are all factors.

Let each child choose a small object from the classroom to test. Place an electric fan (with a security guard) on a table or the floor and gather students around it. Make sure they stand at a safe distance from the fan. Take the objects one at a time and place them in front of the fan. Turn the fan on low. *Does the object move? How about at medium or high speed?* Continue with other objects.

As you test each object, sort them into two piles: those that moved and those that didn't. Follow up by asking: *Is there anything similar about the objects that moved?* Students might notice that objects that are very light, such as a sheet of paper or a plastic bag, as well as those that are round or cylindrical, were easily moved.

**Book Break**

# The Wind Garden

by Angela McAllister and Claire Fletcher (Lothrop, Lee & Shepard, 1995)

Grandpa can't get around so well and misses visiting the park and all its flowers. He and his granddaughter, Ellie, plant a rooftop garden, but the wind is too strong and the seedlings don't survive. One night, Ellie is magically lifted to the "place where the wind goes," where she finds many things lifted away by the wind, including kites, hats, and laundry. She returns with an idea—she and Grandpa can plant a "wind garden!"

SCIENCE

## Grow a Wind Garden

Observe the presence of the wind by creating a "wind garden" outside your classroom. Send home a letter asking each student to bring in an item to "plant" in the garden. It must be something that will stick into the ground and will move with the wind—for example, a pinwheel or flag. Let students "plant" their objects outside. *What does their garden tell them about the wind each day?*

# Teacher Share

SCIENCE, LANGUAGE ARTS

## I Spy the Wind!

As "wind detectives," your students' mission will be to detect the presence of moving air! Give each student a pencil with a strip of tissue paper taped to one end. Lead them to different locations inside and outside your school building, and encourage them to pay close attention to the strip of tissue paper. Can they "spy" the wind? When and how often? Mark directions in an outside area (North, East, South, West). Guide students in identifying which direction the wind is coming from.

*Pat McMonagle*

## Calendar Pieces

## Backpack Snacks Collaborative Banner

Discuss why it is important to bring healthy snacks to school. (*So students have energy to work and play.*) Explain that sugary snacks only provide short bursts of energy, while foods such as cereal bars and peanut butter and crackers offer longer-lasting results. Let students suggest other favorite snacks. (Or let students list the snacks they have in school that day.) Together, decide which snacks are "healthy." Give each student a copy of page 203. Have students fill in the frame with the name of a healthy snack they can bring to school, then draw a picture of that food inside the backpack. Tape the backpacks side to side to create a collaborative banner that will serve as a healthy reminder.

LANGUAGE ARTS, DRAMATIC PLAY

## May I Take Your Order?

Students create a balanced menu and use it for pretend play.

◎ Make a "menu" by dividing a sheet of posterboard into four sections. Label each section with a different food group—for example, Dairy; Breads and Grains; Meat, Fish, Soy; and Fruits and Vegetables.

◎ Assign each child a category. Have children draw or cut out a picture of a food that belongs to that group. Laminate each food and attach it to the board using Velcro®.

◎ Label the pictures on the posterboard menu and display it in the dramatic play center along with a table, chairs, plates, paper, and pencil.

◎ Let students take turns being "servers," "customers," and "cooks." The customer orders a meal that contains something from each food group. The server writes down the order (using the menu as a resource) and gives it to the cook. The cook prepares the meal by reading the order, removing the foods from the chart, and placing them on the plate. The server then brings the meal to the customer.

**Book Break**

## Showdown at the Food Pyramid
### by Rex Barron (Putnam, 2004)

In this colorful introduction to healthy eating, personified foods fight for space at the top of the food pyramid. Junk food pushes out the fruits and vegetables, but not for long.

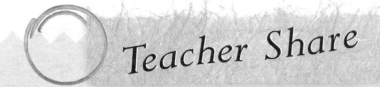

## Teacher Share

# Snack Pack Graph

**D**uring the month of March, collect empty bags from the snack-size (one ounce) chips, crackers, popcorn, pretzels, and so on that students bring in their lunches. Glue bags from three or four different types to the horizontal axis of a graph. Label the vertical axis to represent the number of fat grams per bag.

Pass out the extra bags you've collected, and show students how to read the nutritional information on the package. Explain that "g" is an abbreviation for *grams*, and help students locate the number of fat grams in each bag. Record the fat grams for each snack on the graph, then ask the following questions to guide a discussion.

- How many grams of fat does the bag of _____ have? Repeat for each snack.

- Which snack contains the highest amount of fat?

- Which snack contains the least amount of fat?

- Which snack do you think is the healthiest? Why?

*Elizabeth Wray*

Most snack-size chips come in one-ounce packages. If you are using bags that contain more or less than that amount, you will need to calculate the number of grams in a one-ounce serving.

# The Fat Test

Show students how they can tell if a food contains fat, using this test. Give each student a brown paper towel, a potato chip, and an apple slice. Have children tear the paper towel in half and write "Chip" on one half and "Apple" on the other. Show them how to rub each food on the towel until a spot appears. (They may have to break the chip into pieces to make it easier to rub against the towel.) Let the towels dry, then have students hold them up to the light. The spot left by the apple should have disappeared, while the chip mark is still there. Explain that if a food has fat in it, it will leave a permanent mark.

MUSIC, SCIENCE

# What's Inside My Lunch Box?

Are your students bringing healthy lunches to school? Use this song (see right) and activity to find out.

Ask each child to draw and color pictures of healthy foods. Work together to sort the pictures into different food groups. Place one food from each group into a lunch box. Sing the song again and substitute the foods placed in the box for "crackers, peanut butter, carrots, and yogurt." Take the pictures out of the box as they are named in the song. Repeat several times using different foods. Ask children to look inside their own lunch boxes. *Can they find a food from each group?* Examine the school menu. *Is the cafeteria serving a balanced lunch?*

### Look Inside My Lunch Box

*(sing to the tune of "The More We Get Together")*

Look inside my lunch box,
my lunch box, my lunch box.
Look inside my lunch box,
What do you see?
Crackers and peanut butter, raisins and yogurt.
Look inside my lunch box,
to see what I eat!

MATH, SCIENCE

# Feed Me!

As children play this counting game, they'll learn about the daily food requirements needed by their bodies. Before playing the game, familiarize children with the number of servings needed from each food group:

Bread: 6—11
Fruits: 2—4
Vegetables: 3—5
Milk: 2—3
Meat: 2—3

Give students game boards. (See page 204.) Show them how to cut apart the game pieces at the bottom of the page. Have them color in the child. Write the minimum number of servings for each food group (what is recommended for younger children) on the chalkboard. Divide the class into pairs and give each pair a die. Let students take turns rolling their die and placing that many servings of food in the child's mouth on the math mat. The servings can be from any combination of food groups. For example, if a child rolls a six, he or she may take two servings of milk and four servings of bread. The object of the game is to be the first player to feed the child the correct number of servings for each food group.

Book Break

## Fast Food

by Saxton Freymann and Joost Elffers (Scholastic, 2006)

This whimsical picture book transforms fruits and vegetables into a
skateboard, wheelchair, bicycle, bus, and other things that go. Rhyming
text makes this a great read-aloud. Other titles in this playful series include
*How Are You Peeling?*, *Baby Food*, and *Food for Thought*.

*Teacher Share*

SCIENCE, MATH

## Counting on Exercise

Set a healthy example by exercising with your
students on a daily basis. Not only will they get
their bodies in shape, but their counting skills, too! Set
aside time each day for a mini-workout. Ask one child
to choose an exercise (toe touches, knee bends, jumping
jacks, etc.) and another to pick the counting pattern (by
ones, twos, fives, or tens). Then, get moving! For example,
if toe touches by fives are chosen, your class will count
aloud each toe touch by fives until they reach 50.

*Sue Frank*

Book Break

## The Kids' Multicultural Cookbook:

by Deanna Cook (Williamson, 2008)

This lively book links recipes from around the world with an introduction
to a child who lives in each place. Cultural sidebars, activities, riddles, fun
facts, and cooking tips add to the appeal.

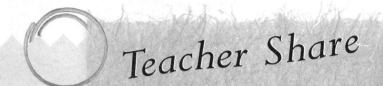

## Teacher Share

SCIENCE

# The Building Blocks of Healthy Eating

Introduce the various food groups to children by building your own pyramid. Gather different-sized blocks and let children watch as you stack them to resemble a food pyramid. (See illustration, left.) Label the blocks accordingly. (You can use sticky-notes.)

Explain to students that the foods in the pyramid work together to create a balanced diet. Show what happens when a few of the blocks are taken away. (*The pyramid crumbles.*) Like the pyramid, their bodies need a variety of foods to remain strong and healthy.

*Pat McMonagle*

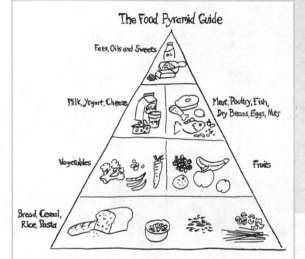

The Food Pyramid Guide

Fats, Oils and Sweets

Milk, Yogurt, Cheese

Meat, Poultry, Fish, Dry Beans, Eggs, Nuts

Vegetables

Fruits

Bread, Cereal, Rice, Pasta

SOCIAL STUDIES, MATH

# Snacks of Yesteryear

**TIP**

Be sure to check with parents concerning food allergies before serving food.

Native American Indians and early settlers were always on the move. They often took long trips through the woods to hunt for food. As they traveled, they ate snacks such as *Pemmican*—a trail mix made from dried beef, suet (animal fat), raisins, berries, and sugar. Follow this recipe to create a modern version of this long-ago snack.

### Trail Mix

Combine equal amounts of two or more of the following ingredients:

raisins
peanuts
sunflower seeds
pretzels
chocolate chips
fish-shaped crackers

Name _____

Date _____

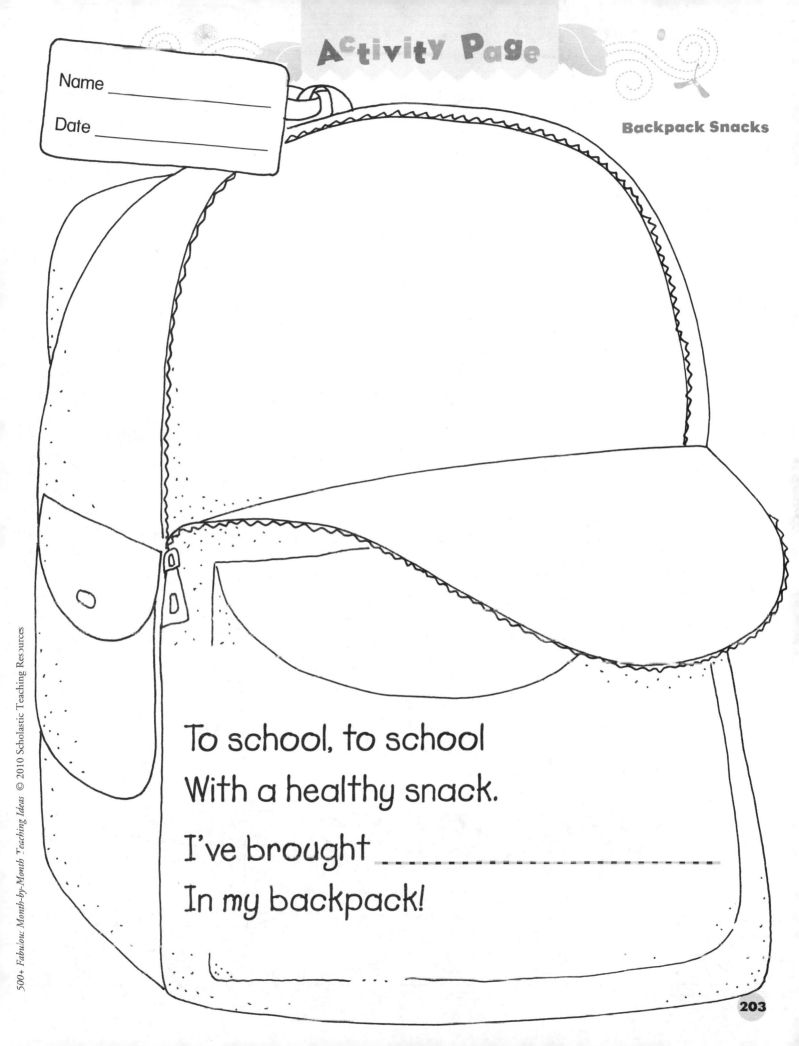

To school, to school
With a healthy snack.
I've brought _____
In my backpack!

Name _____ Date _____

## Feed Me!

LANGUAGE ARTS, SCIENCE

# Collaborative Seed Catalog

*What does a bean seed look like? How about a sunflower seed?* Children learn to identify a variety of seeds as they contribute one page to a seed catalog.

Explain to students that people read seed catalogs to help them decide what to plant. Give each student a different seed, an index card with the name of the seed written on it, and a copy of "Seeds for Sale." (See page 210.) Show children how to glue the seed on the paper in the left box and draw a picture of what it will grow into on the right. Let them complete the frame using their index card as a spelling resource. Bind the pages together and attach a construction-paper cover that reads *Room ____'s Seed Catalog.* Place a small piece of clear packing tape over each seed for durability. Children will enjoy reading the book during their free time and identifying each seed.

## Book Break

### **Seeds** (Plant Parts Series)

by Vijaya Khisty Bodach (Capstone, 2007)

With simple text and close-ups of seeds in recognizable states (such as peas in a pod and seeds inside a sunflower), this nonfiction selection is a perfect choice for teaching reading skills for informational text. A table of contents, glossary, and index are among the nonfiction features included.

MATH, SCIENCE

# Plant Rulers

Let children make rulers to measure plants as they grow. Each child will need a tongue depressor, ruler, and fine-point marker.

◎ Show children how to draw a line across the tongue depressor at the one-inch mark. The area below this line will be inserted into the soil.

◎ Demonstrate how to match up the edge of the ruler with the one-inch line on the tongue depressor. Have children draw four additional lines in one-inch increments and label them from one to four. (You may also have them mark half inches.)

◎ Let children plant seeds in small containers and stick their rulers in the soil. Provide plant journals for children to draw pictures of their plants at different stages and to record the heights.

**TIP**

For plants that will grow taller than four inches, use paint sticks instead of tongue depressors.

**TIP**

Stock a center with extra copies of page 211 so that students can add to the seed house book or banner on their own.

LANGUAGE ARTS, SCIENCE

# Lift-the-Flap Seed Houses

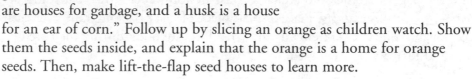

Children will look at plants differently after they explore the way fruits, flowers, vegetables, and cones are houses for seeds.

If possible, begin by reading the book *A House Is a House for Me* by Maryann Hoberman (Scholastic, 1986). This book gets children thinking about objects as houses for other objects. For example, "a glove is a house for a hand, trash cans are houses for garbage, and a husk is a house for an ear of corn." Follow up by slicing an orange as children watch. Show them the seeds inside, and explain that the orange is a home for orange seeds. Then, make lift-the-flap seed houses to learn more.

◎ Give each child a copy of page 211. Invite children to color the house and cut the window on three sides as indicated to make a flap. Have children glue the paper to a sheet of light-colored construction paper, being careful not to put glue beneath the flap.

◎ Have children draw a picture of a seed on the outside of the window flap. (They may glue a real seed here, if available.)

◎ Under the window flap, have children draw a picture of what the seed will grow into.

◎ Have children complete the sentence frame at the bottom of the page. Put the pages together to make a book or a banner.

**Book Break**

## The Plant That Kept on Growing
by Barbara Brenner (Bantam Doubleday, 1996)

Twins plant a seed in hopes of winning a prize at the 4-H fair. They're surprised when their plant keeps growing, growing, growing!

## Teacher Share

MATH, SCIENCE

## Big Seeds, Big Plants?

**D**o big seeds grow big plants? Do little seeds grow little plants? Try this experiment to find out. Gather five seeds and measure their length. Create a chart that lists (in order from big to little) the name of each seed and its measurement. Plant each seed separately. Keep all conditions (pot, soil, water, sunlight) the same. As the plants grow, measure their height. (See Plant Rulers, page 205.) Do the big seeds grow the biggest plants?

*Judy Wetzel*

### Book Break

## The Big Seed

by Ellen Howard (Alladin, 2007)

Bess is the smallest girl in her class. When the teacher lets her choose which seed to plant, she picks a BIG one. Expecting a marigold, she's surprised to find the big seed grows into a sunflower.

LANGUAGE ARTS, SCIENCE

## "Seeds on the Move" Mini-Play

As children participate in the rhyming play on page 214, they'll learn how seeds travel. This play is best done in a Readers Theater format. Place children in groups of four. Assign each member of the group a different part and let them practice their lines independently, then take turns reading aloud. Create simple costumes by cutting strips of construction paper to form headbands. Let children color and cut out either a flower or a seed and glue it to the front of the band.

**TIP**

Add more "seed" parts to the play by creating new lines using the repetitive frame for seeds 1, 2, and 3. This will give children an opportunity to think of other ways that seeds travel.

SCIENCE

# Mystery Garden

Everyone loves a mystery, so why not plant a mystery garden? Plant ten different kinds of seeds in separate containers. Place them all in a sunny window and water regularly. Display the seed packets in random order nearby. As the plants grow, challenge children to match the plants with the pictures on the seed packets. *Can they identify all ten?*

## Book Break

# The Surprise Garden
### by Zoe Hall (Scholastic, 1999)

The children in this story plant and care for some mysterious seeds, and are surprised to find a "picnic of plants" by summer's end.

MATH

# For the Birds Math Story Mat

Give children practice with addition, subtraction, fair shares, and number combinations by letting them "feed the birds" on a math story mat. Prepare for the activity by giving each child a copy of the math mat on page 212. Let children color the flower and the birds (one red and one blue). Give them 12 sunflower seeds to place in the center of the flower. Let them "feed the birds" using the following story problems:

◎ The red bird ate five sunflower seeds. The blue bird ate two. Which bird ate more? How many more did he eat? (Repeat as needed, substituting different numbers.)

◎ The red bird ate three sunflower seeds. The blue bird ate six. How many seeds did they eat all together? (Repeat as needed, substituting different numbers.)

◎ Place eight seeds in the center of the sunflower. If the red bird and the blue bird ate the same number of seeds, how many did each bird eat? (Repeat as needed, substituting different numbers.)

◎ Place seven seeds in the center of the sunflower. The birds ate all of the sunflower seeds. How many did the red bird eat? How many did the blue bird eat? Ask children to share their answers. Record the different number combinations on the chalkboard. (Repeat, substituting different numbers.)

SOCIAL STUDIES, SCIENCE

# Meet the Other George Washington!

Incorporate some history into your study of plants by introducing students to George Washington Carver. Each day share one fact about George, using the reproducible activity page as a guide. (See page 213.) Let children respond by recording information about themselves. Plan a mini-research project to learn more about this inspirational African-American scientist. Students will discover that his history-making career went well beyond discovering hundreds of uses for the peanut plant.

## Book Break

# A Weed Is a Flower: The Life of George Washington Carver

## by Aliki (Aladdin, 1988)

*Did you know that George Washington Carver was a sick, weak baby? Or that he never cashed many of the checks he received for his work? Like other nonfiction books by Aliki, this biography of Carver combines detailed illustrations and simple text to bring its subject to life.*

MUSIC, MOVEMENT

# Seed Dance

Students will enjoy using movements to act out the following poem:

### Little Cradles

In their little cradles,     [*Squat down and wrap arms
Packed in tight,     around legs*]

Baby seeds are sleeping,
Out of sight.

Mr. Wind comes blowing,     [*One child weaves in and out of
With all his might,     the others making wind noises*]

The baby seeds are scattered,     [*Pop up and scatter around the
Left and right.     classroom*]

—*Anonymous*

Name _____ Date _____

A _____ seed

grows a _____ plant.

Name _____  Date _____

Lift-the-Flap
Seed Houses

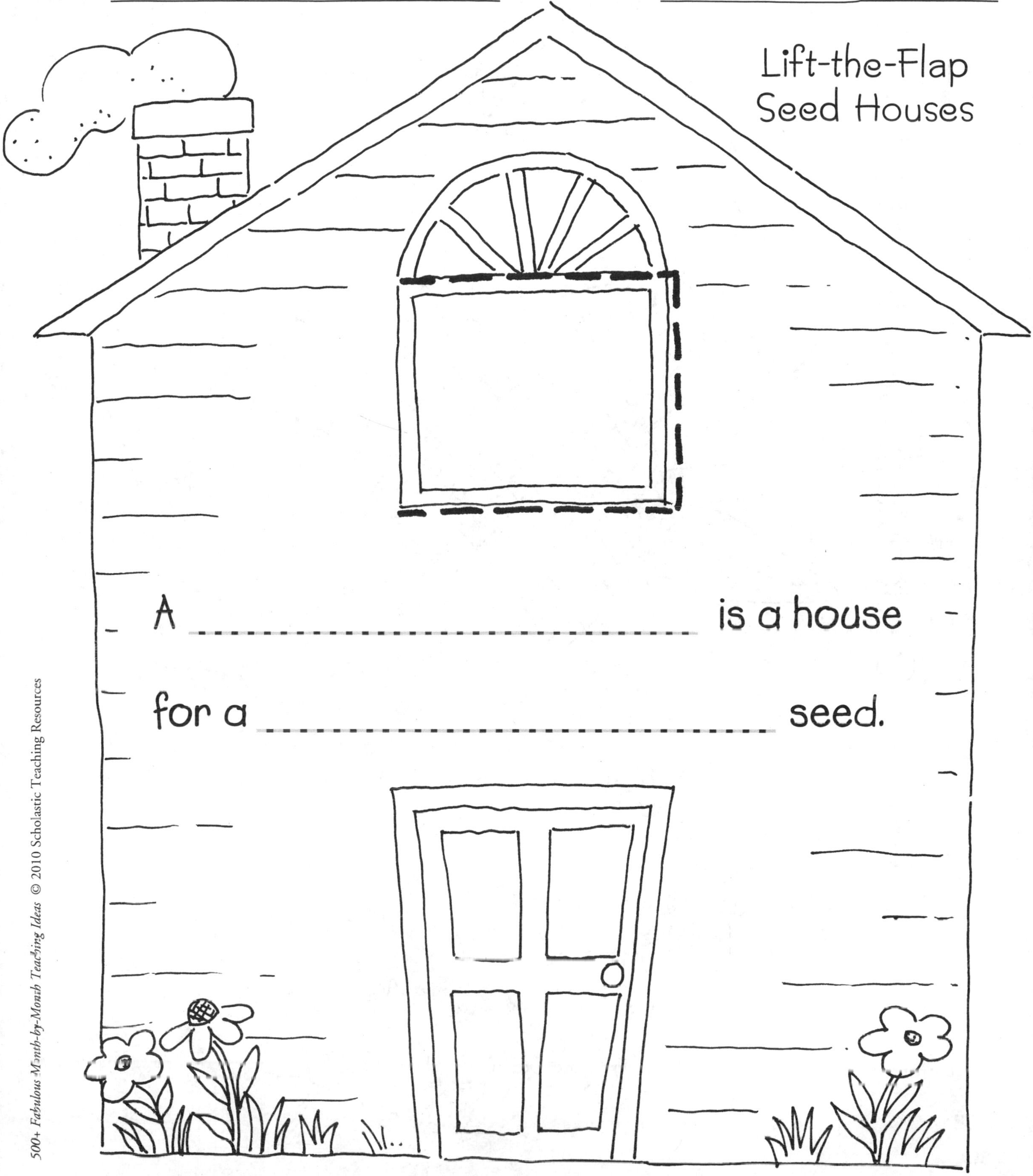

A _____ is a house

for a _____ seed.

Name _____

Date _____

# For the Birds Math Story Mat

*500+ Fabulous Month-by-Month Teaching Ideas* © 2010 Scholastic Teaching Resources

Name _____ Date _____

# Meet George Washington Carver–and Me!

Paste your picture here.

## All About George

## All About Me

George Washington Carver was born in 1860 in Missouri.

I was born in _____
Year
in _____ .
State

When George was young, he kept a garden. He made sure all the plants were healthy. His neighbors called him the Plant Doctor.

My nickname is _____

_____ .

George could play the piano, sing, and paint. But his love of plants led him to study agriculture.

I like to learn about

_____ .

When George finished college, he began to teach. He taught others how to make crops grow better.

I can teach someone how to

_____ .

George discovered many uses for the peanut plant.

I discovered _____

_____ .

# Seeds on the Move

## A Rhyming Mini-Play

by Jaqueline Clarke

**Characters:** Flower  Seed 1  Seed 2  Seed 3    **Setting:** a Garden

**Flower:** My little seeds,
It's time to go,
To find your place
In the Earth below.

**Seeds:** But how will we move
From here to there?

**Flower:** Seek a friend in nature
In this world we share.

**Seed 1:** I'll ask the wind
For a ride.
We'll travel the sky
Far and wide.

**Seed 2:** I'll ask the water
For a ride.
We'll travel the ocean
Far and wide.

**Seed 3:** I'll ask the child
For a ride.
We'll travel the Earth
Far and wide.

**Flower:** Wherever you land
When your trip is through,

**Seeds:** Is where we'll grow
To be just like you!

*500+ Fabulous Month-by-Month Teaching Ideas* © 2010 Scholastic Teaching Resources

# April

# April
## Teaching Ideas

April is a busy month! Spring cleaning, science fairs, sports practices, parent-teacher conferences…the list goes on and on. Yet, there are some wonderful events and seasonal changes that beg to be celebrated.

April brings you creative activities for teaching with four favorite spring themes and topics. NATIONAL POETRY MONTH invites us to discover a new favorite poem or even the poet within! EARTH DAY encourages us to show appreciation for the plants and animals (see "Endangered Animals Scrapbook," page 219) that share our world. RAIN AND THE WATER CYCLE may keep us indoors, but they also teach us about rain and the water cycle with activities like "What Makes a Puddle?" (page 231). Finally, EGGS AND LIFE CYCLES reminds us of how we continue to grow and change.

Activities and ideas for this month cover all areas of the curriculum, many naturally integrating more than one subject. Here are some of April's other highlights:

- a reproducible send-home activity calendar
- a rhyming mini-play
- literature connections
- pocket chart poetry
- a reproducible mini-book
- hands-on math and science activities
- a classroom "museum" project
- a collaborative banner
- computer connections
- poems and "piggyback" songs
- movement activities
- and more!

Name _____

# April Activity Calendar

Choose _____ activities to do each week this month.
Ask an adult in your family to initial the square in the box of each activity
you complete. Bring this paper back to school on _____ .

| Monday | Tuesday | Wednesday | Thursday | Friday |
|---|---|---|---|---|
| Write the word *April* on a sheet of paper. Cut apart the letters. Make new words! | Ask someone to tell you a joke. Tell someone you know a joke. | Look at this ladybug. Find a matching ladybug on this page. | April is the fourth month of the year. Name the third month. Name the fifth month. | What do you think "It's raining cats and dogs" means? What are other ways to describe rain? |
| Use your hands to make the sound of rain. Slide your palms back and forth, tap and snap your fingers, clap your hands. | Pretend you're an earthworm. Show how you move. What words describe how you move? | Go outside with an adult in your family. Look at clouds. Tell each other about a picture the clouds make. | List the foods you ate today. List the fruits. List the vegetables. | Estimate how long it will take you to get ready for bed. Have someone time you. |
| Tell someone at home a story about your day. Include a beginning, a middle, and an end. | Make a picture time line of your day. Show what happened first, next, and so on. | Close your eyes. What sounds do you hear? See if you can name ten. | Ask a family member five questions about him- or herself. Use the answers to write a story or poem about that person. | Circle the dates for each Monday on a calendar this month. What pattern do the numbers make? |
| Look for signs of spring around you. Record your observations in a picture. | Look for weather information in a newspaper. List words that describe weather. | Compare yourself to someone in your family. Tell how you are alike. Tell how you are different. | Look at the words on this calendar. Can you find two that rhyme with *cake*? | Turn *April* into a tongue twister! Make up a sentence using as many words as you can that start with *a*. |

500+ Fabulous Month-by-Month Teaching Ideas © 2010 Scholastic Teaching Resources

Book Break

# Endangered Animals
### by Faith McNulty (Scholastic, 1996)

This book provides a great introduction to this topic. In simple terms it explains how some animals become endangered and some become extinct. An invitation at the end of the book encourages children to think not only of their needs, but of those with whom they share the planet.

SCIENCE, LANGUAGE ARTS

## Endangered Animal Scrapbook

Looking for a class pet to adopt? How about an endangered animal? After reading about several, let children vote on one to study. Create a scrapbook to display the information students gather. Encourage them to find and record the following:

- ◎ the animal's classification (mammal, reptile, etc.)
- ◎ drawings and/or photographs of the animal
- ◎ maps illustrating where the animal can be found
- ◎ reasons why the animal is endangered
- ◎ products made from the animal
- ◎ population statistics
- ◎ conservation efforts
- ◎ related newspaper and/or magazine articles

Let students take turns sharing their scrapbook with other classes to build awareness in your school.

## ComPuter Connection

Endangered Animals
Many organizations will allow you to sponsor an endangered animal for a small donation. In return, they'll send a packet of information about the animal. For a list of links visit

http://geocities. com/Heartland/ Farm/5353/ endg.html

TIP

If possible, locate a stuffed version of your endangered animal and let students vote on a name.

Book Break

## The Sun in Me: Poems About the Planet
### Compiled by Judith Nicholls (Barefoot Books, 2003)

From the rainforests of Africa to the mountains of Japan, the poems in this exceptional collection take readers around the globe, celebrating the beauty of the natural world. Charlotte Zolotow, Rabindranath Tagore, Mary Kawena Pukui, and David McCord are among those whose works are included.

## Stuff! Reduce, Reuse, Recycle
### by Steven Kroll (Marshall Cavendish, 2009)

As a packrat, Pinch stashes all sorts of stuff. When his friends decide to have a tag sale, at first he naturally wants no part of it. He soon changes his mind, and his actions will reinforce for readers reasons to reduce, reuse, and recycle.

## Teacher Share

MATH

## Trash Basket for a Day

It is estimated that each American generates more than four pounds of trash per day. Make children aware of just how much trash they produce daily by inviting them to carry their trash with them.

Ask each child to come to school wearing a pair of pants with belt loops and to bring a plastic grocery bag with handles. Assist children in tying the handles of the bag to one of their belt loops. As children go through the day, ask them to throw any nonfood garbage into their bags. Encourage them to continue doing this in the evening while at home. The next day have children bring their trash bags back to school. Let each child weigh his or her bag of garbage. Create a graph to show how much garbage each child produced. Discuss the data: Who produced the most garbage? Who produced the least? Was the average close to four pounds?

*Bobbie Williams*

**TIP**

Help children learn more about the problem of trash by sorting the contents of the classroom wastebasket into four groups: Recycle, Reduce (items to use less of), Reuse (items to use again or turn into something new), and Reject (could replace with more environmentally sound products). Repeat the activity the next day. Ask: *Was there less trash in the basket than the day before?* Have students share ways they were able to cut down on the amount of garbage that went into the wastebasket.

## Hey! Get Off Our Train
### by John Burningham (Crown Publishers, 1999)

A boy and his dog take an imaginary journey on a train. At each stop they meet an endangered animal looking to be rescued. This is a great book for children to act out. Create a train by lining up boxes or chairs, and let children take turns being one of the endangered animals, the boy, or the dog.

SCIENCE, LANGUAGE ARTS

# Going, Going, Gone

As children play this variation of Duck, Duck, Goose, they will learn the difference between the terms *threatened*, *endangered*, and *extinct*.

◉ Gather children in a circle on the floor. Tell them they are a species or group of animals called the "Foo Foos."

◉ Walk around the circle tapping each Foo Foo on the head while saying, "going, going, gone." Each Foo Foo that is tapped on the word "gone" must leave the circle.

◉ When approximately one half of the species has "disappeared," explain that the Foo Foos are now *threatened*.

◉ Continue playing until about one half of the remaining Foo Foos have left the circle, leaving approximately one quarter of the original group. Tell children that the species is now *endangered*.

◉ Resume action until all Foo Foos have disappeared, making them an *extinct* species.

◉ Follow up with a discussion on how animals become threatened, endangered, and extinct. Ask children to suggest ways they could make a difference.

SCIENCE, SOCIAL STUDIES

# Friends of the Earth

Rachel Carson was a good friend to the Earth! Work with children to find out why this was true. Create a chart listing the many ways she cared for the Earth. (For suggested resources, see Book Break, page 222, and Computer Connection, right.)

Using her life as an example, encourage children to become "Friends of the Earth." Create a large flower and staple all but the petals to a bulletin board. Paste a photo or drawing of each child in the center of the flower and title the display "Friends of the Earth." Each time a student does something to help Earth, such as picking up litter or planting a seed, record it on a petal along with his or her name and add it to the flower. Soon your flower will be blooming with environmentally friendly deeds!

## Computer Connection

The Life and Legacy of Rachel Carson www.rachel carson.org This Web site features a biography of the biologist, nature writer, and ecologist, and provides links to related materials.

## Book Break

# Rachel: The Story of Rachel Carson

(Reprint Edition)
by Amy Ehrlich (Harcourt, 2008)

This picture-book biography introduces young readers to the life and work of the leader of the environmental movement.

**TIP**

Once you close the museum, use the objects for math activities such as counting, weighing, and sorting.

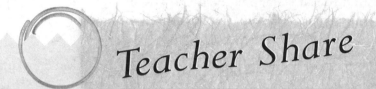

*Teacher Share*

LANGUAGE ARTS, SCIENCE

## A Piece of the Earth

Celebrate Earth Day by helping your students create a "piece of the Earth" museum! Introduce the activity by sharing the poem "Who Am I?" (See page 223.) Explain that as "pieces of the Earth," we share our planet with many other natural objects such as rocks, flowers, leaves, and seashells. Send home a letter requesting that each child bring in a "piece of the Earth."

Display the objects in the classroom on a table or bookshelf. Help children see the impact these objects have on our natural environment by creating a chart that lists each object, tells why it is important, and what would happen if it disappeared. Transfer this information to index cards to serve as museum notes for each object. Invite other classes to visit your museum, and let children take turns being tour guides.

*Sue Frank*

Name _____ Date _____

# Who Am I?

The trees ask me,
And the sky,
And the sea asks me
    *Who am I?*

The grass asks me,
And the sand,
And the rocks ask me
    *Who I am.*

The wind tells me
At nightfall,
And the rain tells me
    *Someone small.*

  *Someone small*
  *Someone small*
  *But a piece*
    *of*
    *it*
    *all.*

—Felice Holman

# April Bubbles Chocolate:
## An ABC of Poetry

Selected by Lee Bennett Hopkins (Simon & Schuster, 1994)

Organized in A–Z fashion, this anthology offers one poem for each letter of the alphabet. It includes work by well-known poets such as Charlotte Zolotow, Eve Merriam, Aileen Fisher, X. J. Kennedy, and Langston Hughes.

**TIP**

Let students add poems they have written to the class A-Z Poetry book!

LANGUAGE ARTS, ART

## A–Z Poetry

Create an alphabet book of poetry by collecting poems for each letter of the alphabet. Write each letter of the alphabet on a sheet of 11- by 18-inch (or larger) card stock. Add a cover and bind the pages together using loose-leaf binder rings (also called *O-rings*). Work with children to collect poems for the book in one of the following ways:

◎ Include poems by authors whose last names start with each letter of the alphabet.

◎ Include poems with one-word titles and arrange in alphabetical order, one poem per letter of the alphabet.

◎ Include favorite poems and arrange in the book according to the first letter of the first word in the title.

Copy each poem on the appropriate page. Let children take turns illustrating the poems. Share the book regularly by letting children take turns choosing a page to read. Make the book available for children to enjoy on their own and at home, too!

LANGUAGE ARTS

## Pocket Poetry

Wouldn't it be nice to always have a "poem in your pocket"? Here's how you can have one handy to read in celebration of seasonal changes and special events in the classroom. Purchase a shoe organizer with several pockets. Label each pocket with a different category such as "Rainy Days," "Birthdays," "Lost Teeth," "Fall," or "New Students." Copy poems onto index cards that correspond to the categories you've selected and place them in the pockets. The next time someone loses a tooth or has a birthday, you'll be ready to celebrate with a "poem in your pocket"!

ART, LANGUAGE ARTS

# Poet Tree

*Who was Robert Frost? How about Langston Hughes?* Introduce children to these poets and others by creating a Poet Tree. Begin by having children create a large tree on a bulletin board. Choose a favorite poet and gather pictures, information, and sample poems. Display the collection on the tree and share the poet's life and work with children. Change the tree regularly and involve students in your search for items to add to the display. Be sure to highlight a wide variety of poets with many different styles. Children will also enjoy using the Poet-Tree to highlight their own work. Share a few young poets each week to give everyone a chance to shine!

**CoMPuter**
Connection

Academy of American Poets
www.poets.org
Browse an index of poets, find poems for special occasions, listen to recordings of poems, and more.

## Teacher Share

LANGUAGE ARTS, ART

## Off the Wall Poetry

Create a poetry-rich environment by posting poems on the walls of your school and classroom. Challenge children to search anthologies for poems that relate to objects or people found in your school. For example, "Band-Aids" by Shel Silverstein (Where the Sidewalk Ends, HarperCollins, 1974) could be hung outside the nurse's office, while "Table Manners" by Gelett Burgess (Random House Book of Poetry, Random House, 1983) would be appropriate in the cafeteria. Copy each poem on posterboard and let children add illustrations. Display the posters in the appropriate places around the school, and soon your walls will be alive with poetry!

*Charlotte Sassman*

Book Break

# Riddle Road: Puzzles in Poems and Pictures

by Elizabeth Spires (Margaret McElderry, 1999)

In this sequel to *With One White Wing* (McElderry, 1995), riddles about clocks, pillows, shoes, and other everyday objects are accompanied by pictures that provide clues to the answers.

SCIENCE, LANGUAGE ARTS

# Insect Riddle Poems

Kids love riddles and insects! By combining the two you'll have an activity they'll also love!

- Tell children that the poem you are about to read is a riddle poem. It is about an insect; however, the poet does not come out and tell you which one. Instead, she wants you to use the clues given in the poem to guess.

- Read the poem aloud. (See page 228.) Ask children to guess the insect. Once "firefly" is guessed, ask them to identify the clues that helped them to discover the subject of the poem.

- Let children create a collaborative riddle poem. Ask each child to write down the name of an insect on a slip of paper. Place the slips in a box and choose one at random. This will be the subject of your poem. Ask children to write down what comes to mind when they think of this insect. Elicit one word or phrase from each child, and record each response on a separate line on a sheet of chart paper. Title the poem "Who Am I?" and let the last line read, "Who am I?" Write the name of the insect next to the poem and cover it with a flap of paper. Write the words *I am a…* on the flap. Post the poem in the hallway for other students to enjoy.

- Encourage children to write their own riddle poems about other insects. Let them take turns sharing their poems with the class. Give students time to guess each insect's identity before letting the poet reveal the answer.

Book Break

# Skip Across the Ocean: Nursery Rhymes From Around the World

collected by Floella Benjamin

(Francis Lincoln Children's Books, 2007)

This multicultural collection of poetry includes verse from China, Nigeria, Peru, Sweden, Australia, and Greenland. In some cases, poems are written in both the original language and English.

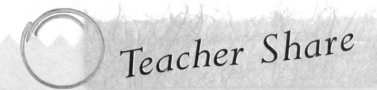

## Teacher Share

SCIENCE, LANGUAGE ARTS

### Sensational Poetry

Spending time outdoors in the springtime can be a feast for children's senses as well as an inspiration to write poetry. Take your students on a quiet walk and encourage them to explore the outdoors using their senses. Invite them to record what they see, touch, smell, and hear in the spaces on a record sheet.(See sample, right.) Return to the classroom and let children write simple poems about spring using the following frame:

| see 👁 | touch 🖐 |
|---|---|
| ants clouds | flower petals bark |
| smell 👃 | hear 👂 |
| cut grass pine trees | birds |

**Welcome Spring!**

I see _____

I hear _____

I smell _____

I touch _____

Spring is here!

*Sue Lorey*

SOCIAL STUDIES, LANGUAGE ARTS

### Fishing for Feelings

In order for children to express their feelings, they need to know the words associated with various emotions. In this bulletin board activity, children will learn this vocabulary and realize that behind every poem are the author's feelings.

Read "Poets Go Wishing" to children. (See page 229.) Explain that writing poetry is one way to express feelings, and that it's a poet's job to "fish" for the right words to match what they're feeling inside.

On the left side of a bulletin board, post a drawing of a child fishing. Brainstorm "feeling words" with children and write each one on a fish pattern. (See page 229.) Staple the fish to the bulletin board and title it "Poets Go Fishing."

As you interact with children, ask them to share how they're feeling, and encourage them to use the board as a resource to find the appropriate words.

**TIP**

For students who are familiar with basic "feeling words," extend the activity by choosing one word, and labeling a new set of fish with words or phrases that name other ways of telling about that feeling. For example, in the case of the word *excited*, students might volunteer *bursting with joy, bubbling,* or *jumping up and down.*

Name _____ Date _____

Have you ever watched a lighthouse
flashing in the dark?

Have you ever seen a flashlight
turning on and off?

Now think of something smaller
that blinks from dusk to dawn.

There I am! Catch me.
Catch me if you can.

firefly

—Elizabeth Spires

500+ Fabulous Month-by-Month Teaching Ideas © 2010 Scholastic Teaching Resources

Name _____   Date _____

# Poets Go Wishing

Poets go fishing
with buckets
of words,
fishing
and wishing.

Using a line
that's loose or
tight
(Maybe this time
a rhyme is
right.)

Unreeling
unreeling
the words till they
match
the feeling the poet is
trying to
catch.

—Lilian Moore

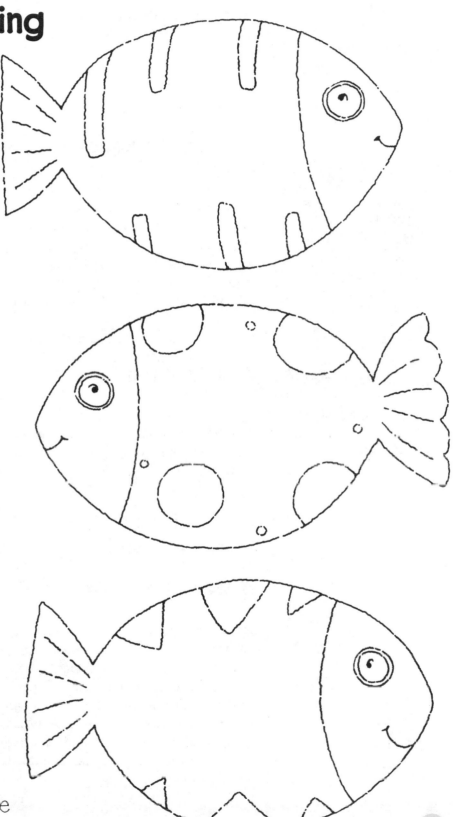

# Little Cloud
### by Eric Carle (Putnam, 2001)

As Little Cloud moves through the sky, he changes into a sheep, an airplane, and two trees. Then he joins the other clouds and makes rain.

SCIENCE, ART

## Cloud Parade Collaborative Banner

Take children outside on a day when there are lots of clouds in the sky. Invite them to lie on the grass and watch the "cloud parade." What pictures do they see in the sky? Back in the classroom, give children a sheet of white paper. Ask them to tear the paper into the shape of one of the pictures they saw during the "cloud parade," then paste it to light-blue construction paper. Have children copy each line of the following rhyme on their cloud pictures and complete the last sentence.

> Hooray for the cloud parade!
> Marching pictures through the sky.
> What will we see today?
> There goes a _____ floating by!

Create a cloud parade banner by gluing pictures side by side on a long sheet of banner paper. Display the banner up high so students can look up and watch the clouds go by!

**TIP**

Use the rhyme for a pocket chart activity. Copy the rhyme on sentence strips and place in the pocket chart. Give each child a piece of a sentence strip. Have children write the word for their cloud picture on the sentence strip. Read the rhyme aloud, again and again, letting children take turns completing the last sentence.

SCIENCE, LANGUAGE ARTS

## Where Do Animals Go When It Rains?

As children participate in this rhyming play, they'll learn how animals seek shelter on rainy days. Organize the play in small groups as a Readers Theater or as a whole-class performance.

For Readers Theater, place children in groups of five. Assign each member of the group a different part and let children take turns reading aloud. To use the play as a whole-class activity, adapt the dialogue to reflect groups of squirrels, birds, spiders, and bees (rather than one of each). Choose one student to play the child, and divide the rest of the class into the four animal parts.

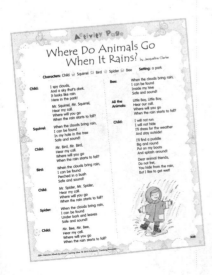

# Teacher Share

MATH, SCIENCE

## April Showers Calendar Activity

Is April really a rainy month? Present this research question on the last day of March (or as early in April as possible) and let students collect, record, and interpret weather data to find the answer. Make copies of the umbrella calendar squares (see right) and let students color and cut them out. As part of your calendar routine, ask children if there was any rain on the previous day. If the answer is yes, choose a student to tape an umbrella cutout to the calendar for that day. At the end of the month, restate the research question. Let students look at the data collected on the calendar to determine whether there were more days with or without rain in April.

***Judy Meagher***

Umbrella Calendar
Cutout

SCIENCE

## What Makes a Puddle?

Children love puddles! In this activity, they'll explore water and discover how puddles form.

◎ Give each child a sheet of waxed paper, a toothpick, an eyedropper, and a cup of water tinted with blue food coloring.

◎ Show children how to use their eyedropper to put five separate drops of water onto the waxed paper. Ask them to observe and describe the shape of the drops.

◎ Demonstrate how to pull one drop over to another. Ask children to describe what happened when the drops touched. Explain that this is how a puddle forms. Invite children to pull the rest of their drops over to the larger one. Ask: *How many drops make up your puddle?* Challenge children to pull the five drops out of the puddle. *Was it easy or difficult to pull each drop away? Did you pull out more or less than five drops?* Provide extra time for children to continue exploring the water. Ask them to share any observations they have made.

MOVEMENT, SCIENCE

# Raindrop Relay

As children participate in this relay race, they'll follow a raindrop through the water cycle.

◉ Divide the class into two teams. Each team will need a set of three cones set up as shown, approximately eight feet apart. Use construction paper to label the cones "Puddle," "Cloud," and "Rain."

◉ Line up each team up behind the PUDDLE cone. Give the first player on each team a blue balloon on a string to represent a raindrop. On the word *Go*, the first player carries the raindrop from PUDDLE to CLOUD to RAIN and then back to PUDDLE. The next player in line then takes the raindrop and repeats the actions of the first player. The first team to get all its players through the water cycle wins the game!

SCIENCE

# Absorb or Repel?

Have you ever noticed how rain rolls off an umbrella or raincoat? This is because nylon and rubber both repel water. In this activity, children test different kinds of materials to discover whether they absorb or repel.

◉ Place a sponge in a shallow tub. Ask children to predict whether it will absorb or repel water. Show them where to record their predictions on the record sheet. (See page 236.)

◉ Pour water over the sponge. Ask: *Did the water roll off or did the sponge soak it up?* Have children record the results on their record sheet. Repeat the activity using other objects, such as a paper towel, plastic wrap, soil, and a nylon or polyester sock.

◉ Once you've tested all the objects, ask children to examine the objects that absorbed water. Challenge them to place them in order from most to least absorbent. Continue to observe the objects periodically while they are drying. *Which object was the first to dry completely? the last?*

## Book Break

# Wiggling Worms at Work
(Let's-Read-and-Find-Out Science 2)
by Wendy Pfeffer (HarperCollins, 2003)

Readers are invited to explore earthworms—their habits, anatomy, diet, movement, and life cycle—and learn about their importance to soil health.

SCIENCE, ART

# Earthworm Mural

*Why do worms come out when it rains?* Post this question on a bulletin board or wall space in the hallway outside the classroom. Challenge children to use books and the Internet to find the answer. Have them create a mural to illustrate the answer. (*When worms' homes underground are flooded, they come out for air, which has been displaced by the water.*)

◉ Draw a line across the middle of a large sheet of craft paper to indicate ground level. Divide the class into two groups. Assign one group to illustrate the "aboveground" portion while the other does the "underground" scene.

◉ Have children record the answer to the question on chart paper or sentence strips and post this along with the mural in the hallway display. Children will take pride in sharing their knowledge with others, while fellow students and staff will enjoy learning something new!

**TIP**

Assist each group in brainstorming what the scene needs to include—for example, worms above ground and flooded passageways below ground.

# Teacher Share

SOCIAL STUDIES, ART

## Make a Rain Stick

**N**atives of the Amazon jungle believed they could coax water from the sky with rain sticks. Show children this location on a map and discuss the climate. Ask: Why might these people need rain? Let students make their own rain sticks. Give each child a cardboard tube from a roll of paper towels or gift wrap. Show children how to poke straight pins into the tube at equal distances, approximately every inch. Assist them in winding masking tape around the tube to secure the pins. Cut two 6-inch circles from the bottom of a grocery bag. Demonstrate how to place one circle over one end of the tube and secure it with a thick rubber band. Give each child a handful of rice. Have children pour the rice into their tubes and secure the open end with the remaining circle and a rubber band. Invite children to decorate their rain sticks with colorful patterns and designs. Let children experiment with using their rain sticks to create the sound of rain.

*Bob Krech*

# Let's Make Rain!

Lead children in the following movements to simulate a rainstorm. Make each sound for five to ten seconds:

- Slide palms back and forth.
- Tap fingers together.
- Snap fingers.
- Clap hands.
- Slap thighs.
- Stomp feet.

- Slap thighs.
- Clap hands.
- Snap fingers.
- Tap fingers together.
- Slide palms back and forth.
- Rest hands quietly in lap.

# Teacher Share

## Move Like Water

Watch children move through the water cycle with this interactive poem.

### Surprise!

| | |
|---|---|
| I'm a puddle. Splash me! | (stamp feet up and down) |
| I'm water vapor. Watch me rise! | (squat with arms around knees and slowly stand up) |
| I'm in a cloud, Condensing. | (pull arms into chest) (students huddle together) |
| I'm raining down. | (stand with arms overhead— wiggle fingers and lower body down) |
| SURPRISE! | (jump up) |

*Natalie Vaughn*

# Where Do Animals Go When It Rains?

by Jacqueline Clarke

**Characters:** Child 🌧 Squirrel 🌧 Bird 🌧 Spider 🌧 Bee      **Setting:** a park

**Child:**
I spy clouds,
And a sky that's dark.
It looks like rain
Here in the park!

Mr. Squirrel, Mr. Squirrel,
Hear my call.
Where will you go
When the rain starts to fall?

**Squirrel:**
When the clouds bring rain,
I can be found
In my hole in the tree
Safe and sound!

**Child:**
Mr. Bird, Mr. Bird,
Hear my call.
Where will you go
When the rain starts to fall?

**Bird:**
When the clouds bring rain,
I can be found
Perched in a bush
Safe and sound!

**Child:**
Mr. Spider, Mr. Spider,
Hear my call.
Where will you go
When the rain starts to fall?

**Spider:**
When the clouds bring rain,
I can be found
Under bark and leaves
Safe and sound!

**Child:**
Mr. Bee, Mr. Bee,
Hear my call.
Where will you go
When the rain starts to fall?

**Bee:**
When the clouds bring rain,
I can be found
Inside my hive
Safe and sound!

**All the Animals:**
Little Boy, Little Boy,
Hear our call.
Where will you go
When the rain starts to fall?

**Child:**
I will not run
I will not hide
I'll dress for the weather
And stay outside!

I'll find a puddle
Big and round
Put on my boots
And splash around!

Dear animal friends,
Do not fret,
You hide from the rain,
But I like to get wet!

Name _____  Date _____

# Absorb or Repel?

| Object | My Prediction | | Results | |
|--------|--------|-------|--------|-------|
|        | Absorb | Repel | Absorb | Repel |
| ① |  |  |  |  |
| ② |  |  |  |  |
| ③ |  |  |  |  |
| ④ |  |  |  |  |
| ⑤ |  |  |  |  |
| ⑥ |  |  |  |  |

*500+ Fabulous Month-by-Month Teaching Ideas* © 2010 Scholastic Teaching Resources

# Teacher Share

## Who's Hiding? Mini-Book

Use this repetitive mini-book to give your students practice reading and to introduce them to a variety of animals that hatch from eggs.

❧ Make one book for each child by folding two sheets of 8- by 11-inch paper into four sections and cutting on the folds. Give each child a copy of the riddles on page 242. Ask children to cut out the egg-shaped riddles. Show them how to glue down just the tip of each egg to create one flap per page (excluding the front and back covers). Have children add a front and back cover, and staple the pages together.

❧ Read each riddle aloud with children. See if they can guess the animal's name. Ask them to tell you which clues helped them to figure out the answer. Invite them to use crayons or markers to draw a picture of that animal under the flap. Repeat these steps with the remaining riddles.

❧ Give children time to practice reading their mini-books with partners. Let them take the books home to share with their families, too.

*Natalie Vaughn*

**Answers**, clockwise from the top left of the activity page are: *caterpillar, penguin, sea turtle, ostrich, frog, chick.*

## Out Popped a....

You'll get a surprise every time with this interactive rhyme! Prepare for the activity by sending each child home with a plastic egg. Ask children to place something inside (either an object or a picture) that wouldn't ordinarily hatch from an egg. Tell them the sillier the better!

Copy the rhyme at right onto chart paper or sentence strips. When children return to school with their eggs, teach them the rhyme. Let them take turns reading the rhyme aloud and filling in the blanks. When they get to the first blank, they should name an adjective that describes their egg. When they complete the second blank, they should open their egg to reveal what's hidden inside.

I went for a walk
and what did I find?
A _____ egg,
someone left behind.

It started to crack
before my eyes.
Out popped a _____ .
What a surprise!

MATH, SCIENCE, TECHNOLOGY

# Internet Egg Hunt

*How many eggs does a swan lay? How about a frog?* Give children (or partners) a copy of the Internet Egg Hunt. (See page 243.) Challenge children to search the Web to find out how many eggs each animal lays. (You might begin at the Smithsonian National Zoological Park Web site: nationalzoo. si.edu/.) When a child finds an answer, invite him or her to share it with the rest of the class so everyone can record it on their sheets. Talk about which animal lays the most eggs and which lays the least. Happy hunting!

SCIENCE, MATH

# How Big Is This Egg?

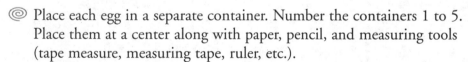

*Which animal lays the biggest egg? the smallest?* In this activity, children measure and compare five different animal eggs.

◎ Make five eggs out of clay, using the following dimensions as a guide. (These are in mm—25 mm per inch.)

**Ostrich:** 175 X 145     **Platypus:** 18 X 15
**Chicken:** 50 X 30      **Hummingbird:** 12 X 8
**Pigeon:** 40 X 24

◎ Place each egg in a separate container. Number the containers 1 to 5. Place them at a center along with paper, pencil, and measuring tools (tape measure, measuring tape, ruler, etc.).

◎ Invite children to visit the center and measure the length and circumference of each egg. Have them record the measurements.

◎ On the chalkboard, list the animals that go with the eggs. Challenge children to match each egg with an animal. After sharing the answers with children, ask them if they think the size of an animal has anything to do with the size of the egg it lays. Have them explain their answers.

**TIP**

Challenge children to find egg sizes for other animals. Dinosaur eggs, for example, ranged in size from a grain of rice to bigger than a bowling ball!

**Book Break**

# An Egg Is Quiet

by Dianna Hutts Aston (Chronicle, 2006)

From hummingbird eggs to fossilized dinosaur eggs, the eggs pictured in this book come in many shapes, sizes, and colors. Elegant and detailed illustrations and informative text will keep children coming back to this book.

# Teacher Share

### SCIENCE

## How Are These Animals Alike?

**C**olor and cut out pictures of animals that lay eggs, such as those pictured here. Fold them in half and place each inside a plastic egg. One by one, have students "crack" the eggs. After they open all the eggs, ask children to tell you what the animals have in common. Explain that these animals are all oviparous, which means they produce eggs that hatch outside the body. Challenge students to name other animals that hatch eggs. Let them draw and label new pictures to put inside the eggs.

*Mary Rosenberg*

### MATH

## Egg Count
## Math Story Mat

As children manipulate jelly bean eggs between two bird's nests, they'll gain practice in counting, addition, and equal shares. Prepare by giving each child a copy of the math story mat (see page 244) and 20 jelly beans. Guide them in using the jelly beans as manipulatives to find the answer to the following story problems:

◎ Place three eggs in the robin's nest and five eggs in the blue jay's nest. Which nest has more eggs? How many more eggs are in the blue jay's nest? (Repeat as needed, substituting different numbers.)

◎ Place five eggs in the robin's nest and four eggs in the blue jay's nest. How many eggs are in the nests all together? Can you find a different way to show nine eggs? (Repeat as needed, substituting different numbers.)

◎ Using eight eggs, give each bird an equal share. (Repeat as needed, substituting different numbers.)

SCIENCE

# Breathing Room

In this experiment, children discover that an eggshell has tiny holes in it so air can reach the animal growing inside. Place an egg in a jar half-filled with warm water. Ask: *Does the egg sink or float?* Have students observe the bubbles coming from the egg. What do they tell us? (*The eggshell is porous—it has holes in it—so air can go in or out of the egg.*) Discuss why it is important for an eggshell to have holes in it. (*to provide air to the baby growing inside*)

## Book Break

# Guess What's Growing Inside This Egg

## by Mia Posada (Millbrook, 2006)

A question and answer format engages readers in learning about the animals featured (penguins, alligators, ducklings, sea turtles, spiders, and octopuses). For each egg, a clue-filled rhyming verse invites readers to identify what is growing inside. A section at the back of the book shows a cross-section of a duck developing inside the egg.

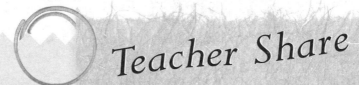

*Teacher Share*

SCIENCE

# Watch Me Grow!

Children create life cycle wheels to reflect on the past, present, and future.

◎ Give each child two paper plates and a brass fastener. Assist children in using a pencil and ruler to divide one plate into four equal sections. Have children label the sections with the four stages of life: baby, child, adult, and senior citizen, then draw pictures or paste photos of themselves at each stage.

◎ Demonstrate how to cut out one section from the second paper plate. Help children push the brass fastener through the center of the two paper plates (with the life cycle wheel on the bottom). Children can turn the bottom plate to share their life cycle with classmates, friends, and family.

**Sandy Hoff, Heather Kurtenbach,
Stephanie Bushjahn**

MUSIC, MOVEMENT

# From Caterpillar to Butterfly

As children act out the life cycle of a butterfly, they'll learn what happens at each stage of metamorphosis. You'll need a sleeping bag and a brightly colored beach towel.

Demonstrate how to move through the life cycle, using the movements and props described. (See right.)

Let each child take a turn. Extend the activity by letting children come up with ways to act out the life cycle of a frog and chicken.

| Stage | Movement |
|-------|----------|
| Egg | scrunch body into a ball |
| Larva | crawl across the floor |
| Pupa | crawl into the sleeping bag |
| Adult | pop out of the sleeping bag wearing butterfly wings (beach towel) |

SNACK

# Edible Nests

Tell children they should never touch a nest if it is still home to a family of birds. Then, follow this recipe to create bird's nests children can not only touch, but also eat! (Note: The following recipe makes about 20 nests.)

◎ Melt 1 stick margarine in a large saucepan over low heat. Add a 10-ounce bag of large marshmallows and stir until melted. Turn off the heat and stir in 12 crumbled shredded wheat biscuits.

◎ After the mixture has cooled slightly, place 1 tablespoon of the warm mixture on a sheet of waxed paper for each child. Let children shape the mixture into a bird's nest.

◎ When the nests are completely cool, add a few jelly bean "eggs."

Check for food allergies before serving the edible nests.

MOVEMENT, SCIENCE

# Chicken Dance

As children create movements to go with the following song, they'll explore the "dance" that chickens do as they hatch from eggs.

Once students memorize the song, ask them to come up with movements for each line. Sing the song several times using the children's movements.

**I'm a Little Chicken**
(sung to "I'm a Little Teapot")

I'm a little chicken,
Ready to hatch,
Pecking at my shell,
Scratch, scratch, scratch.
When I crack it open, out I'll leap,
Fluff up my feathers and cheep, cheep, cheep!

—by Susan Peters

# Activity Page

## Who's Hiding? Mini-Book

This baby's so tiny,
It would fit in a spoon.
Before it grows up,
It'll spin a cocoon.

This baby keeps warm
On its daddy's feet.
It will be black and white
And have fish to eat.

This baby is yellow,
And covered with fluff.
It pecks at the ground
'Til it's eaten enough.

This baby has flippers
And swims very well.
It doesn't have teeth
And carries a shell.

This swimmy baby
Will get a surprise.
It'll grow four long legs
And eat lots of flies.

This baby's eggs
Are the biggest around.
It has two small wings,
But can't leave the ground.

Name _____  Date _____

# Internet Egg Hunt

| Animal | Number of Eggs |
|---|---|
| ① Swan | |
| ② Woodpecker | |
| ③ Lizard | |
| ④ Frog | |
| ⑤ Turtle | |

◎ Which animal lays the most eggs? _____

◎ Which animal lays the fewest eggs? _____

500+ Fabulous Month-by-Month Teaching Ideas © 2010 Scholastic Teaching Resources

Name _____

Date _____

# Egg Count Math Story Mat

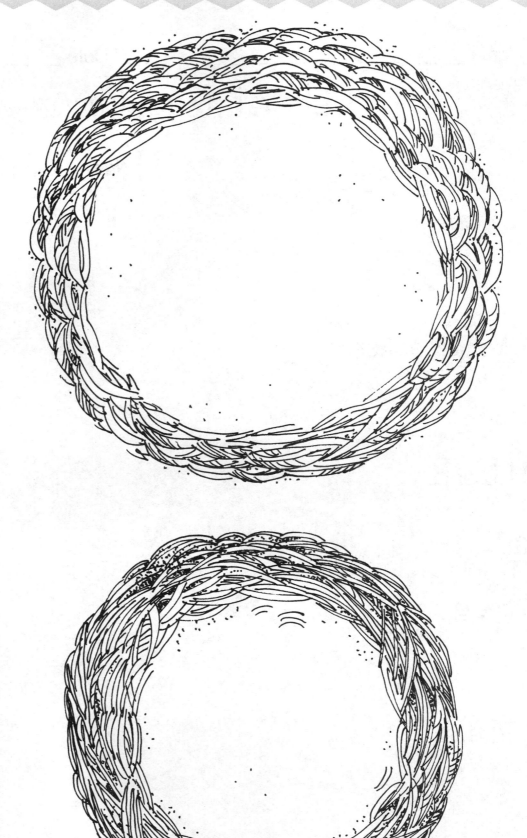

# May

## Safety

## Seeds and Flowers

## Be Kind to Animals Week

## All About Me

# May
## Teaching Ideas

May delivers several invitations for celebrating and learning! Take advantage of these seasonal changes and events with these activities, organized by four topics that are just right for this time of the year: SAFETY, SEEDS & FLOWERS, BE KIND TO ANIMALS, and ALL ABOUT ME.

As you begin to spend more time outdoors, recognize the need for SAFETY by introducing children to bicycle, water, playground, and traffic safety rules. Coordinate activities in SEEDS AND FLOWERS with the blooms of your school garden or neighborhood to let children discover their state flower, their birthday flower, the world's biggest flower, and the meanings of several flower names. Honor BE KIND TO ANIMALS WEEK with activities that introduce fictional and real animals, such as "Who's Afraid of the Big Bad Wolf?" (page 263) and "Welcome to the Pet Show" (page 266). Use the ALL ABOUT ME section to reintroduce children to themselves and celebrate Personal History Month. Here are other special features you'll find in the pages that follow:

- a reproducible send-home activity calendar
- literature connections
- pocket chart poetry
- a reproducible flower dictionary
- a math story mat
- a no-cook recipe
- hands-on science activities
- collaborative collage activities
- collaborative banner
- easy-to-learn poems and songs
- movement activities
- a rhyming mini-play
- and more amazing activities for May!

Name _____

# May Activity Calendar

Choose _____ activities to do each week this month.
Ask an adult in your family to initial the square in the box of each activity
you complete. Bring this paper back to school on _____.

| Monday | Tuesday | Wednesday | Thursday | Friday |
|---|---|---|---|---|
| Write the word May on a sheet of paper. List as many words as you can that end in -ay. | Look at this flower.  Find a matching flower on this page. | Write down the foods you ate today. Count the fruits. Count the vegetables. | May is the fifth month. Name the fourth month. Name the sixth month. | A robin can beat its wings two times every second. How many times can it beat its wings in a minute? |
| Pretend you're a bird. How many times can you flap your wings in a minute? | Look for weather information in a newspaper. Find a weather prediction for tomorrow. | Tell someone at home a story about your day. Include a beginning, a middle, and an end. | Circle each Thursday on the calendar this month. The numbers make a pattern. Add three numbers to continue the pattern. | Look around you. Find something that comes in twos. Find something that comes in fives. What comes in tens? |
| List the foods you ate today. Draw a picture that shows how you feel about the foods you ate. | Make a map of the place you live. Draw what is in front, behind, to the left, and to the right of your home. | What do you think this means: April showers bring May flowers. Do you think this is true? Why or why not? | Look at the words on this page. Find one that sounds the same as the word two but has a different spelling. | Plan a pet show. (You can use a stuffed animal if you like.) Tell how you care for your pet. Tell what is special about your pet. |
| Look at the words on this calendar. Can you find one that rhymes with May? | Look out a window. Describe or draw ten things that you see. Use lots of detail. | Use your senses! List the sights, sounds, tastes, smells, and textures (the way things feel) that remind you of home. | Put an object in a sock. Let a family member try to guess what it is by feeling the object through the sock. Trade places. Play again. | Turn May into a tongue twister! Make up a sentence using as many words as you can that start with m. |

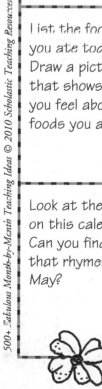

500+ Fabulous Month-by-Month Teaching Ideas © 2010 Scholastic Teaching Resources

Book Break

# Please Play Safe!

### by Margery Cuyler (Scholastic, 2006)

Penguin and his friends teach the do's and don'ts of playing at the playground. Young readers can join in the fun and reinforce their own playground safety knowledge by responding to the questions throughout the book.

LANGUAGE ARTS

# Rebuilding the Rules

Reinforce playground safety rules with this sentence-building activity.

◎ Write each playground rule on a sentence strip. Place the rules in the pocket chart and share them with children.

◎ Cut apart each rule word by word. Place one of the mixed-up rules in the pocket chart. Read it aloud to children. Ask: *What's wrong with this rule?* Let them help you rebuild the rule by putting the words back in the correct order. Encourage them to use clues such as capital letters and punctuation to identify the first and last word in the sentence.

◎ Write each rule on the outside of an envelope and place the cut-up words inside. Let children practice rebuilding the rules independently.

**TIP**

This activity may also be used to reinforce water, bicycle, and traffic safety rules.

Book Break

# I Read Signs

### by Tana Hoban (HarperCollins, 1987)

Striking photographs invite children to explore signs in their world. As you share the book with children, invite them to read the signs with you. Have them be on the lookout for signs on their way home that day, then share their findings with the class the next day. Discuss the connection between various signs and safety.

# Safety in Numbers

Share the poem "Safety in Numbers" (see page 254) to teach children that when playing outdoors they should use the buddy system and travel in groups. Guide children in following these directions to make an accordion-fold chain of paper people to use with the poem.

◎ Using an 8- by 11-inch sheet of construction paper, make four 2-inch accordion folds from left to right.

◎ Draw the outline of a person on the folded paper, making sure that the arms extend to the sides of the paper. Cut out the person, leaving the sides intact (so the chain will stay joined together when the paper is unfolded).

◎ Open up the paper chains. Color the first paper person (front and back) to look like you. Color the rest (front only) to look like your friends.

◎ Have children fold up the paper chains. As you read the poem aloud, have them open up the chain to reveal first themselves, then a buddy, and then a group. Let children bring their paper chains home with a copy of the poem to share with families.

ART

# Dressed for Safety

Outdoor activities such as bike riding and roller-blading require children to wear protective equipment and clothing that allow them to be easily seen. Help children learn to dress for safety by designing clothes and equipment for a one-dimensional figure.

◎ Give each child a sheet of brown craft paper that covers the length and width of their body. Ask them to lie down on the paper while a teacher, parent volunteer, or classmate traces around them.

◎ Have them cut out the figure and add features such as eyes, nose, mouth, ears, and hair.

◎ Provide materials such as reflector tape and brightly colored (or fluorescent) paper, paint, and markers for children to dress the figure. Have children equip their figure with a helmet, knee pads, elbow pads, and other safety equipment and clothing. Display "safety kids" in the hallway to remind others how to dress while playing outdoors.

## Book Break

# Franklin's Bicycle Helmet
### by Paulette Bourgeois (Scholastic, 2000)

Beaver makes fun of Franklin's new bicycle helmet. Now he's ashamed to wear it. Rabbit comes to the rescue with words of encouragement and helps Franklin put things into perspective.

# Teacher Share

### SCIENCE

## Why a Helmet?

Our skull protects our brain in the same way that a shell protects an egg. Sometimes, however, this protection is not enough. Demonstrate the need for a helmet with this experiment.

◎ Take children outdoors. Drop a hard-boiled egg from a height of ten inches. Ask children to describe what happened to the egg. Explain that our skulls can crack, just like the egg, and that is why we wear helmets for additional protection.

◎ Back in the classroom, form small groups and give each group an egg. Challenge them to use recycled materials (e.g., egg cartons, polystyrene, tape, paper, cotton, and so on) to create a safety device that will protect the egg when dropped on a hard surface.

◎ Take children outdoors and let them test their devices. Discuss the results. Compare and contrast the materials used with those found in a bike helmet. Invite children to share some of the activities for which they wear helmets (such as bike riding, skating, skateboarding, horseback riding, skiing).

*Bob Krech*

SCIENCE

## Staying Afloat

Children know that some objects sink while others float. Help them discover why this is true and how floating objects contribute to water safety.

◎ Gather children around a tub of water. Show them an empty, capped 20-ounce soda bottle. Ask them to predict whether it will sink or float. Place the bottle in the water and push it below the surface. Ask children to describe what happens.

◎ Fill the bottle halfway with water, cap it, and place it back into the tub. Again, let children predict whether it will sink or float, then describe what happens when you push the bottle under water.

◎ Finally, fill the bottle completely with water and cap it. Let children make their predictions. Place the bottle in the tub and observe the results.

◎ Ask children why the bottle sometimes floated and sometimes sank. Explain that for something to float, it must contain enough air to make it less dense than the water. As the air in the soda bottle was replaced with water, it became more dense, and, therefore, began to sink.

◎ Objects that float—such as kickboards, inner tubes, and life jackets— are important for water safety because they can help save someone from drowning. Our bodies are also able to float. Let children share their experiences learning to do a back float.

**Book Break**

## On Your Bike
### by Ruth Thomson (Franklin Watts, 2008)

From checking the bike before a ride to signaling turns, this book covers the basics of bike safety. Other titles in the series look at safety at home, at school, on the road, near water, and with strangers.

SOCIAL STUDIES

# Simon Says, "Stop!"

Help children practice the hand signals for bike riding by playing Simon Says. Begin by teaching them the signals for left turn, right turn, and stopping/slowing down. (See right.) Once children know the signals well, play Simon Says by naming a signal for them to make. Children should follow only those commands preceded by the words "Simon Says."

Stopping/Slowing Down

Right Turn

Left Turn

SOCIAL STUDIES, SNACK

# Stop-and-Go Snacks

*Red, yellow, green! What do they mean?* As children prepare this snack, they'll learn the significance of the colors in a traffic light. Each child will need a graham cracker, one tablespoon peanut butter, and three M & M's® (red, yellow, and green). Have children spread peanut butter on the graham cracker and place the M & M's® in a vertical position, with red on top, yellow in the center, and green at the bottom. Discuss what each color means, then "give the green light" to go ahead and eat the snack!

**TIP**

Check for allergies before serving.

MUSIC AND MOVEMENT

# Left or Right?

Many of the safety rules children must follow require them to know the difference between right and left. Share this poem and let children follow the actions as indicated in the rhyme to reinforce these directions.

**Right Hand, Left Hand**

This is my right hand,
I'll raise it up high.
This is my left hand,
I'll touch the sky.
Right hand, left hand,
Roll them around
Left hand, right hand,
Pound, pound, pound.

—Author Unknown

# Activity Page

## Safety in Numbers

Sometimes it's great,
to play all alone,
building houses of blocks,
in a room of my own.

But when I go out,
to swim, skate, or ride,
I bring along a buddy,
to be by my side.

Then there are times,
When one buddy won't do,
I travel in groups,
to the park, mall, or zoo.

There's safety in numbers,
you can't go wrong.
When you leave the house,
bring your friends along!

—Jacqueline Clarke

### Try This!

Draw a picture of you and a buddy. Write a sentence about what you are doing together.

_____

_____

LANGUAGE ARTS

# Flower Dictionary

Flowers have a language all their own. In the old days, if you knew each flower's meaning, the gift of a bouquet might hold a secret message. Let children create a dictionary to learn the language of flowers.

◎ Give each child a copy of page 261. Tell children to color and cut out the flowers, then glue each to a sheet of paper. Have children make a cover that says "Flower Dictionary" and put their pages together to make a book.

◎ Have children use their dictionaries to name the best flower for each occasion:

- ✿ Valentine's Day
- ✿ Fourth of July
- ✿ A new neighbor has just moved in
- ✿ A friend lost a pet
- ✿ A friend did something nice for you

◎ Challenge children to search for the meanings of other flowers. Let them add new pages to their flower dictionaries.

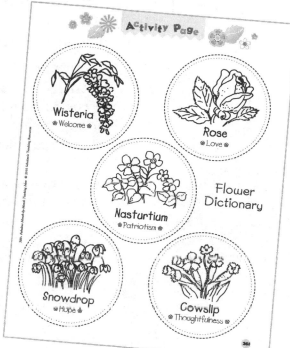

Activity Page

Wisteria ✿ Welcome ✿

Rose ✿ Love ✿

Nasturtium ✿ Patriotism ✿

Flower Dictionary

Snowdrop ✿ Hope ✿

Cowslip ✿ Thoughtfulness ✿

261

---

**Book Break**

# Alison's Zinnia

by Anita Lobel (HarperCollins, 1996)

In this alphabet of flowers, "Alison acquired an amaryllis for Beryl. Beryl bought a begonia for Crystal," and so on until the circular pattern brings us back to the beginning with, "Zena zeroed in on a Zinnia for Alison."

MUSIC, LANGUAGE ARTS

# If I Could Be a Flower

Introduce children to an assortment of flowers with this pocket chart song.

**TIP**

Turn the pocket chart activity into an interactive chart by gluing the sentence strips to a sheet of posterboard. Laminate the chart and the flowers. Place a piece of Velcro® in the blank space in the song and on the back of each flower. Store the flowers in a resealable bag and staple it to the back of the posterboard. At a center, children can choose flowers to fill in the blank and practice reading the song.

◎ Collect pictures of flowers from magazines or seed catalogs. Make sure you have at least one per student. Show the pictures to children and share each flower's name. Ask: *If you could be a flower, which one would you be?*

◎ Let each child choose one flower picture. Have children paste a picture of themselves in the center of their flower. Glue the flowers to sentence strips and record each flower's name.

◎ Write the words to the following song on sentence strips and place them in the pocket chart:

> If I could be a flower,
> A flower, a flower,
> If I could be a flower, what kind would I be?
> A daisy, a pansy, a tulip, a lilac,
> If I could be a flower, I would be a _____.

Sing the song with children to the tune of "The More We Get Together." Let children take turns placing their flowers in the blank space and leading the song.

## Book Break

# Flower Garden
## by Eve Bunting (Harcourt, 1994)

Told in rhyming verse, and set in an urban neighborhood, the story tells of a girl and her father as they shop for the makings of a "garden box," which becomes a birthday surprise for her mother.

# Teacher Share

## Flower Sort

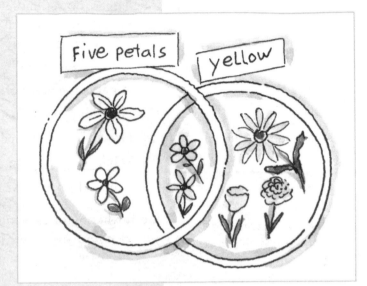

Flowers come in a wide variety of colors, shapes, and sizes. Teach children about these attributes through this sorting activity.

◎ Have each child bring a flower to school. (Have extras on hand to share.) Provide time for children to examine their flowers closely. Ask them to name attributes that tell about their flower. Record each attribute—for example, *scented, red, yellow, orange, five petals, six petals, thorns, leaves*—on a separate index card.

◎ Gather children in a seated circle. Place two hula hoops in the center so they overlap to create a Venn diagram. Place one attribute card next to each circle. Invite children to place their flowers in the Venn diagram accordingly. For example, if the two cards chosen were "red" and "scented," red flowers would go in the red circle, scented flowers would go in the scented circle and red, scented flowers would go in the space where the circles intersect. All other flowers would be placed outside of the diagram.

◎ Once the flowers are sorted, ask children what information they can gather from looking at the Venn diagram. Repeat the procedure several times using different attribute cards.

*Natalie Vaughn*

**TIP**

Check with local florists who may be willing to donate slightly aged flowers for educational use.

---

### Book Break

## The Reason for a Flower

by Ruth Heller (Putnam, 1989)

Rhyming verse and elaborate illustrations explain plant reproduction and the purpose of a flower in this charming book.

# A Flower SO Big!

The largest flower in the world is the *Rafflesia*, which can be found in Indonesia. Help children discover just how big this flower is by going on an Internet scavenger hunt. Start at **www.didyouknow.com/flowers.htm**. Help children navigate the site to find answers to these questions:

- What is the name of the biggest flower in the world? (*Rafflesia Arnoldi*)
- How long are the petals? (*1 foot 6 inches long*)
- How thick are the petals? (*1 inch thick*)
- What does it weigh? (*15 pounds*)
- Where does it grow? (*Sumatra Island in Indonesia*)

Go further by investigating the smallest flower. (*Duckweed*) Ask: *How could you see a flower this tiny?* (with a microscope)

**TIP**

Help children visualize the length of the Rafflesia petals by giving them a piece of string that is 1 foot 6 inches long. Challenge them to find other objects in the classroom the same length. Place books on a bathroom scale until it reads 15 pounds so children can conceptualize the flower's weight.

*Teacher Share*

## Flower Puzzles

Teach children about the parts of a flower. Then, let them show what they have learned by creating a flower puzzle.

- Draw a flower on a sheet of chart paper. Work together with children to label the roots, stem, petals, sepals, pistil, and stamens.

- Give each child a 6- by 12-inch piece of oaktag. Ask children to draw, color, and label a flower of their own design.

- Demonstrate how to draw and cut out six to eight intersecting lines on the reverse side to form puzzle pieces. Have children label each piece with their name and place the puzzle pieces in a resealable bag. Invite them to exchange puzzles and use their knowledge of the parts of a flower to put them back together.

*Kathy Gerber*

## My Name Is Georgia: A Portrait

by Jeanette Winter (Voyager, 2003)

Written in first person, this picture-book portrait tells the story of Georgia O'Keeffe, a strong-minded girl who grew up to be a famous artist.

# Teacher Share

ART

## Let's Paint Flowers!

Georgia O'Keeffe painted BIG flowers so other people would notice! Use her work to inspire children to create their own mural of flowers. Begin by reading books about her life (see Book Break, above) and sharing some of her artwork.

Collect several pictures of flowers from magazines or seed catalogs. Let each child choose one flower to study and paint. Tape a long piece of mural paper to the wall. Let children take turns painting their BIG flowers on the mural. Have them sign their name under their flower just as an artist would. When they are finished, you'll have a beautiful classroom garden too big for anyone to miss!

*Frank Murphy*

# Teacher Share

MUSIC AND MOVEMENT

## Watch Us Grow!

In this movement activity, children "grow" from a seed to a flower and then become part of a bouquet. Start by asking children to scrunch down with their hands covering their faces. Explain that they're seeds that have just been planted. Pretend to cover the seeds with dirt and water them. Hold up an orange ball (or orange construction-paper sun) and let the sun shine on the seeds. The "flowers" should start to sprout by slowly standing and then bloom by removing their hands from their faces and spreading their arms open wide. As you pick the "flowers," let children form a bouquet by gathering together in a bunch.

*Pam Snyder*

LANGUAGE ARTS, SCIENCE

## "How Does Our Garden Grow?" Mini-Play

Introduce children to the concept of pollination with this easy-to-read play. The play is best done in a Readers Theater format. Place children in small groups of six. Assign each member of the group a different part and let them take turns practicing their lines. Have each group create simple props for a performance. For example, create simple flower masks by cutting the center from paper plates and gluing petals all around. Add pipe cleaner antennae to construction-paper headbands for bee and butterfly costumes. Wings for all three creatures can be cut from paper bags and taped to the child's back.

**Wisteria**
❀ Welcome ❀

**Rose**
❀ Love ❀

**Nasturtium**
❀ Patriotism ❀

Flower
Dictionary

**Snowdrop**
❀ Hope ❀

**Cowslip**
❀ Thoughtfulness ❀

# How Does Our Garden Grow?

by Jacqueline Clarke

**Characters:** Hummingbird ✿ Bee ✿ Butterfly ✿ Columbine ✿ Marigold ✿ Daylily

**Setting:** a Garden

**Bee, Butterfly, Hummingbird:** Let's visit the garden
For something to eat.
We'll search for flowers
With nectar so sweet.

**Bee:** Bright YELLOW flowers
Are my favorite kind.
I'll buzz around and around
And see what I find.

**Marigold:** Look no further,
I'm yellow as can be!
My name is Marigold.
Pick me! Pick me!

**Hummingbird:** Bright RED flowers
Are my favorite kind.
I'll dart around and around
And see what I find.

**Columbine:** Look no further,
I'm red as can be!
My name is Columbine.
Pick me! Pick me!

**Butterfly:** Bright PINK flowers
Are my favorite kind.
I'll flutter around and around
And see what I find.

**Daylily:** Look no further,
I'm pink as can be!
My name is Daylily.
Pick me! Pick me!

**Bee, Butterfly, Hummingbird:** We've each met our match.
Now it's time for a drink.
To our friends the flowers—
Dressed in yellow, red,
and pink.

**Marigold, Columbine, Daylily:** Sip your nectar right here,
But take the pollen to go.
Carry it to the next flower,
So new seeds will grow!

**Bee, Butterfly, Hummingbird:** Together we'll work
With our flower friends
To create a garden
That never ends!

*500+ Fabulous Month-by-Month Teaching Ideas © 2010 Scholastic Teaching Resources*

LANGUAGE ARTS, SCIENCE

# Who's Afraid of the Big Bad Wolf?

Children's literature isn't always kind to animals. Coyotes, wolves, and foxes are often portrayed as villains or tricksters. In this activity, children examine the stereotype of the wolf as seen in traditional tales. They will then read nonfiction to discover what wolves are really like.

◎ Create a T-chart with the headings "Storybook Wolf" and "Real-Life Wolf." Read books with wolves as characters and list adjectives to describe them in the "Storybook Wolf" column. Read nonfiction books about wolves and list adjectives to describe them in the "Real-Life Wolf" column.

◎ Compare the two columns. How are storybook wolves different from real-life wolves? How are they the same? Is the stereotype of the "big bad wolf" accurate? Write a fictional tale with children about a wolf. Base the character on the information they have learned about real-life wolves.

## Book Break

## First Animal Encyclopedia
(DK First Reference Series)
(DK Children, 2004)

Spectacular photographs and fascinating facts will bring young readers back again and again to build knowledge of the animal world.

SCIENCE, ART

# I Spy Endangered Animals Collage

Create a collage with children to bring about awareness of endangered animals.

◎ Collect pictures of endangered animals from magazines, coloring books, or the Internet.

◎ Let children work together to glue the pictures to posterboard to create a collage. They can add details and a background to complete the picture.

◎ Display the collage entitled "I Spy Endangered Animals," outside the classroom. Post the following line on a sentence strip beneath the collage: *I spy a/an* _____.

◎ You might invite other classes to come and view the collage and search for animals.

MATH

# Five Little Goldfish Math Story Mat

Pet owners have a responsibility to the animals in their care. As you share this number rhyme with children, they will quickly realize what can happen when pets don't receive the care they need.

Give each child a fishbowl math story mat (see page 268) and five fish-shaped crackers. Read aloud the following rhyme while children manipulate the crackers accordingly:

### Five Little Goldfish

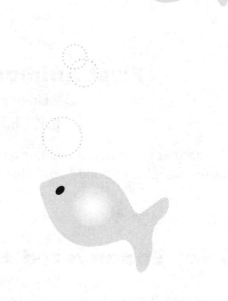

Five little goldfish
From the pet store,
Mother forgot to feed them
And then there were four.

Four little goldfish
As hungry as can be,
Father fed them too much
And then there were three.

Three little goldfish
With bellies full of food,
Brother forgot to clean the bowl
And then there were two.

Two little goldfish
Not having any fun,
Sister dropped one in the sink
And then there was one.

One little goldfish
Left all alone to swim,
The family learned their lesson
And took good care of him!

Create other addition and subtraction story problems for children to solve using the crackers and math story mat. Let children snack on their goldfish as you share five final subtraction stories. Watch them all disappear this time!

**TIP**

Check for allergies before allowing students to snack on the crackers.

MATH

# Dog Biscuit Bakery

Let children take turns measuring and adding the ingredients
in the following recipe to make dog biscuits to donate to a
local animal shelter.

## Dog Biscuits

2 cups whole wheat flour    1/4 cup sunflower seeds
1/4 cup cornmeal    2 tablespoons vegetable oil
1/2 cup soy flour    1/4 cup unsulfured molasses
1 teaspoon bone meal    2 eggs mixed with 1/4 cup milk
1 teaspoon sea salt

- Mix dry ingredients and sunflower seeds in a large bowl.

- Add oil, molasses, and egg mixture (all but one
  tablespoon). Add more flour if the dough is not firm enough.

- Knead dough for 5 minutes. Let it rest for 30 minutes.

- Roll out dough to a 1/2-inch thickness. Use cookie cutters
  to cut the dough in shapes. Brush biscuits with remaining
  egg mixture.

- Bake on an ungreased cookie sheet at 350 Fahrenheit for 30
  minutes (or until lightly browned). For harder biscuits, turn
  off the oven and leave the cookie sheet in for another hour.

- Store the biscuits in a tin, tie with ribbons, and deliver to
  the animal shelter.

**TIP**

You may want to
coordinate a tour
of your local animal
shelter with the
delivery of the dog
biscuits.

---

## Book Break

# Arthur's Pet Business

by Marc Brown (Little, Brown, 1990)

Before Arthur can get a pet, he must prove he is responsible. He starts a pet
business in hopes that his parents will see that he is not only responsible,
but knows how to handle animals. His business is a success, and in the end
he makes a profit *and* gains a puppy.

# *Teacher Share*

## SCIENCE

## Welcome to the Pet Show!

Try this fun alternative to a live pet show!

◎ Ask each child to spend time observing and researching a pet (one of their own or someone else's). Have children draw and color a life-size cutout of the animal, write about the care and feeding habits of the pet, and record the information on the back of the picture.

◎ On the day of the pet show, act as the host and introduce each pet and his or her owner as they "lead" or carry their pet onstage.

*Judy Meagher*

## SOCIAL STUDIES

## Do Animals Have Feelings?

Children might be surprised to find that animals have feelings, too. Ask them how they can tell what a cat is feeling. How about a dog? Write scenarios such as the following on slips of paper and place them in a box.

> You are a cat and someone has stepped on your tail.
> You are a dog and your water bowl is empty.
> You are a rabbit. Someone places you in his or her lap and pets you.

Let children take turns acting out scenarios. Have other students try to guess what is happening.

## Book Break

## Be Gentle With the Dog, Dear!

### by Matthew Baek (Dial, 2008)

Young Elisa loves her dog, Tag, and shows it in familiar ways—by squeezing him, pulling his tail, tackling him. Tag loves her, too, "especially when she is sleeping." Inspired by "events that take place almost daily" in the author's household, this book offers a comic look at learning to care for a pet.

LANGUAGE ARTS, SCIENCE

# Handle With Care

*How should bugs be treated?* Explore this question with children by sharing the following poem and a technique for safely removing insects from their home.

Ask children what they think the poet does when she sees a bug. Let them share how they feel about bugs outside and bugs inside. Teach them this technique for removing a bug from their home. Place a cup over the bug and slip an index card or piece of cardboard gently underneath. Carry the bug outdoors and let it go. Give each child a cup, an index card, and a plastic bug and let them practice this technique.

### Hurt No Living Thing

Hurt no living thing;
Ladybird, nor butterfly,
Nor moth with dusty wing,
Nor cricket chirping cheerily,
Nor grasshopper so light of leap,
Nor dancing gnat, nor beetle fat,
Nor harmless worms that creep.

—*by Christina Rossetti*

# Teacher Share

SOCIAL STUDIES

## Comparing Animals and Humans

**B**y using a Venn diagram to compare animals and humans, children realize that their needs and wants are similar.

◎ Create a Venn diagram on a sheet of posterboard by drawing an outline of a paw print and a handprint so they intersect in the middle. Label the paw print "Animal Needs" and the handprint "Human Needs." Discuss the difference between a "need" and a "want."

◎ Ask children to name different needs. Sort them accordingly using the Venn diagram. How many needs do animals and humans share? What needs belong to animals alone? humans? Repeat this activity with animal and human "wants."

*Bob Krech*

Name _____

Date _____

## Five Little Goldfish Math Story Mat

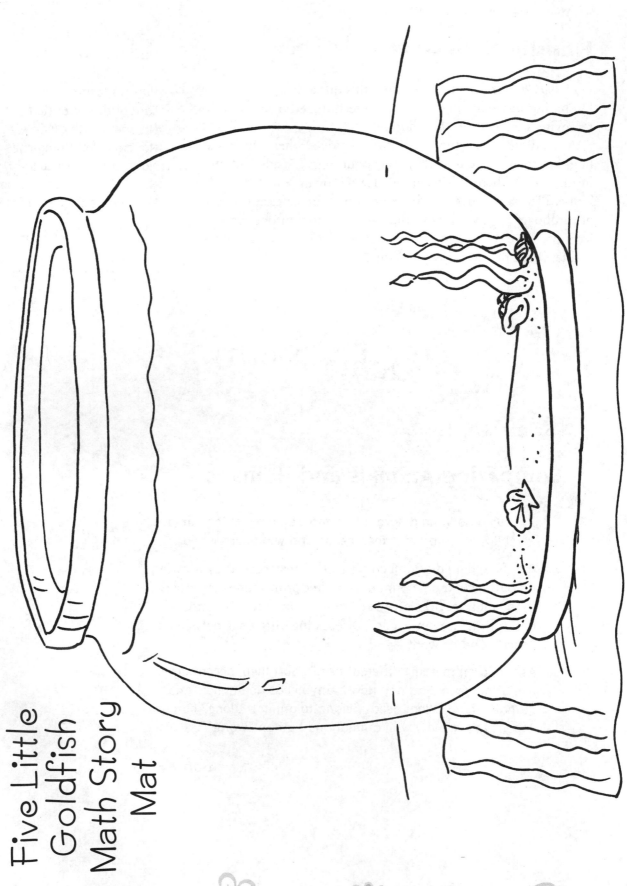

*500+ Fabulous Month-by-Month Teaching Ideas* © 2010 Scholastic Teaching Resources

LANGUAGE ARTS

# I'm in the Dictionary!

Interviewers often ask, *What one word describes you?* Pose this question to children, then have them use a dictionary to learn more about the word they choose (its meaning and part of speech). Let children share their words on a collaborative banner. Give each child a copy of page 272. Have children complete the rhyme, then color and cut out the pattern. Tape the patterns side by side so that "hands" touch. Display on a wall, then invite children to read aloud their rhymes. Ask them to share the word's meaning and part of speech with the class. Did more children choose nouns, adjectives, or verbs to describe themselves?

## Teacher Share

SCIENCE, MATH

## Fingerprint Detectives

**E**ach person's fingerprint is unique. However, fingerprints generally fall into three categories: *arch*, *whorl*, and *loop*. In this activity, children discover their dominant fingerprint type and compare it with classmates'.

Place washable-ink pads, a roll of paper towels, and copies of the record sheet (see page 273) at a center. Let each child use the ink pad to stamp a fingerprint in each box (one for each finger). Help children identify and record each fingerprint type using the illustrations at the bottom of the page. Have them determine their dominant fingerprint type (the one that occurs most often) from the data they collected. Create a graph to determine which fingerprint type is the most and which is the least common in the class.

*Andrea Page*

## COMPUTER Connection

Students can use some great online dictionaries to look up their words. Here are a few to check out:

www. wordcentral.com

http://new. wordsmyth.net

www. merriam-webster. com

Children can also make fingerprints with this fun method: Press your finger on a smooth surface, such as a file cabinet, and sprinkle with powder. Gently blow the powder away to reveal a fingerprint!

## Book Break

# Chrysanthemum

### by Kevin Henkes (Greenwillow, 1991)

Chrysanthemum believed she had the perfect name. Then she started school and her friends made flower jokes and pointed out that her name was as long as half the alphabet. But with the help of Miss Delphinium, the music teacher, Chrysanthemum blooms once again. Follow up with "Names Add Up," below.

 Teacher Share

MATH

## Names Add Up

Names make great mathematical data for counting and graphing!

- Give each child a copy of the record sheet. (See page 274.) Ask children to record their first, middle, and last name in the spaces provided. Have them calculate the total for each name.

- Challenge children to write a number sentence based on the number of letters in their first and last name. Can they find another student with the same sum but a different combination?

- Use the data collected on their first names only to create class graphs. Which name has the most letters? Do more children have an odd or even number of letters?

*Colleen Huston*

SOCIAL STUDIES, ART

## Calendar Sticks

Native Americans of the Southwest recorded history using calendar sticks: pictures drawn or carved on flat sticks. Invite children to create their own calendar sticks. Give each child a flat stick or strip of posterboard. For each of seven days, let children draw one picture to mark an important event. At the end of the week, let children share events on their calendar sticks.

# Another Important Book

## by Margaret Wise Brown (HarperCollins, 2006)

This sequel to *The Important Book* examines the "important" things about ages one to six. For example, "The important thing about being one is that life has just begun," and "The important thing about two is all the things that you can do." Have children think back to their "younger" days and recall one important event for each age. Let them record these events in pictures and words on a time line. Set aside time for each child to share with the class.

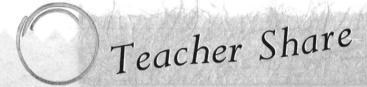

# Teacher Share

SOCIAL STUDIES

## My Life in a Suitcase

We carry our personal histories with us wherever we go. In this activity, children will literally pack theirs into a suitcase to share with others. Begin by sharing your own personal history with children. Gather several items from home that symbolize different aspects of your life—for example:

- photographs
- diplomas and teaching credentials
- favorite books
- objects that represent hobbies/interests
- a recipe for a favorite family food
- maps showing where your family came from

Place the items in a suitcase and bring it in to school. Invite children to listen as you unpack your suitcase and reveal each object's significance. Throughout the next few weeks, set aside time for each student to fill and share his or her own "suitcase." To simplify the procedure, you may have students select items that will fit in a paper lunch bag. Explain that although we each have things in common with others, our personal histories are unique.

*Marianne Chang*

**I'm in the Dictionary!**
**Collaborative Banner**

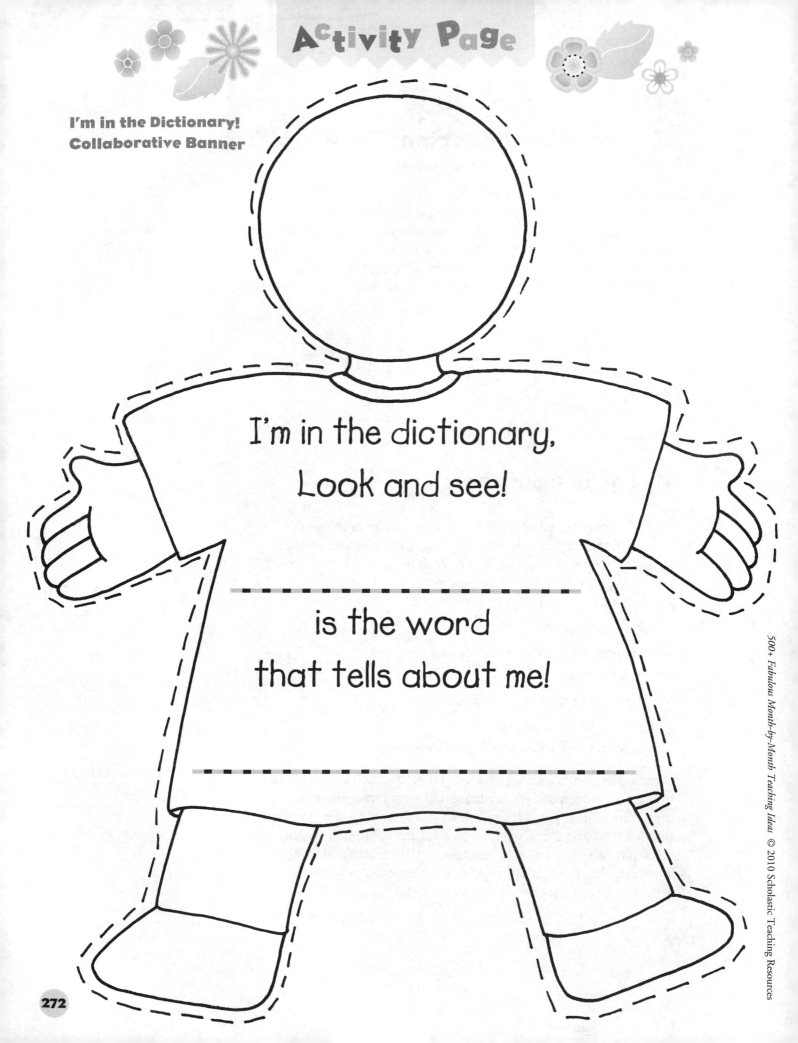

I'm in the dictionary,
Look and see!

_____

is the word
that tells about me!

Name _____ Date _____

# Fingerprint Detectives

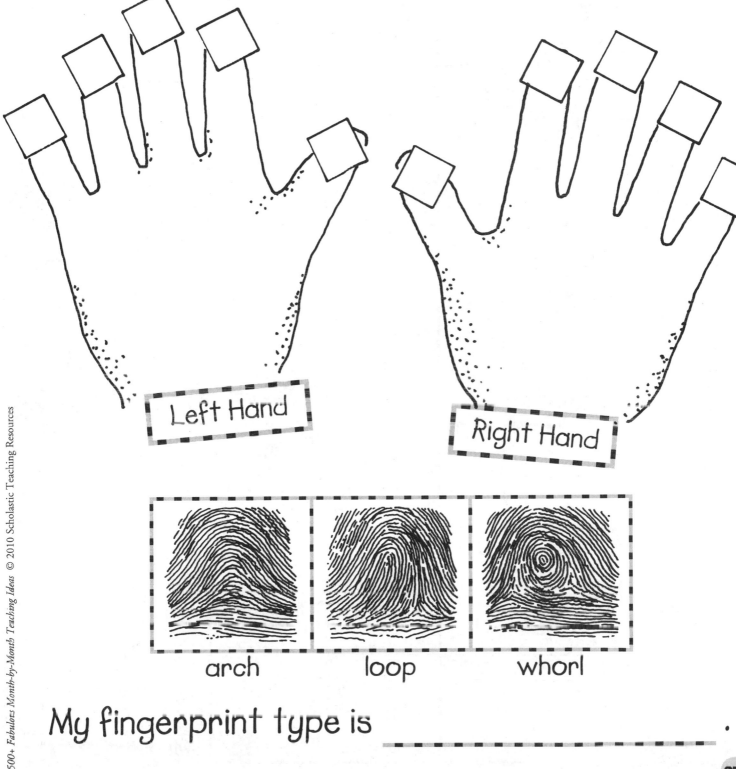

Left Hand

Right Hand

arch          loop          whorl

My fingerprint type is _____.

Date _____

# Names Add Up

| | Number of Letters | Odd or Even? | Number of Consonants | Number of Vowels |
|---|---|---|---|---|
| First Name | | | | |
| Middle Name | | | | |
| Last Name | | | | |

◎ Write a number sentence to represent the number of letters in your first and last name:

_____

◎ Find another student with the same sum but a different combination.

Name _____

# Summer

# Summer
## Teaching Ideas

When most people hear the word *summer*, they think of sandy beaches, swimsuits and sunglasses, vacations, barbecues, and so on. And summer does, in fact, include many of these pleasures. However, the one thing people (especially small ones) usually do *not* associate with summer is the word *school*. Well, if you are reading this, it probably means you are teaching children this summer. And whether you are teaching at a year-round school, summer school, summer camp, or in any other summer program, you will find that the summer months can be loaded with learning that's full of fun, too.

These activities are organized by great summer topics: BUGS, because they seem to be everywhere this time of year; PATRIOTISM, because nothing could be more American than Independence Day; OLD FRIENDS, NEW FRIENDS, because children are getting ready to leave one class and enter another; and SUMMER FUN, because…well, that one is pretty obvious. The activities and teaching ideas cover math, science, music, art, social studies, history, movement, language arts, and literacy, often combining a few areas in one activity. For example, "Collaborative Bug Banner" (see page 283) includes research, reading, writing, science, and art. "Friendship Hearts" (see page 298) combines math, language arts, social studies, and movement. On the pages that follow, you'll also find:

- a reproducible send-home activity calendar
- a fun and easy no-cook recipe based on a favorite story
- a reproducible mini-play
- easy-to-learn songs children will love to sing again and again
- a Bug Bingo game
- a computer pen pal program
- a fun transition-time movement activity
- literature links from old favorites to new classics
- an interactive mini-book for children to make and keep
- a friendship pocket calendar
- and many more summertime treats!

Name _____

# Summer Activity Calendar

Choose _____ activities to do each week this month.
Ask an adult in your family to initial the square in the box of each activity
you complete. Bring this paper back to school on _____ .

| Monday | Tuesday | Wednesday | Thursday | Friday |
|---|---|---|---|---|
| Write your first and last name on a sheet of paper. Cut apart the letters. Use the letters to make new words. | Look at a calendar. Find the first day of summer. How many days until autumn? | Go on a rainbow hunt. Find something for each color of the rainbow: red, orange, yellow, green, blue, purple. | Make up a story about how the sun came to be. Share your story with someone. | People can *walk, skip,* and *run.* Name other words for ways people can move. |
| What word describes you? Ask a family member to help you look it up in a dictionary. What does this word mean? | Think of a word that describes a family member. Look it up together in a dictionary. What does it mean? | What are the dates for each Wednesday in July? The numbers make a pattern. Add four numbers to the pattern. | Pretend you're a caterpillar. Act out your life cycle! | Talk about sun safety with a family member. Draw a picture that shows how to stay safe in the sun. |
| Look at this butterfly. Find a matching butterfly on this page. | Veins carry food and water through a leaf. Look at a leaf. Trace the path the food and water take. | Read a book with someone in your family. Take turns retelling the story. Include as many details as you can. | Look at a calendar. How many months until your birthday? How many weeks? | Make a musical instrument. Place sand or uncooked rice in a paper cup. Tape paper over the top. Shake it while you sing! |
| Fire + fly = firefly! Can you make three more words that start with *fire?* | Collect 20 small stones or shells. (Ask a grownup in your family to help you.) How many ways can you sort them? | Use your pebbles or shells to make number sentences. How many ways can you show the number 20? | Look at the words on this page. Can you find two that rhyme with *play?* | Turn *Summer* into a tongue twister! Make up a sentence using as many words as you can that start with *s.* |

## SCIENCE

# Bug Bingo

Build science vocabulary with a game of Bug Bingo. Make copies of the Bug Bingo activity sheets on pages 285 and 286. Cut out the insect cards and place them in a paper bag. Make multiple copies of the four game boards, cut them apart, and give one to each child. Give each child several Bingo markers—any small manipulative will do—from math unit cubes to dried beans. Reach into the bag and pick a card. Read the name of the bug and show the picture to children. Children with matching bugs on their game boards put a marker on the bug. Continue until someone has a line of four markers in a row: vertical, horizontal, or diagonal. The child then calls out "Bug Bingo!" and the game can begin again.

**Bug Match**
Use Bug Bingo insect cards to play a matching game. Mix up the cards and place them facedown in rows. Let children take turns flipping two cards faceup. If the cards match, the player keeps them. If not, the cards go facedown again and it's the next player's turn.

## Book Break

# The Bugliest Bug
by Carol Diggory Shields (Candlewick, 2005)

Stink bugs come to the rescue at the Bugliest Bug contest when the judges turn out to be arachnids in disguise who drop a web instead of a curtain to capture the contestants.

## SCIENCE

# Insect or Not?

Explore how creepy-crawly creatures are alike and different. Start by asking children to call out names of bugs and other creepy crawlies they know. Record children's suggestions on sentence strips and cut so that each creature is on a separate piece. Make a two-column chart labeled "Insects" and "Non-Insects." Ask children what they think insects have in common. Discuss common attributes: three body parts (head, thorax, and abdomen), six legs and wings.

One at a time, hold up each sentence strip piece and read the name of the creature. Ask children if they think the creature is an insect or not. Place the sentence strips in the columns children suggest, using removable wall adhesive. Follow up by looking for pictures of each creature in books or on the web. Have children look carefully for the insect attributes: *Does it have six legs? three body parts?* Have children reorganize the chart according to what they discover. Leave the chart up for reference and exploration. Children can remove the creatures' names and try re-sorting them.

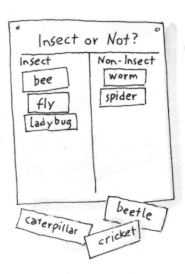

**279**

# The Very Hungry Caterpillar

### by Eric Carle (Putnam, 1994)

This classic story introduces children to many concepts, including the days of the week, numbers, and the life cycle of a butterfly. After reading the story for pure enjoyment, let children plan and prepare a snack fit for a hungry caterpillar—and hungry children! (See Caterpillar's School-Day Snack, below.) To further explore concepts introduced in the book, see A Caterpillar's Calendar, below.

SCIENCE, LANGUAGE ARTS, ART

## A Caterpillar's Calendar

After sharing *The Very Hungry Caterpillar*, try this story-mapping activity to learn more.

◎ Make a story map by dividing a sheet of craft paper into seven sections—one for each day of the week. Let children tell you the days of the week, in order, using the book for help. Write them across the top of the story map.

◎ Invite a child to draw a picture to show what happened on Sunday. (*The caterpillar came out of the egg.*) Have other volunteers use words and pictures to record what the caterpillar ate from Monday to Saturday.

◎ Let children use this graphic organizer to retell the story to you and one another. Follow up by asking children to point out each stage in the caterpillar's life. Introduce the word *metamorphosis* and use the activity as an introduction to a lesson on life cycles.

MATH, SOCIAL STUDIES

## Caterpillar's School-Day Snack

**TIP**

Check for allergies before serving.

After reading *The Very Hungry Caterpillar*, ask children to tell you what the caterpillar ate on the days they go to school. Review what the caterpillar ate on these days and list the foods on chart paper: 1 apple, 2 pears, 3 plums, 4 strawberries, 5 oranges. Gather the ingredients and prepare them for children to work with (remove plum pits, peel oranges, cut away strawberry tops, core apple and pears). Give children blunt or plastic knives and let them work on paper plates or cutting boards to cut up the fruit. Have children place the fruit in a big bowl, then serve and enjoy their snack!

LANGUAGE ARTS, SCIENCE

# "The Riddle of the Bugs" Mini-Play

Explore rhyming words and give children a chance to express their dramatic flair with the mini-play on page 288. Copy the play on chart paper. Read it through with children, then invite them to find rhyming pairs, such as *sting* and *thing*. Give each child a copy of the play, assign parts, and create simple costumes—for example, attach pipe cleaners to a construction-paper headband for antennae. Let children rehearse, then perform their play for an audience. Repeat the play several times so that children can play different parts.

*Teacher Share*

Elliott

2 ladybugs + 3 ants = 5 bugs

SCIENCE, MATH, LANGUAGE ARTS

## Closeup on Bugs

Take a nature walk to investigate insects. Use "bug-catchers" (available at science and teacher supply stores) if you can, but regular jars with holes poked in the lids will also do. Encourage children to try to catch bugs they recognize. The best way to do this is to creep up quietly, gently place the jar on the ground, and let the bug crawl in. (Be sure to caution children to steer clear of bugs that might sting or bite, such as bees and fire ants.) When children have several insects in the jar, return to the classroom for a closer look: *What are the bugs doing?*

Make a math connection by letting children write number sentences and stories about their bugs. Children can draw the bugs, then write number sentences beneath the pictures—for example, 2 ladybugs + 3 ants = 5 bugs. (See sample, left.) Go further by having children turn their number sentences into short stories—for example, *I went on a nature walk to collect bugs and I found a ladybug. Next I found two ants. I found another ladybug and one more ant. All together, I found five bugs.* Be sure to return the insects to their natural habitats before too long.

*Bobbie Williams*

If you live in an area that makes it difficult to look for insects outside, consider purchasing little plastic bugs (sold in toy and school-supply stores). Let children pick a handful without looking and place them in a jar. They can complete the activities as described using the toy bugs.

# Teacher Share

## MUSIC, SCIENCE

### The Buggy Song

Children (and adults!) tend to learn facts better when there's a tune to go with them. To help children learn the criteria needed to classify a creature as an insect, sing this song to the tune of "The Farmer in the Dell." (Note that not all insects have antennae.)

Antennae and six legs
Antennae and six legs
Insects can have them both you know
Antennae and six legs.

Head, thorax, abdomen
Head, thorax, abdomen
An insect has three body parts
Head, thorax, abdomen.

You can make up little teaching songs easily: The words don't need to rhyme, they just need to fit roughly into the rhythm of a familiar children's tune. How about "Old MacDonald"?

Old MacDonald had some bugs, E-I-E-I-O.
And one of these bugs, it was a bee, E-I-E-I-O.
With a *buzz-buzz* here, and a *buzz-buzz* there...

That's a start...you (and the children) do the rest!

*Rita Galloway*

## Book Break

# National Audubon Society First Field Guides: Insects
by Christina Wilsdon
(Scholastic, 1998)

Easy-to-read text and more than 450 photographs help students get to know the insects around them. A removable, water-resistant "spotter's guide" makes it easy to identify insects anywhere.

SCIENCE, LANGUAGE ARTS, ART

# Collaborative Bug Banner

Make copies of the bug banner activity sheet on page 287 and give one to each child. Ask children to choose a bug they'd like to learn more about. Some suggestions might be ladybugs, butterflies, beetles, dragonflies, grasshoppers, bees, and so on. Have children write the name of their bug on the sheet, then conduct research to learn more—for example, *What does the bug eat? What is something special it can do?* (See Book Break, below, for suggested resources.) Have children use words and pictures to record information.

To create the banner, cut out a simple circle shape for a head, and draw a smiling face. Tape two pipe cleaners to the top, and attach the head to the wall. As children complete their bug banner pages, have them cut out the shapes along the dashed line, and tape them one after another to the bug's head. Soon you will have a beautiful bug banner crawling around your classroom!

······ **Book Break** ·······

## Bugs Are Insects
### (Let's-Read-and-Find-Out Science I))
by Anne Rockwell (HarperCollins, 2001)

What makes a bug a bug? This book explains the answer and clarifies differences between insects and spiders. Suggestions for further exploration are provided for young entomologists who want to learn more.

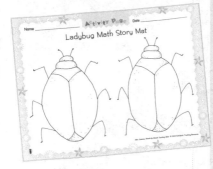

# Teacher Share

## Ladybug Math Story Mat

**M**ake copies of the math story mat on page 289. Give children red crayons or markers, and let them color in their ladybugs without adding spots. Make a set of small black construction-paper circles, about ten for each child. Share math stories that students can act out with the black spots on their story mats. Look at different ways children solve the problems. Samples follow.

◎ **For addition:** The first ladybug had three dots. The second ladybug had four. How many did they have all together?

◎ **For subtraction:** The first ladybug had five dots. The second ladybug had three, but then she lost one. How many do they have all together?

◎ **For logical thinking:** The two ladybugs had nine dots all together. The ladybug on the right had fewer than the ladybug on the left. How many dots could each ladybug have?

*Bob Krech*

## TIP

Before serving, check for milk or honey allergies.

SCIENCE, MATH, SNACK

## One Honey of a Treat!

Talk about bees with children. A lot of people don't like bees because they can sting. But bees can also do a wonderful thing—make honey! Older honeybees suck *nectar*, a sweet liquid, out of flowers. They feed the nectar to younger bees. The bees have a "honey machine" right inside their stomachs! It's called a *honey sac*. Inside the honey sac, the nectar gets thicker and turns into honey. When it's ready, the honey comes out the bee's mouth and is stored in the hive. Celebrate bees with this delicious and nutritious treat.

◎ Measure 4 cups of milk and pour into a blender or bowl. Add 4 scoops frozen yogurt and 3 tablespoons honey.

◎ If blending by hand, let children take turns stirring the mixture with a wire whisk. If using a blender, blend on high speed until the mixture is frothy. Pour the mixture into small drinking cups. Enjoy the honey milkshake, and don't forget to thank the bees!

Praying Mantis

Ladybug

Beetle

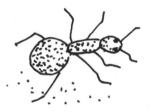

Butterfly

Mosquito

Grasshopper

Ant

Bee

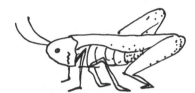

Fly

Dragonfly

Moth

Wasp

Katydid

Cicada

Cricket

Locust

Treehopper

Water Strider

# Activity Page

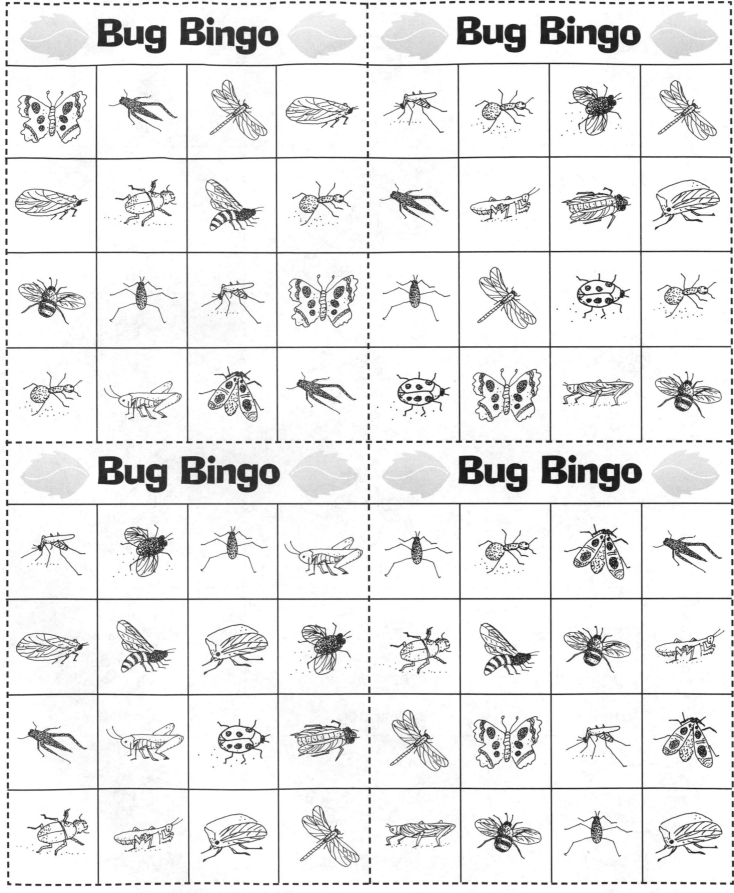

500+ Fabulous Month-by-Month Teaching Ideas © 2010 Scholastic Teaching Resources

**Collaborative Bug Banner**

Name _____

My bug's name is

_____

My bug eats _____

My bug can _____

My bug looks like this:

# The Riddle of the Bugs

by Pamela Chanko

## Characters
(to be played by small groups of students)

Children ❧ Bees ❧ Mosquitoes ❧ Caterpillars/Butterflies ❧ Ladybugs

**Children:** Where did all
These bugs come from?
Listen to them
Buzz and hum.

**Bees:** We are bugs,
We can sting.
But we make honey,
A yummy thing!

**Mosquitoes:** We are bugs,
We sting, too.
Better watch out.
We might sting you!

**Children:** Where did all
These bugs come from?
Listen to them
Buzz and hum.

**All Bugs:** Summer is here!
Summer is here!
We all come out
This time of year.

**Caterpillars/
Butterflies:** We are bugs,
We don't sting.
We crawl now
But we'll grow wings.

**Ladybugs:** We are bugs,
Red with spots.
The spots are small,
But we've got lots!

**Children:** Bugs are playing
Little games.
They want us
To guess their names.

Bees make honey.
Mosquitoes sting.
Ladybugs have spots.
Caterpillars grow wings.

**All Bugs:** They guessed
our secret names,
Oh no!
No time for games.
It's time to go!

*500+ Fabulous Month-by-Month Teaching Ideas* © 2010 Scholastic Teaching Resources

Name _____

Date _____

# Ladybug Math Story Mat

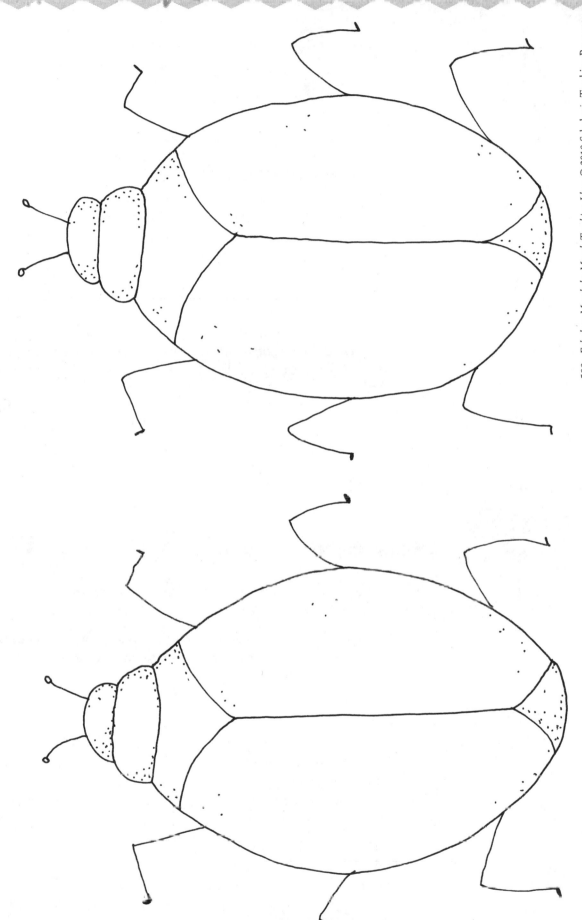

500+ Fabulous Month-by-Month Teaching Ideas © 2010 Scholastic Teaching Resources

## TIP

For a variation on the Independence Day Parade, plan an Appreciation Parade to celebrate America. Initiate a discussion about what is special about our country's people and places. Have children create flags to carry in a parade, using words and pictures to tell something they appreciate about their country. They can use sturdy paper for the flags, then attach them to yardstick-length dowels.

# Teacher Share

### ART, SOCIAL STUDIES

## Independence Day Parade

Children will have fun making mini "floats" for an Independence Day Parade. Give each child a shoebox (lids not needed) to decorate with paint, markers, crayons, feathers, stickers, glitter, and, of course, anything red, white, or blue! Have children bring a stuffed animal or doll to school on parade day and place it on the float. String the boxes together by stapling one to the next with pieces of yarn. On the day of the parade, play a march (Sousa marches always work well) and have children march through the halls, leading their floats to the beat of the music and a cheering audience!

*Mary Jane Banta*

### SOCIAL STUDIES

## Secret Ballot Box

Explore the concept of voting—one of the ways Americans participate in the political process—by setting up a class ballot box.

◎ Introduce the activity by asking children what they know about voting. Explain that this is how the president and other people in our government get their jobs.

◎ Make a class ballot box to give children an opportunity to vote on class decisions. Have children decorate a shoebox top and bottom with a patriotic theme. Cut a slit in the top and place it on the box bottom.

◎ Give each child a copy of the secret ballot slips on page 293. Have children cut apart the ballots and complete the first one to vote on a class snack. (Depending on the size of your class, you may wish to write two or three choices—such as crackers, pretzels, and fruit—on the chalkboard.)

◎ When everyone has placed their ballots in the box, remove the lid and take a count.

◎ Use the other ballots as you choose: every few days, once a week, and so on. Make new ballots to take votes on other class decisions, such as when to have free-choice time.

**Book Break**

# Betsy Ross

by Alexandra Wallner (Holiday House, 1998)

Set in Colonial Philadelphia, this charming book tells the story of Betsy Ross's life, including her most famous accomplishment—the sewing of the first American flag. Children will love the details of eighteenth-century American life and the descriptions of Revolutionary times. After reading, let children follow Betsy's directions in the back of the book as she teaches them how to make a five-pointed star in just one snip!

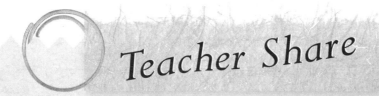

*Teacher Share*

· SOCIAL STUDIES, MATH ·

## Measure the Statue of Liberty

Almost all children have seen pictures of the Statue of Liberty, but not many have seen it up close. This measuring activity will help children understand just how big this national symbol is.

◎ On green paper, draw the outline of an eye measuring 2 feet, 6 inches across. (You may need to tape two sheets of paper together.) Do the same for the lips: The correct measurement is 3 feet across. Set these aside.

◎ Give children non-standard units of measurement. (Unifix cubes work well because they can be counted by tens.) Show children a photograph of the statue and point to one of the eyes. Ask: *On the real statue, how many units would it take to get across the eye?* Have children record estimates. Do the same for the mouth.

◎ Display the actual-size drawing of the eye and mouth. Let children revise their estimates, then measure! *If just one eye is that large, how big do they think the whole statue is?*

*Mitzi Fehl*

**CoMPuTer Connection**

National Park Service

www.nps.gov/stli This informative site features facts about the Statue of Liberty (including measurements), stories, and curriculum materials.

## Computer Connection

Learn more about the American flag, and the flags of other countries, at these Web sites:

Betsy Ross House

www.ushistory.org (hosted by the Independence Hall Association of Philadelphia) Select "Betsy Ross House" to take a tour of the Betsy Ross House, read a biography, view a picture gallery of the flag at different times in history, find flag facts and trivia, even learn about theories about what the colors represent.

International Flags

www.w3f.com/gifs/flag/country/index.html

ART, SOCIAL STUDIES

## Design a Class Flag

*What does America's flag stand for?* Invite children to share their thoughts, then read *The Flag We Love* to learn more. (See Book Break, below.) Investigate other countries' flags (see Computer Connection, left), then work together to create a class flag. Discuss what the class flag will stand for, then brainstorm colors, designs, symbols, and so on. Make a sketch, then create the flag. Hang your class flag proudly outside your door. Children may want to salute it each day as they come in!

### Book Break

## The Flag We Love (10th Anniversary Edition)
### by Pamela Munoz Ryan (Charlesbridge, 2006)

Each right-facing page of this inventive book is a colorful painting of the American flag under different circumstances: being raised in front of a log schoolhouse, at the Vietnam memorial, even on the moon! Each left-facing page includes a smaller picture, and facts about the flag and the event.

MUSIC, SOCIAL STUDIES

## Singing and Signing the Red, White, and Blue

Part of being a patriotic American lies in appreciating the diversity of our nation. This includes showing respect and consideration for people who speak different languages and have special needs. You can touch on these concepts while teaching about the American flag with this song.

*(Sing to the tune of* "Three Blind Mice."*)*

| | |
|---|---|
| Red, white, blue, | Oh what a wonderful sight to see, |
| Red, white, blue, | A flag for you and a flag for me, |
| I love you, | It means we live in a land that's free, |
| I love you. | Red, white, blue. |

Write the words to the song on chart paper, and sing it a few times with children. Once children are familiar with the song, teach them the hand signs that go along with it. (See illustrations, below.)

I love you          red                    white                blue

# Secret Ballot

I think
we should have

----

for snack.

# Secret Ballot

I think
we should read

----

at story time.

# Secret Ballot

I think
we should do

----

for our group project.

# Secret Ballot

I think our class
show-and-tell theme
should be

----

# Best Friends for Frances

### by Russell Hoban (HarperCollins, 1976)

This classic story has all the "Frances" trademark elements: funny, repetitive, childlike dialogue; seemingly endless food lists; a conflict resolved in an interesting way; and, of course, plenty of offbeat ditties sung by Frances. In this one, Frances ignores her little sister in order to gain the attention of her "best friend" Albert. For a fun follow-up, why not make up a Frances-style "song" together? Remember—the last few lines don't always have to rhyme. Frances likes her freedom!

**TIP**

Remind children never to give out personal identity information (such as home addresses or phone numbers), and be sure to review other rules for Internet and e-mail safety with your learners.

LANGUAGE ARTS, SOCIAL STUDIES, TECHNOLOGY

# Twenty-First Century Pen Pals

A great way to make new friends is to get a pen pal. And the most modern way to do this is, of course, on the Internet! Set up an e-mail pen pal program for your class. These programs can be a wonderful way to make new friends, learn about different cultures, and get children writing! There are plenty of web sites to help you get started. Suggestions follow.

- **www.ks-connection.org/** Pen Pal Box is a wonderful site designed especially for children. It features pen pals sorted by classrooms and age groups.

- **www.ozkidz.gil.com.au/rm/student/surfe.html** Surf-E-Mates includes a link to the Kid City Post Office, as well as a link called "Class Projects: Intercultural E-Mail Classroom Connections," specifically designed to coordinate e-mail projects with classrooms around the world.

- **www.worldwide.edu/planning_guide/Pen_Pals/PenPals.html** World Wide Classroom Pen Pals provides a host of links to pen pal program resources around the world.

# Best Friends

### by Steven Kellogg (Penguin Putnam, 1986)

Kathy and Louise are best friends, but that doesn't mean they always get along. After sharing the story, let children talk about times they've experienced difficulties, such as jealousy, in their friendships. What did they do about it? Depending on the age level of your students, you might want to have a group discussion or use the question as a writing prompt.

MATH, SOCIAL STUDIES

# Friendship Pocket Calendar

This class calendar will encourage acts of friendship every day!

- Write the month and year across the top of a sheet of tagboard. Underneath, write the days of the week left to right, Sunday through Saturday. Write numbers (1–31) on the outside of empty library card pockets for the dates. (Check school-supply stores and catalogs.)

- Glue the pockets to the tagboard in numerical order, starting with the first day of the month. Display the calendar.

- Give each child an index card. Discuss things people do to show love and caring for friends—for example, with a hug, by doing someone a favor, by giving someone a compliment, and so on. Have children write an "act of friendship" on one side of their index card. (To fill out the calendar, you may want to add a few cards of your own, or have some children write two cards.)

- Place the cards in the pockets with the blank side facing out. Each morning, turn over the card in that day's pocket. It is each child's "mission" to accomplish the act of friendship written on the card at least once by the end of the day.

**TIP**

You might want to write the "friendship mission" of the day on the chalkboard and have children write their initials next to it once they have accomplished it. At the end of each day, children can describe the situation and what they did.

Teacher Share

LANGUAGE ARTS, SOCIAL STUDIES

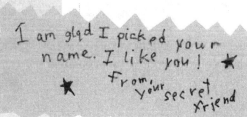

## Secret Pal Messages

This "secret pal" activity is a great way for children to make new friends. On a Monday, put children's names in a paper bag and have each child pick one. The name they picked will be the person they will write secret messages to. Talk with children about writing positive messages and let them suggest some—for example, "I like you because...you are a good friend." Have children write and deliver (to classroom mailboxes and cubbies) their secret messages (no names!) each day from Monday through Thursday. On Friday, have children write their last message, signing it with their first initial only. Allow extra time for children to guess their secret pals.

**Bobbie Williams**

LANGUAGE ARTS

# Old Friends and New Friends Mini-Book

In advance, ask parents and children to find photos of one old friend and
one new friend to bring in from home. Give each child a copy of page 299.
Have children cut along the dotted lines and tape A to B. Guide children in
completing each page to tell about their old friends. Have children flip the
paper and tell a story about a new friend, using the "old friend" sentences as
a model. (Have them substitute the word *new* for *old*.) When children are
finished, they can add illustrations, and fold their pages back and forth to
make accordion books.

## Teacher Share

SOCIAL STUDIES

## Facts About Friends

Use this giant Venn diagram to let
children explore the many ways
they can be friends.

◎ Have children write several facts
about themselves on index cards, one
fact per card. Encourage children to
stick to such things as likes and dislikes,
favorite hobbies, and so on, rather than
facts such as "I have red hair" or "I'm wearing
a green shirt." Have children write their names on an
index card, too.

◎ Gather children in an open area and overlap two hula-hoops
on the floor. Invite two children to try the activity. Have
them place their name cards above the circles. Then let them
take turns sharing their fact cards aloud. If both children
"share the fact" it goes in the overlapping section. Otherwise,
children put their cards in their individual circles.

*Rita Galloway*

MUSIC

# Silver and Gold Friendship Circles

This is a great activity for transition times, such as finding partners or preparing to go home. Practice the following traditional song with children:

> Make new friends and keep the old,
> One is silver and the other gold.

Once children are familiar with the song, divide the group in half and have them form two circles by holding hands. One circle should be inside the other, so that children in the inside circle are facing those in the outside circle. Have them sing the song as the circles move in opposite directions. When children reach the word "gold," they must stop moving. Whomever they are facing is their partner! If using the activity to prepare for going home, keep repeating the song after each pair goes to their cubbies. This is both a lovely way to end the day and a great way to avoid the cubby crush!

SOCIAL STUDIES

# Old Friends...Young Friends!

One nice aspect of intergenerational friendships is the capacity they have to teach. Older people can teach younger people things they have learned from experience. Younger people can teach older people new ways of looking at the world. Have children write and/or dictate a story about something they have learned from an older friend—for example, a special way to make cookies, something about their friend's hometown, or even how to take care of a pet parakeet. Repeat the activity for something they have taught their older friends. Have children illustrate their pages and bind them together to create a class book about these special friendships.

## Book Break

# Wilfrid Gordon McDonald Partridge
### by Mem Fox (Kane/Miller, 1989)

"There was once a small boy named Wilfrid Gordon McDonald Partridge and what's more he wasn't very old either. His house was next door to an old people's home and he knew all the people who lived there." Miss Nancy is Wilfrid's favorite. But one day Wilfrid overhears his parents saying that Miss Nancy has lost her memory. Wilfrid asks all his friends at the home what a *memory* is...something warm, something as precious as gold, something that makes you laugh. Wilfrid collects his interpretations of these things, and gives them to Miss Nancy one by one. And bit by bit, she begins to remember.

# Owen & Mzee: The True Story of a Remarkable Friendship

### by Isabella Hatkoff (Scholastic, 2006)

This is the true story of a baby hippopotamus orphaned by the 2004 tsunami in Southeast Asia. The rescued hippo is brought to an animal sanctuary in Kenya, where it forms an unexpected and astonishing friendship with a giant tortoise.

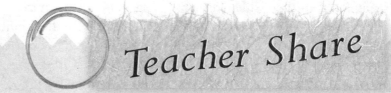

*Teacher Share*

MATH, LANGUAGE ARTS

## Friendship Hearts

This activity can strengthen a range of skills and will get children together who may not ordinarily spend time with one another.

◎ Make sets of matching hearts to pair up children in your class. Your matches can reflect any skill you'd like to reinforce. For example, you can strengthen addition skills by writing number sentences with the same sum on matching hearts. Or make matches to practice word families—for example, write words that contain the same phonogram on matching cards (*pack, quack; dog, frog*).

◎ Use removable wall adhesive to stick the hearts in children's cubbies. You may do this randomly, or you may want to take this opportunity to pair up children who don't often spend time together.

◎ When children come to school the next morning, have them stick their hearts to the fronts of their shirts or sweaters. Then have them find their matching heart! Explain that children with matching hearts are "Fast Friends"— they will do special things together that day. (You can plan a special activity or project in advance, have partners sit with each other for lunch or snack, make a simple gift, and so on.) At the end of the day, gather children together to exchange their gifts and talk about the experience.

*Catherine Wenglowski*

# My Old Friend

by .....................................

**1**

Put a picture
of your friend here.

**A**

I have an old friend

named ..................... .

**2**

**B**

I like .....................

because .....................

..................... .

**3**

We like to .....................

.....................

..................... .

**4**

# Teacher Share

MATH

## Beach Ball Math

This activity is fabulous for adding summer fun to math practice, and it couldn't be easier! Pick up an ordinary beach ball, the kind with different-colored stripes. On each color (or every other), place a strip of masking tape with a different number sentence on it (2 + 3, 7 − 4, 3 x 2...the level of difficulty depends on the age group you are working with). Indoors or out, gather children in a circle. Toss the ball to one of them. Ask this child to choose the color under one of his or her hands, then read the number sentence on that color, give the answer, and toss it back to you. Continue, tossing the ball to a different child each time until everyone has had a turn. As children become familiar with the number sentences, you can try to make the game go faster and faster! Then you can change the math problems on the ball and start over.

*Deborah Rovin-Murphy*

MATH, SCIENCE

## Hide-and-Seek With Shells

This game is sure to delight children of any age group. Follow these steps to play.

◎ Fill your sand and water table with sand. (You can also use a sandbox or large plastic tub.)

◎ Give each child a large-size crayon, a plain piece of paper, and a shell. (Try to make the shells as different as possible.) Have children make shell rubbings. Collect the rubbings and post them on a bulletin board near the sand table.

◎ Now the mystery begins! Collect all the shells and have children turn their backs as you hide them in the sand. Then let children turn around and start digging! The object of the game is to find shells and match them to rubbings. Remind children that careful observation, not speed, is the key.

# How I Spent My Summer Vacation

by Mark Teague (Dragonfly Books, 1997)

When Wallace Bleff's teacher assigns a report on "How I Spent My Summer Vacation," his imagination takes over and turns a visit to his aunt's into a cowboy fantasy.

SCIENCE, MATH, HISTORY

## Sun Shadow Clock

Explain to children that long ago, the sun had a very important job: It was the only way people were able to tell time! They used the shadows the sun made on a device called a *sundial* to keep track of time. Then try this experiment to let children see how sundials work.

- Fill an empty coffee can with wet sand. Stick a ruler in the middle of the sand.

- Find a sunny spot on blacktop or a sidewalk where you can draw with chalk. Make sure the spot is in open sunlight so that other shadows don't interfere.

- Place the can on the sidewalk and look for the line of the ruler's shadow. Trace over the line with chalk.

- Go out again in an hour or two and find the ruler's shadow. Again, trace the line with chalk. Continue checking and tracing every hour or two throughout the day. *In what direction are the lines moving? How far apart are they?* Compare the lines to those on the clock in your classroom. You just might see a similarity!

**Remind children not to look directly at the sun.**

## Lemonade Sun and Other Summer Poems

by Rebecca Kai Dotlich (Boyds Mills, 2001)

From bumblebees and butterflies to jump-rope rhymes and jacks, these poems celebrate what's special about summer—in the city and the country.

## TIP

For a simpler (though not quite as dramatic) version of this activity, have children collect collage materials and/or natural objects and place them on dark-colored construction paper. (Stick lightweight objects to the paper with removable wall adhesive.) Set the collages in direct sunlight and move them as needed so that they stay directly in the sun. Do this for a period of a few days (be sure to pull them indoors quickly if it rains) until the color of the construction paper has faded quite a bit. (You can tell by comparing it to a new piece.) Remove the objects and see the print!

## Teacher Share

ART, SCIENCE

## Sun Prints

Making sun prints is both a technological and natural activity that results in spectacular outcomes. Materials for sun prints are available from several educational companies at surprisingly low prices. Using these kits is simple, and involves no chemicals. Children simply select collage items (lace, leaves, flowers, feathers, thin branches, paper cutouts, and so on) they'd like to print. Then they place them on the sun-sensitive paper and set it out in the sun for a short time. The paper develops in plain water in just a few minutes and produces a beautiful blue and white image! Following are two resources for sun print supplies.

◎ EDUCATIONAL INSIGHTS: **www.ierc.com/** (800) 933-3277.

◎ THE LAWRENCE HALL OF SCIENCE: **www.lhs.berkeley.edu/store** (510) 642-1016.

*Catherine Wenglowski*

## Book Break

# The Way to Start a Day

by Byrd Baylor (Simon & Schuster, 1986)

In this Caldecott Honor book, Byrd Baylor describes the way to start the day in many places all over the world and throughout history: by greeting the rising sun with special words, gifts, and rituals. After reading, ask children how they like to greet the new day. Ask: *What is the first thing you do when you get up in the morning?* Together, decide on a ritual to greet each new day in the classroom. It can be very simple, such as looking out the window, finding the sun, and waving "hello" to it.

# Teacher Share

ART, SCIENCE

## Sun Safety Puppets

**M**ake copies of the sun safety puppet activity sheet on page 304. Have children cut out the puppet and color it in, then glue on yarn to make hair. Ask children to draw a favorite bathing suit (or make one out of construction paper and glue it on), then glue the back of the puppet to a craft stick.

Tell children that their puppets are taking an imaginary trip to the beach. Ask: *What do they need to do before they go?* (Have them look at the remaining pictures on the activity sheet for clues.) Talk about how sunblock, sunglasses, and a shirt can help keep them safe in the sun. Have children cut out the other three items and color them in. They can use removable wall adhesive to put the sunglasses and shirt on their puppets, then place the sunblock in its hand.

*Deborah Rovin-Murphy*

SCIENCE, MATH

## Where Do Puddles Go?

Children are drawn to puddles—and are naturally curious about where they go. Introduce the water cycle with this activity.

- Find or make a puddle in a sunny spot outdoors. Find or make a puddle of approximately the same size in a shady spot. Ask children what happens to puddles after a rain shower. Record ideas on chart paper.
- Take different colors of yarn and scissors outside to measure the puddles. String the yarn around the perimeter of each puddle and snip it off where it completes the circle. Use a different color for each puddle.
- Use the yarn lengths to measure the puddles each day. Keep snipping the yarn as the puddles grow smaller. Compare the two colors of yarn each time: *Which puddle is growing smaller faster?* Keep the experiment going until one or both of the puddles is entirely gone.
- Discuss children's observations and record new ideas about what happens to puddles. Children may now recognize that the warmth and light of the sun helps to dry up water.

**TIP**

Encourage children to take their puppets and props home and share a sun safety lesson with their families.

## Computer Connection

Kids Health

kidshealth.org/
kid/watch/out/
summer_safety.
html

With separate areas for kids, teens, and parents, this site offers information on sun safety, including pronunciation keys and definitions for important terms.

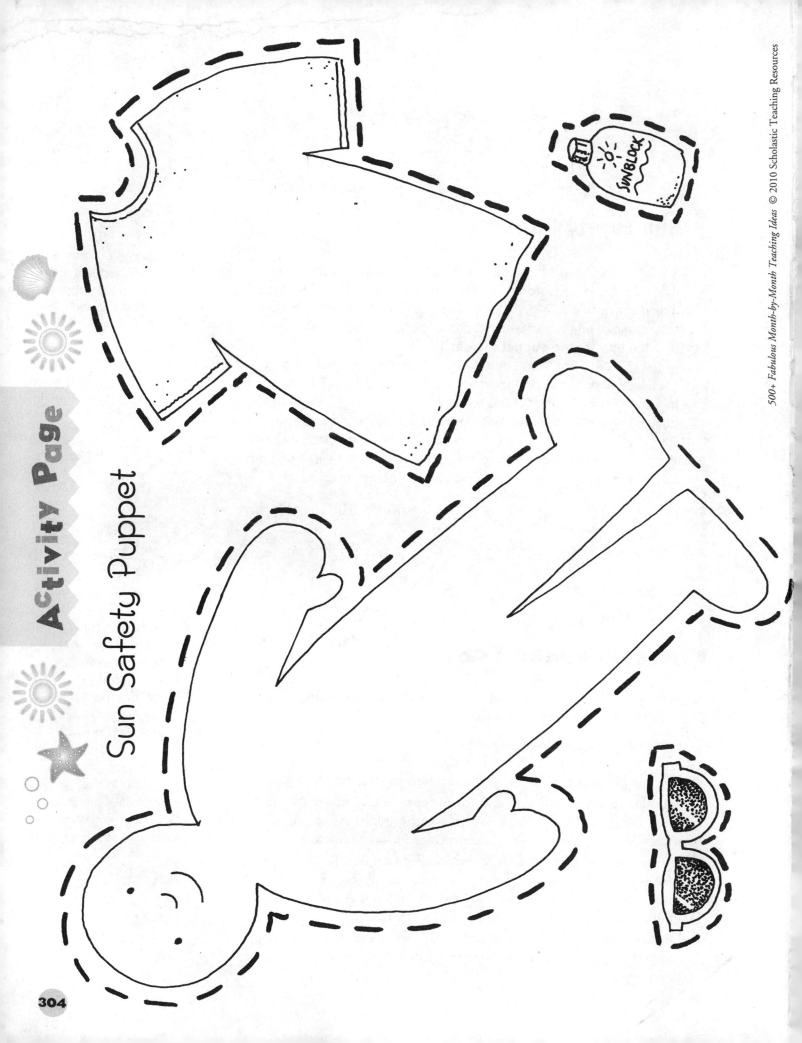

Sun Safety Puppet

SUNBLOCK

500+ Fabulous Month-by-Month Teaching Ideas © 2010 Scholastic Teaching Resources